I0878617

May Irwin

MUSIC IN AMERICAN LIFE

A list of books in the series appears at the end of this book.

May Irwin

Singing, Shouting, and the Shadow of Minstrelsy

SHARON AMMEN

UNIVERSITY OF ILLINOIS PRESS
Urbana, Chicago, and Springfield

© 2017 by the Board of Trustees
of the University of Illinois
All rights reserved
Manufactured in the United States of America
1 2 3 4 5 C P 5 4 3 2 1
∞ This book is printed on acid-free paper.

Publication of this book was supported by the AMS 75 PAYS Endowment of the American Musicological Society, funded in part by the National Endowment for the Humanities and the Andrew W. Mellon Foundation.

Library of Congress Cataloging-in-Publication Data
Names: Ammen, Sharon, 1951– author.
Title: May Irwin : singing, shouting, and the shadow of minstrelsy / Sharon Ammen.
Description: Urbana : University of Illinois Press, [2017] | Series: Music in American life | Includes bibliographical references and index.
Identifiers: LCCN 2016024718 (print) | LCCN 2016040566 (ebook) | ISBN 9780252040658 (hardback) | ISBN 9780252082153 (paperback) | ISBN 9780252099090 (e-book)
Subjects: LCSH: Minstrel shows—United States—History. | Irwin, May, 1862–1938—Criticism and interpretation. | Minstrel music—United States—History and criticism. | BISAC: MUSIC / History & Criticism. | PERFORMING ARTS / Theater / History & Criticism. | SOCIAL SCIENCE / Ethnic Studies / African American Studies.
Classification: LCC PN1969.M5 A46 2017 (print) | LCC PN1969.M5 (ebook) | DDC 791/.120973—dc23
LC record available at https://lccn.loc.gov/2016024718

Dedicated to the memory of Dana McCleod,
whose strength and grace in the face of adversity
inspired everyone whose life she touched.

Contents

Acknowledgments

I have lived for many years with May Irwin. Sometimes she has been the object of most of my attention and research. At other times, she has receded into the background. I am forever indebted to the faculty at the University of Maryland who assisted me in my early research: Harry Elam, who introduced me to black theater aesthetics; Jane Donawerth, whose enthusiasm and suggestions for further publications have been a welcome addition to my work; and Catherine Schuler, whose scholarly guidance, wit, and friendship kept me on track. I owe a great deal to those individuals at libraries and archives who worked patiently with me, and although it is impossible to include them all here, my heartfelt thanks goes to them all. I received invaluable help from the research specialists at the Library of Congress, the New York Library of the Performing Arts, and Houghton Library at Harvard University.

I am particularly grateful for the generous support of the people in and around Clayton, New York, where Irwin spent much of her life. Harold Kendall at Clayton Museum and "Ragtime Bob" Darch, both deceased now, shared memories, scrapbooks, and valuable sheet-music collections with me. The staff at Hawn Library in Clayton was welcoming and generous with their special collections. Robert Bertrand wrote to me of his memories of May, and retired archivist Brian Winter, from Irwin's hometown—Whitby, Ontario, Canada—sent valuable papers. Jack Brown's scrapbook of clippings from Mallorytown, Ontario, was also especially helpful.

When I left the University of Maryland to work as a theater professor at Saint Mary-of-the-Woods College (SMWC) in Indiana, I found new ways to explore May Irwin's influences through performance combined with scholarship. I thank Linda Harold of the Clayton Museum for obtaining a New York State Arts Grant for the mounting of *May Irwin Is Back* in the late 1990s at the Clayton Opera House. Kathleen Golden graciously invited me to her home in Edinboro, Pennsylvania, to appear in her documentary *Three Vaudeville Women,* which focused on the careers of Eva Tanguay, May Irwin, and Marie Dressler and was released in 2008. Elizabeth Surles visited me to discuss information for her liner notes on Aerophone's recording of the songs of May Irwin and Clarice Vance in *The High Priestess of Jollity and the Southern Singer,* produced by Richard Martin and Meagan Hennessey in 2011. During these years, I adapted many scripts of May Irwin's work to perform with students from Depauw University and Saint Mary-of-the-Woods College at a variety of national associations' conferences, including the National Communication Association and the Popular Cultural Association/American Culture Association. I want to especially thank my dear friend Professor Susan Anthony for her help in organizing and performing at these conferences.

I thank SMWC for granting me a semester sabbatical to work on research, and I extend heartfelt thanks to Dr. John McIntyre of SMWC and Sherri Wright of Arts Iliana in helping to secure a grant for the presentation of the program *Reconstruction to Ragtime* at SMWC. This valuable program would also not have happened without the excellent work of professional actress Anita Dashiell-Sparks of Los Angeles; student actresses Valentine Soposky, Elizabeth Ortiz, Danielle O'Connor, and Betsy Baer; pianist Ronald Maurey; and technical director Tyler Hutcheson and his wife, Lisa Hutcheson. I would be remiss if I did not also offer thanks and eternal gratitude to my first mentor, Dr. Lee Potts, University of Colorado–Boulder, who taught me how to adapt materials for performance and whose lessons have always stayed with me.

I am heavily indebted to the continual work and encouragement of Laurie Matheson at the University of Illinois Press for her years of editing suggestions and help and also to her two assistants, Marika Christophides and Julie Laut, as well as the rest of the outstanding staff at the press. Readers Gillian M. Rodger and Andrew L. Erdman are especially appreciated for their in-depth scholarly reviews of my work and suggestions for improvements. I am also grateful to Sharon Bourquin at the Thousand Island Museum (formerly the Clayton Museum) for her support and the Lester S. Levy Collection at the Sheridan Libraries at John Hopkins University for their generous usage policy. For their kind guidance in procuring photographs, I thank Chelsea Weathers of the Harry Ransom Center at the University of Texas; Sarah Ferensz at Whitby Archives, Whitby Library in Whitby, Ontario, Canada; and the staff at Houghton Library at Harvard University.

Finally, I owe a special tribute to three people without whom this project would never have even gotten off the ground. First, I offer my eternal gratitude to my mentor Patti Gillespie for the countless hours of work (over several years) that she spent reviewing my research and writing. Second, I thank the remarkable May Irwin collector Karen Killian for her continual help as my primary guide in Clayton. She always kept in touch and faithfully sent me new material and information that she discovered. Finally, I thank the love of my life who has always supported me in every way possible, my husband of forty years, Ron Moore.

May Irwin

INTRODUCTION

May and Me

> May Irwin is a famous fun-maker; of jolly, rotund figure, and with a face that reflects the gaeiety of nations, she is the personification of humour and careless mirth. . . . Her good-fellowship is infectious, and she has a great facility for getting on intimate terms with her audiences, making herself, for the time being, the personal friend of every man, woman, and child in the theatre the instant she appears on the stage.
>
> —Lewis C. Strang, *Famous Actresses of the Day*

Before Sophie Tucker "corked up" to entertain her audiences with ragtime songs in "Negro dialect" and before Fanny Brice stumbled into the footlights in her rendition of the "Dying Swan," the reigning queen of comedy and song on the American stage was May Irwin. A performer both in vaudeville and on the legitimate stage, Irwin was also known as an accomplished homemaker and loving mother, a political activist, a real estate tycoon, and a prolific writer of articles, composer of songs, and author of a popular cookbook.

Georgina May Campbell was born on June 27, 1862, in Whitby, Ontario, Canada, but moved to New York in 1875.[1] In the course of her career, she became an enormously successful and popular entertainer, variously described as the "high priestess of jollity," "a female Falstaff," "the dean of comediennes," and, in her younger days, the most "artistic soubrette" in Augustin Daly's distinguished company of actors.[2] At the height of her fame, May Irwin was acknowledged as having "no rivals on the American stage" and as filling a singular position in the minds of the popular audience, "carved out for herself with no other instrument than her own genius."[3] Enthusiastic critics maintained that there was "hardly another comedian on our stage with so much of natural unction, of convincingly assumed jocularity," and that Irwin was "a far finer artist than the average auditor imagines."[4] English critic Clement Scott declared that "if May Irwin wore trousers she would be one of the greatest actors of the age."[5]

Irwin's significance as a comic entertainer is difficult to overestimate. During a long career, her comic appeal never flagged. Her work encompassed the variety and changes in American theater from the 1880s to the 1920s. She was successful in Tony Pastor's homespun variety theater, as an ensemble actor in Augustin Daly's prestigious company, as a major star in comedies produced by her own company, and as a touring vaudevillian in the large circuits developed by managers such as B. F. Keith and Edward F. Albee (adoptive grandfather of the Pulitzer Prize–winning playwright). She embodied the American dream—rising from poverty to wealth and fame. The songs she sang were overnight sensations, and the sheet music for them appeared in parlors all across America. (Many of these numbers were "coon songs," composed of racist lyrics set to ragtime music. May Irwin has the dubious honor of being the singer most closely associated with the creation of "coon shouting.") In her heyday, rarely did a week pass without media coverage of Irwin's activities, whether it was an advertisement for sheet music, a review of one of her latest performances, a personal interview on her home life, or her own essays on popularity, the "woman question," homemaking, and humor.

Although many female stars of the era used the media to their advantage, Irwin's appearances in the *New York Times* far exceeded others. A complete online search of the paper reveals 493 news items on May Irwin compared to 122 for Trixie Friganza, 306 for Eva Tanguay, and 304 for Marie Dressler for all years of publication. Of vaudevillians who left their native Ontario to try their luck in America, Canadian historians list May Irwin and Marie Dressler as the two who "achieved international stardom."[6]

Nevertheless, despite the great fame she achieved during her lifetime, Irwin has been largely forgotten, and when she is not forgotten, she is likely to be mischaracterized: "It is perhaps a sad reflection on our times that if May Irwin is remembered at all it is not as a vaudevillian or even as a star of the legitimate stage and musical comedy, but as a plump, somewhat unattractive actress, bestowing an amorous kiss in a flickering film from the cinema's infancy."[7] This refers to one of the first bits of silent film, *The Kiss* (1896), in which May Irwin and John C. Rice re-created a kiss from her hit farce *The Widow Jones.*

I first encountered May more than twenty years ago. My husband and I had just returned from five years working and living in Europe. Prior to going abroad, I was making a rather poor living as a comic actress and singer in Washington, D.C.—I fled just after completing a three-month run as Ruth in *The Pirates of Penzance.* In Europe I was able to teach, direct, perform, run a theater program for U.S. military personnel, and, finally, study acting for a year in London. When I returned to Washington, I slowly got back into the performance swing, eventually ending up in a run of the musical *Do Black Patent Leather Shoes Really Reflect Up?* In case any musical theater aficionados are reading this, I believe I only need say that I played the "cookie nun" in order to give an idea of my "type."

That's when I faced an important career crossroads. I applied for a fellowship offered through the University of Maryland and simultaneously signed up for the National Theatre Auditions. As luck would have it, I was offered money for research studies the same week I was offered three separate dinner-theater roles. The roles were the same as those I'd been pigeonholed in for years. Suddenly, I saw before me a life spent playing the domineering battle ax in *A Funny Thing Happened on the Way to the Forum* or the wicked-witch stepmother in *Robber Bridegroom.* As my character (in a creaky melodrama) Calamity Jane said every single night for ten long months, I had a "feelin' of forebodin.'"

As I considered my own life as a performer, I became increasingly intrigued by how riddled with contradictions it was. My experiences with seemingly self-deprecatory, even misogynistic, comic material had made me feel powerful as an actor. Here I was—an ardent feminist, betraying my own values in my work onstage! Concurrently, I became eager to try my hand at historical research. So although I continued earning extra money directing freelance and performing in musical skits of political satire (reliably steady work in Washington, D.C.), I was also spending time researching at the Library of Congress and making frequent trips to the Billy Rose Collection at the New York Library of the Performing Arts. As a beginning scholar, I loved critical analysis when connected to practical performance. My first publications in peer-reviewed journals included an analysis of Simone Benmussa's adaptation of a story by George Moore and a study of audience response to a production of Caryl Churchill's *Top Girls* that I was hired to direct.[8] Both of these articles drew on my interest in feminist studies as well as in performance.

As often happens to me when I am open to new knowledge or experience, a fluke event occurred that helped me take the plunge. A book someone had recently given me fell off the shelf and opened to an entry on May Irwin. The book was *Women in Comedy,* by Linda Martin and Kerry Segrave, and I noticed as I picked it up that this woman named May Irwin had given a command performance in Washington, D.C., for Woodrow Wilson, who promptly dubbed her "America's Secretary of Laughter." I thought I could begin by looking in Washington archives and finding out more about this event.

Although my first effort researching the "Secretary of Laughter" did not turn into anything earthshaking, I developed an abiding interest in May Irwin. I found her mentioned in nearly every encyclopedia and dictionary covering vaudeville or popular music, but there were no major studies of her life or her performance history and no major archival collections.[9] Slowly gathering information, I began to put together a picture of a woman who was not only a formidable presence in American theater and popular culture for more than thirty-five years, but also an outspoken activist in support of a variety of social causes, including animal rights, pacifism, and suffrage. She was known as a woman of great strength, one who, when she was still in her early twenties, would stand up to and argue with the great Augustin Daly and later in life even speak her mind to President Woodrow Wilson when she thought the country was in danger of entering World War I.

Yet this woman, who expressed her opinions on a number of issues and wielded enormous power, never acquired a reputation for being temperamental. In fact, her behavior was compared favorably to the tantrums of Nora Bayes and Eva Tanguay and the lavish lifestyle of Sophie Tucker.[10] Instead, she seemed to be universally loved and accepted. She could bluntly claim that women really have a greater sense of humor than men, but men "haven't enough sense of humor to recognize the truth of it" and still be praised by men for her wit.[11] She could openly take an unconventional stand against the double standard applied to working mothers and fathers and not bring down the wrath of critics.[12] Indeed, Irwin was noted for her good nature *and* her outspoken opinions. Her contemporaries felt that "on and off the stage her geniality distinguished her like a halo." Irwin was said to have "an absolutely perfect sense of humor—from a man's point of view." However, she was also lauded as "most popular with the women, she is their champion and exemplar, the weapon in domestic arguments on this subject [of women's alleged lack of humor]." Historians of vaudeville often repeated praises of her equable character: "In all the exhumations incidental to this book, with the cross-current comment, the sometimes laughable displays of temperament, the almost inevitable disparagement of one actor for another, this writer has not once read or heard one word against May Irwin, as a person or a performer."[13]

Although it became clear to me that Irwin was a formidable entertainer who was able to embrace the contradiction of being powerful and well liked, I was well aware that many female comics and singers from the time were lauded in a similar manner. In truth, Irwin had strong similarities to leading ladies of her day and built upon many trailblazers who lived before her. I also knew that women had learned to employ a variety of strategies to maintain their popularity in a society in which they were still not accepted in the public sphere, as well as one in which female performers were considered morally shady and even equated with prostitutes. But this was a changing society, and the success of women comics reflected these changes.

May Irwin lived in an America that was rapidly developing from a rural society into an urban one. In 1880 28 percent of the population of the United States dwelled in urban areas, while 72 percent lived in rural areas; by 1920 things had dramatically shifted, with more than half (51 percent) of Americans living in urban areas and only 49 percent in rural.[14] This new urban culture was supported by immense technological advances and the growth of the world's largest consumer-based capitalist economy. In 1880 the streets of New York City were first lit by electricity, and twenty-eight hundred New Yorkers subscribed to the new telephone system; by 1896 the number of New Yorkers with telephones had already grown to fifteen thousand.[15] In 1880 most transportation consisted of a horse and buggy, but by 1900 extensive streetcar lines connected people with businesses in forty-one major cities. Soon the United States would become a land dominated by automobiles. Already by 1916, Ford had sold 1.7 million of the new Model T cars.[16]

During her career, Irwin witnessed both the creation of powerful financial trusts and the reform movements directed against those trusts. She lived through a long period of peace and prosperity in America and then beheld the shattering of that peace through America's entry into World War I. She observed the suppression of the rights only recently gained by American blacks, the flowering of the women's movement, and the transformation of the fight for suffrage into a mainstream cause. Additionally, Irwin saw major changes take place within her own profession, including the rise of the star system. She also witnessed the birth of a new art form—the film—that would grow to threaten the popularity of live theater. In the 1890s, the American public enjoyed the first moving picture; by 1912 five million Americans were visiting the cinema daily.[17] Although May was in one of the first moving pictures made, she did not pursue a transition to the new medium, preferring to stay onstage and to begin to slowly retire to her home in the Thousand Islands.

May was fortunate to come to America during a period in which the number of women employed as actors experienced enormous growth. Certainly, acting was a profession in which women had a chance of matching men in their income-earning ability. Actress turned feminist lecturer Olive Logan was a staunch defender of women in the theater, contending, in her book

Apropos of Women and Theatre, that theater and literature were the two occupations in which "men and women stand on an absolutely equal plane in the matter of cash and reward."[18]

Not only was Irwin able to garner enormous wealth, but her combination of star power and talent also enabled her to succeed in show business far longer than the average female performer. Not as many women as men stayed in the theater as they grew older. This was true in other professions as well, for, when women married, they often withdrew to domestic life. The necessity of youthful beauty, however, was more of a factor in the theater than in most other professions. In 1900, for example, about 17 percent of all male actors were over the age of forty-five, compared to 4 percent of female actors.[19]

Several factors combined during this period to create new opportunities for women in show business. First were the greater freedoms and responsibilities granted to women in American society. In addition, the stage itself was gaining respectability as an honorable profession and as a legitimate career choice for young women. This was fueled in large measure by the explosion of theater in the United States. By 1900 there were three thousand theaters across America and 392 touring companies traveling throughout the country performing musicals and dramas.[20] The amazing growth in show business corresponded to the growth of great urban centers, an increase in leisure time, and the rising influence of specialization, affecting both work and recreation. "Entertainment was no longer sought in one's home or place of work, but in specialized venues of pleasure: the billiard parlor, racetrack, dance hall, baseball field, theater. Leisure time, moreover, lengthened considerably. The average work week in nonagricultural industries decreased by almost ten hours between 1850 and 1900, from 66 to 56 hours, then fell even more sharply from 1900 to 1920 to about 45 hours. Both opportunity and inclination, then, encouraged a quickened pursuit of amusement."[21] And so in the late 1800s, women were flocking to careers in the theater: "From 1870 to 1880 the United States census showed an increase in the number of actresses from 780 to 4,652, a rise of about 496 percent. In the period from 1890 to 1910 that number grew by almost 232 percent, from 4,652 to 15,436, and then spurted another 29 percent in 1920 to 19,905."[22]

As Susan Glenn has pointed out in her excellent study connecting women in theater to the birth of modern feminism, many of these women were creating their own brand of humor: "On the turn-of-the-century stage, women, though still the targets of comedy, were increasingly becoming the active agents of laughter, and categories like 'girl comedian' and 'funny lady' were entering the American cultural vocabulary."[23]

Irwin certainly was a major popular star and possessed her own inimitable style, but did she differ from her peers in any significant manner? I maintain that one would be hard-pressed to find a female comic entertainer of Irwin's time who employed such a wide variety of strategies to reach and hold on to success, strategies that so clearly reflect so many aspects of the culture—from domestic feminism to the cults of personality and professionalism to the nativist impulse to the dawn of the Progressive movement.

Like many of her peers, May Irwin was a white female comic and singer of considerable girth, who used her physicality for comedy and gained fame on the vaudeville circuit. However, because she worked for a time as a legitimate actor in Augustin Daly's prestigious company and in her later farces portrayed assertive women who were romantically successful (rather than sad, rejected "fat girls" or sexually aggressive "hot mamas"), her appeal had a level and breadth not often attained by her colleagues. Additionally, her private life was seemingly blameless—helping deflect potential criticism of her behavior. And once she gained financial security, she retained it throughout her life. A brief look at a few of her contemporaries illustrates these differences.

Trixie Friganza (1870–1955) had a long career, first as a slender chorus girl and then, when she grew corpulent, as a song-and-dance vaudevillian, singing self-deprecating songs such as "No Wedding Bells for Me" and often accompanying herself on a tiny ukulele. But Friganza never gained true stardom and encountered major publicity problems when she aligned herself with women's suffrage.[24] Faye Templeton (1865–1939) began her career as a singer of light opera. After she became stout, she delighted her audience with a "comedy skit that featured her being pushed on stage in a rolling chair."[25] Faye's life was plagued by multiple failed marriages and bankruptcy. The inimitable Marie Dressler (1868–1934), an actress of considerable athletic ability despite her weight, made the transition from stage to film in the highly successful *Tillie's Punctured Romance.* Dressler's comedy depended on her unattractiveness and inability to find romance. Her real-life affair and marriage to Jim Dalton were marred by his alcoholism and gross mismanagement of her finances.[26] Eva Tanguay (1878–1947) became the famous "I Don't Care" girl, with her whirlwind dancing and overt sexuality. Tanguay commanded one of the highest salaries in vaudeville, but she also earned controversy with her numerous affairs, marriages, and temperamental outbursts. Long before her death, she had lost all of her considerable fortune and her health. Many of her medical bills and financial needs were met through the generosity of her friend Sophie Tucker.[27]

Sophie Tucker (1884–1966), arguably the most celebrated and well-known early female comic, had a career that overlapped Irwin's. Because Tucker thrived during a later period than Irwin, she was able to bridge the transition to mass media, and her name is more broadly recognized today. Tucker may have been financially successful and able get away with "naughty" jokes by "creating a 'free zone' where the unmentionable could be acknowledged and laughed about," but her aggressive sexual appetite (at least in her public persona) and her tendency to play up her unattractiveness (an oft-repeated story has her donning blackface in her early years because of her ugliness) distinctly place her in a different category than Irwin.[28] Sadly, Tucker's reputation was hampered by her history of three failed marriages and a child she abandoned to be raised by other members of her family.[29]

Why have there been no full-length studies of May Irwin? The reasons are manifold. Entertainers whose roots were in vaudeville have generally been neglected until fairly recently. Both Marie Dressler and Sophie Tucker left autobiographies. However, the first biography of Dressler was published only in 1997, with two more studies appearing in 2006 and 2009.[30] Although an interesting fictional memoir of Tucker exists, Armond Fields's biography of her did not come out until 2003. Despite excellent partial coverage in dissertations, neither Faye Templeton nor Trixie Friganza has received her due. Eva Tanguay, arguably the most popular vaudeville star of her day, received her first biography only in 2012.

May has also been forgotten because, unlike Dressler and Tucker, she never fully made the leap into film, which limited her exposure to later generations. Surely, a third important reason is simply the difficulty in researching Irwin's life. Unlike Sophie Tucker, Irwin did not leave a large amount of private material to posterity, and unearthing her past requires extensive research. Works that include brief sections on Irwin usually simply echo the sentiments expressed again and again during the peak of her fame, dubbing her "the most beloved woman of the period" and a performer with a comic genius "devastating to the vaudeville audience."[31]

The largest body of primary evidence available for a study of May Irwin exists in old newspaper articles and performance reviews and in the many articles that Irwin herself wrote for magazines such as *Green Book* and *Cosmopolitan.* Theater journals from the time also include interviews and short pieces on aspects of Irwin's life. Irwin's cookbook, written in 1904, is readily available in libraries and online.[32]

In the course of my work, I have discovered that there is no single repository of these materials. Irwin herself hinted that she stored a literary manuscript in her luggage, composed of incidents in her "everyday" life, but that work has yet to appear.[33] Instead, information is scattered throughout several archives and private collections, and research requires many hours reading through newspapers and searching for sources in archives. The largest collections are available at the New York Library of the Performing Arts, the Library of Congress, Hawn Memorial Library, and the Thousand Islands Museum, the latter two both in Clayton, New York, where May retired. Many other libraries and archives also have holdings. Over time I was able to peruse and procure hundreds of newspaper articles, playbills, and photographs. Alas, only a few personal letters still exist. The researcher must hope for glimpses of the private May through her highly public image.

My most interesting research, however, proved to be through personal contacts in Clayton and in Canada. For example, Jack Brown, of Mallorytown, Ontario, Canada, has a scrapbook of articles about Irwin clipped from newspapers from upstate New York and Canada, as well as a variety of newspapers in the states. A videotape of one of Irwin's silent home movies, given to me by "Ragtime Bob" Darch (a New York ragtime pianist who has since died), provided invaluable information. This movie, made at Irwin's island home sometime during the late 1920s or early 1930s, shows the older May Irwin impersonating her earlier performance style. (The original of this film is in the Thousand Islands Museum.) Ragtime Bob also shared with me a large selection of sheet music and enjoyed playing selections from Irwin's wide repertoire for me. The wonderful Karen Killian of Clayton has an extensive collection of May memorabilia and has never wavered in her enthusiasm or willingness to share. Many others in the Thousand Islands area and in Canada shared their research and personal memories with me. (Many of these individuals were quite old when I began my research and have since died.)

A final major reason Irwin has been forgotten is also, paradoxically, one of the most important reasons for remembering her. Irwin was closely associated with the birth of the "coon song," a style of ragtime singing replete with racist imagery depicting African Americans. Although many singers of her time—both male and female, black and white—sang these numbers, not only is Irwin one of the most renowned "coon shouters," but she was also tied to a particularly racist, violent number, "The Bully," which had a long hold on the American imagination. Much of the history of these songs and their singers has been erased because of its distastefulness. From at least the mid-1980s, however, scholars have followed Sam Dennison's lead in *Scandalize My Name,* a landmark study of racist imagery in song, published in 1982. Since this period, there has been growing interest in these songs and their connection to race and gender in post-Reconstruction America. Thus, a possible reason for May Irwin's disappearance becomes a reason for a deeper consideration of her performance of this number.

In 1997 I changed locations to become the theater director at a small Catholic women's college in Indiana. Although May went on the back burner for a while, I continued my research as time allowed and would occasionally uncover some new information or receive new material from others.

During this period, I also began performing some of Irwin's music and comedy with colleagues and students. Two of these performances were at the Clayton Museum, a space in which May actually performed. After the success of the first performance, the museum awarded me a New York Arts Grant to put together a second piece. For this performance, I invited two actors to join me in reviving excerpts from some of May's most successful productions, intertwining these pieces with music and commentary. The results were well received—I was surprised by the durability of much of the humor and intrigued by audience questions concerning Irwin's life and times.

As I renewed my efforts and began revisions with a fresh eye, I was quickly able to establish that no significant new research on May Irwin had come to light during my hiatus. In fact, the superficial and sometimes inaccurate accounts on Irwin that I saw in a number of new books on vaudeville and women comics strengthened my resolve to pursue further research. For example, although Armond Fields's collection of biographical profiles of women in vaudeville comprises a much-needed and generally well-documented source, he does have errors in May Irwin's section.[34] She was not, as Fields has reported, the eldest of two girls; she was the youngest of five children (three boys and two girls). Additionally, May's sister, Flo, did not retire early from the stage and remain close with her. In fact, Flo performed for most of her life and had a fierce (and often bitter) rivalry with May. Many studies neglect to note—or remark only in passing—that Irwin did not perform coon songs in blackface. Instead, she is included with women for which "blackface provided an immediate cue to the audience about how to read their acts."[35] In some articles, even the content of Irwin's songs is described incorrectly. Irwin's most famous number, "The Bully," is sung in the persona of a black male bragging about killing the "other Bully," so he can be the "only one boss bully" in town. In her article "First of the Red Hot Mamas: 'Coon Shouting' and the Jewish Ziegfeld Girl," Pamela Brown Lavitt incorrectly notes that

"The Bully" "farcically depicts the vengeful rage of a black *woman* against her adulterous spouse."[36] Short Internet biographies often include errors as well.

Fascinated by Irwin's status as a coon shouter, I began to look closer at African American performance history. How did black Americans react to coon shouting? What coon songs did female African American performers sing? Using some of my findings, I staged a program, *Reconstruction to Ragtime,* that looked at Irwin's work in connection with a black female performer, Belle Davis, who did impressions of Irwin singing "coon songs." Supported by an Arts Grant and the local chapter of the National Association for the Advancement of Colored People (NAACP), I asked a professional African American actress to portray Belle Davis, while I performed May. This hall of mirrors stimulated lively discussions with the audience about race, gender, and the history of the late nineteenth century. I began to think about what audiences laugh at—then and now—and why. Theory and practice bumped against each other, strengthening my understanding of both. Meanwhile, I was contacted by a documentary filmmaker and was able to add my voice to a film about May Irwin, Marie Dressler, and Eva Tanguay.[37]

All of my findings to date have culminated in this book. My study is both critical and historical. In reviewing the life of a major comic entertainer, I look at how her strategies for success—both conscious and unconscious—reflect the culture in which she flourishes and simultaneously contribute to that culture. I compare her to her peers and consider her particular style of comedy and personality, illuminating ways in which women performers have used comedy to enhance their own power, both within their profession and in society at large.

The organization of my study focuses on the major components of Irwin's public persona. Chapter 1 covers Irwin's early years up to her success in *The Widow Jones* in 1895. I examine Irwin's choices and fortunes and how they were aligned with developments in vaudeville, theater in general, and the surrounding economic and social conditions.

Chapter 2, "Stardom," considers the string of farces in which Irwin gained fame and how her stardom connected to her particular audience and her particular talent and physical characteristics. Importantly, I analyze how Irwin internally balanced traits of talent, skill, and attractiveness and how this balance was one of the keys to her overall success.

The third and fourth chapters take on the complicated case of the coon song in American history and Irwin's role as a promoter of coon shouting. These chapters are certainly the heart of my study, for it is in her rendering of

"The Bully" that Irwin achieved her greatest success. The song's relationship to the triumph of Jim Crow and the birth of the image of a new "dangerous" urban black is undeniable. Here I complement research that clarifies how disempowered groups use even less powerful groups to enhance their own status. Additionally, I analyze the possible ramifications of the popularity of a white female's adoption of black personae of both sexes, adding to scholarship on the intersection of race and gender.

Like other strong women of the late nineteenth century, Irwin shrewdly coupled her domestic talents with her professional life. Chapter 5 focuses on the way she was able to create this successful blend, particularly in her publication of a well-received cookbook. In Chapter 6, I discuss the political and social causes that May championed and explore the degree of influence she was able to wield in those areas.

My final chapter, "The Road to Rainbow's End," traces May's later years and summarizes what I have concluded were her five interconnected strategies for success onstage and in public life. I also include an epilogue that raises questions about performing May's material today.

In the late 1970s, I read a short story titled "The May Irwin–John C. Rice Kiss." I had completely forgotten about it until, in 2006, I found an old copy while cleaning out one of my bookcases. The story is about a film buff and his search for love. He writes that movies deny time and death—but never love. Then he lists some of the scenes that have stayed in his mind: "Robert Montgomery entering a restaurant with his topcoat thrown over his shoulders; Joseph Cotton watching Valli walk past him in the autumn Viennese cemetery; Dana Andrew's swiftly suppressed smile at Gene Tierney . . . that long dead couple whose kiss arrested the world."[38]

May should not be remembered, if she is at all, as a fifteen-second flickering image. Her story has long deserved to be told. May this offering serve as a beginning.

1

Never Were There Such Devoted Sisters

> The curtain rose on a group of harvesters, boys and girls, busy about a haystack. Smirks and gestures of purport easily grasped by those in the audience not too drunk to understand were a prelude to the exit of all but one couple. This couple repaired to the back of the haystack. Then the others returned, and the boys, one by one, with simpers, gigglings, and pointings and suggestive calls visited the girl behind the stack. As each returned to the stage his expression registered what had happened. The finale was the exit of one of the boys in disordered clothing.
>
> —Douglas Gilbert, *American Vaudeville: Its Life and Times*

Risqué acts such as "The Haymakers" were at the heart of the new "variety" theater that thrived in America's saloons in the 1860s. An alternative to the legitimate theater, whose prices had skyrocketed after the Civil War, these shows offered male-only audiences a succession of musical numbers peppered with bawdier fare. Men of all social classes intermingled to drink, gamble, and get an eyeful of the "'legmania' dancers who wiggled their hips suggestively or kicked high to expose their 'drawers.'"[1] With increased leisure time, however, women and "respectable" men were clamoring for their fair share of entertainment in a secure environment. Theater managers began to clean up their acts, both figuratively and literally.

The credit for sanitizing variety and ushering in the new age of vaudeville is usually given to Tony Pastor. As a child and young man in the 1850s, Pastor sang at temperance meetings and performed in blackface for minstrel shows. After a stint touring with the circus, Pastor worked in New York as a comic singer and wrote and published some popular songs. He was in his late twenties when he teamed up with Sam Sharpley to open Tony Pastor's Opera House at 201 Bowery Street in New York. As time went on, Pastor began to consider the idea of building a more respectable type of variety show, one that would attract women and a general mix of working- and middle-class audiences who could enjoy good, clean entertainment for less than half the price of a ticket to a Broadway show.

The transition from variety to vaudeville was not an orderly one. The word *vaudeville* was derived from the French *voix de ville*,[2] or "voice of the city," and in the 1700s was loosely applied to musical and comedy entertainment. It became, in late-nineteenth-century America, a term used to describe "a series of individual acts strung together to produce a complete bill of entertainment."[3] From the 1890s until its gradual diminishment in the late 1910s after the birth of the motion picture, vaudeville was the most popular form of entertainment in America.[4] During vaudeville's heyday, a magazine produced for the managers and performers of amusement parks was able to say of vaudeville: "The women and children of America spend the greater part of $900,000 every week in proclaiming it the cleanest and most wholesome form of modern entertainment. No other theatre bears the same relation to the family circle. Cater to the women and children and the men will follow—it is a motto that has made millionaires of the great vaudeville caterers of the United States."[5]

The most complete contemporary analysis of the variety show as the precursor of vaudeville is Gillian Rodger's *Champagne Charlie and Pretty Jemima: Variety Theater in the Nineteenth Century*. Rodger examines how the small "free and easies" of the 1830s and '40s grew into larger venues and "the ways that the performances themselves represented the interests, aspirations, and desires of their audiences."[6] Because Irwin's early success (and, indeed, most of her subsequent work) was based in New York City, Rodger's careful delineation of the use of the terms *vaudeville* and *variety* within Manhattan itself—as opposed to the rest of the theater world—is particularly relevant to May's career.

In the late 1860s and early 1870s, the name vaudeville—often paired with burlesque—could be applied both to legitimate acting companies and to the more risqué performances that historians generally refer to as "variety." Rodger surmises that the latter use of the word *vaudeville* in New York may explain Tony Pastor's preference for *variety* as a label for his clean, family-oriented fare. She underlines the necessity of unpacking the use of the two names because "it illuminates the tensions between sexualized and respectable performance that were present within the form for its entire history."[7]

Tony Pastor's desire to reform variety reflected his keen interest in courting more women to attend the theater. Although Pastor professed great admiration and affection for women as morally superior to men, Sophie Tucker noted, in 1908, that probably "he just figured that if you could sell five tickets to a family you made more money than by just selling one."[8] (Profit had become more important than ever after the panic of 1873. This depression outlasted the previous panics of 1837 and 1857, ending nearly five years after the initial failure of Jay Cooke and Company.)[9]

Of course, women had been in theater audiences before the 1870s. As historian and critic Rosemarie Bank has noted, "The frequency with which women are erased from antebellum theatres at the same time they are identified in antebellum theatrical records recommends a certain caution about accepting the image of reluctant femininity." Many theaters began to include matinees in the 1850s, and the renovation, a decade earlier, of the "pit" to include comfortable seating (not to mention renaming it the "parquet") certainly made theater attendance more welcoming to women. However, troubling financial times surely increased theater efforts to attract women. In 1875–76 free "ladies' nights"—with male chaperones—were introduced in Brooklyn to try to prevent closures caused by economic conditions.[10]

As Rodger has pointed out, the panic of 1873 not only encouraged the "cleaning up" of variety in order to attract more women, but attracted the attention of reformers and temperance leaders as well: "Contemporary thinking connected personal failure to national failure, and in the midst of economic crisis and on the cusp of the centenary, anxiety about the nation's moral health ran high."[11]

Connected to the zeal for reform was an important bill passed in New York City in 1862—the Anti-Concert Saloon Bill—which prohibited alcohol or waitresses in the theater itself as well as in the lobby and connected rooms. The importance of this bill, despite its many infringements,[12] cannot be overstated. The emergence of clean variety and vaudeville owes much to its existence and continual reinforcement throughout the nineteenth century.[13] As reforms grew in significance, Pastor's move to Fourteenth Street in 1881 helped to solidly establish vaudeville as a family affair, prohibiting smoking and drinking in the audience and attracting a broader clientele.[14]

Acts in the vaudeville theater came in a wide array of shapes and sizes. There were the "gold bricks," or acts featuring stars of the legitimate stage, such as one of the Barrymores, or concert musicians, or opera stars.[15] There were the animal acts, such as Fink's Mules or "Rahlander's Pigs" (the trainer wore a butcher's uniform and carried a carving knife as a training baton!).[16] There were magicians, female impersonators, male impersonators, acrobats, and jugglers. Cissie Loftus did impressions. Lew Dockstader performed in blackface. Weber and Fields did physical comedy and supposedly were the first team ever to ask the question "Who was that lady I saw you with last night?"[17]

By the turn of the 1880s and 1890s, vaudeville was at the heart of popular American culture. There was no better place for a city dweller to escape from the frantic pace of American life—the bustling traffic of new electric trolley cars carrying women to department stores such as Marshall's or Wanamaker's, the latest news of mounting labor strife and violence, and the rising voice of suffragettes demanding the vote for women. In the vaudeville theater, the weary customer could enjoy the latest "coon song" (ragtime melodies with lyrics in "Negro dialect") and revel in the fantasy of pastoral skits. And he or she could see any number of sibling acts—brothers and sisters who sang, told jokes, and danced. There were the Dolly Sisters, the Ritz Brothers, the Duncan Sisters, the Cherry Sisters, and the Nicholas Brothers. One of the most successful of the early sister acts was the Irwin sisters, May and Flo.

Born Georgina (Georgia) May Campbell on June 27, 1862, in Whitby, Ontario, Canada, Irwin was the youngest of five children. Her parents, Robert E. Campbell and Sophronia Jane Draper, farmed a 250-acre homestead outside of Whitby, and Robert gained success in the pine lumber business. Robert was a native Canadian, descended from Hugh Campbell of the Scottish Clan Campbell. The Campbell clan originated in the thirteenth century in Argyllshire, Scotland, and was often at war with neighboring clans over cattle theft and territorial holdings. Hugh moved to America in the late eighteenth century and married. After his first two children were born, he relocated his family to the Kingston Township in Upper Canada and raised nine more children. His second son, John, was May's grandfather, who continued the Campbell tradition of large families with a brood of ten children. Most of the Campbells lived uncommonly long lives for the time, well into their seventies and eighties. John was a prosperous mill owner who became a preacher when he "converted to God" and a staunch advocate of temperance.[18] May's family spent some of her early years just outside the town of Whitby at her grandfather's farm, before renting a house owned by her wealthy uncle Chester Draper.[19]

The year before Georgia's birth, the family owned a lot and house valued at $2,000, two carriages valued at $60, and one horse and one cow valued together at $120.[20] Although initially the family prospered, Robert apparently spent money recklessly and led the family into bankruptcy, after which he left the lumber business and became an express agent for the town of Whitby.[21]

Even in her youth, Georgia's talents and personality were noted by her neighbors: "She was always merry and bright. She was short and plump and used to come singing down the street. I remember quite well hearing her sing that song of Topsey's [*sic*] about 'Golly I'se so wicked.'"[22]

Georgia and her older (and only) sister, Adeline Flora (Addie) Campbell, were boarders at St. Cecilia's convent school until their father's failure in business forced them to return home. At home both girls were noticed for their remarkable singing talents in the local church choir. Irwin remembered those early days: "Singing came naturally to me. . . . My voice never had any cultivation. I harmonised as naturally as I talked, my voice was naturally placed, and I produced tones by the law breathing taught me, not by any other rule. All through my childhood I sang in all the cantatas and such folly that is a part of going to school."[23]

When the sisters' father died suddenly in 1874 and left the family without any money, Mrs. Campbell decided to find her two girls a life on the stage in the United States (the older three brothers were all working as clerks in Canada by this time). In an interview in 1908, Mrs. Campbell explained her decision this way:

> When they were little things their father died, and there was trouble about a will. By a technicality of the law we lost everything. In a village a few miles out of Toronto I thought out the problem of how best to earn a living. For six months I tried out a boarding-house. The tradesmen became clamorous. Most of the household furniture went to satisfy their claims.
>
> The girls, who were twelve and fourteen years old, were both bright. They could dance almost as soon as they could walk. They could sing. I thought they had talent for the stage. I had a brother who was wealthy, and wanted to adopt them. I was determined to keep them myself. When I talked to him about putting them on the stage he was shocked. He looked as though he was going to faint. He begged me not to disgrace the family.[24]

And so May's mother—evidently determined to "disgrace the family"—took her two girls, all dressed in black, to a hotel in Rochester, New York, early in 1875, with a total of one hundred dollars. Mrs. Campbell explained her circumstances to the hotel landlord and requested an introduction to a theater manager. She declared that she and her girls would "rather die" than live on another family's charity and that Georgia and Addie could sing and play piano like "angels." From this time on, Mrs. Campbell and her daughters would remain in the United States.[25]

In addition to the multitude of European immigrants, many vaudeville entertainers in late-nineteenth-century America were, like Georgia and Addie, originally Canadians. Top stars on the circuit, such as Marie Dressler and Eva Tanguay, hailed from Canada. Both also suffered financial hardship because of unsuccessful fathers. Marie's father was an abusive parent, unable to earn a living because of his "erratic behavior."[26] Eva's father died early and left his family impoverished.[27]

The fact that many actresses of this period entered show business out of necessity rather than through choice was often publicized to bolster their popularity. Certainly, May was no exception to this rule. She was particularly adept at emphasizing a work ethic honed from hardship and a child's love of her mother, claiming that, during those difficult early years, she had but "one religion . . . and that was to work hard and to help my mother."[28] Her close relationship with her mother continued throughout her mother's life. When Irwin was asked later to reveal the secret of her continual successes, she would nearly always cite her mother: "Why, [I attribute my success] to my mother, of course. Why, I've got the best—yes, sir, the very best mother God ever gave a woman. If there's anything good in me you must blame my mother for it."[29]

Fortunately, Mrs. Campbell's pleas in 1875 to a landlord resulted in the girls landing a tryout for manager Daniel Shelby. After rehearsing the children for a few weeks, Shelby sent them to a small variety house in Buffalo for a six-week trial before signing them to a contract. The girls made their debut in "dresses so short that their home-made and unadorned pantalettes fell far below their skirts" and in "ghastly" pink stockings. When they attempted to sing a duet, Georgia fainted, leaving Addie to sing both parts. However, Georgia quickly recovered and returned to the stage, shouting out to her mother, "Don't be afraid, Mamma, this time I'll be real good and not get sick."[30]

This story was retold innumerable times throughout May's career, with many minor discrepancies among the versions. The major events remained the same, except for the question of *which* sister fainted before that first performance. In later retellings, it was always Addie who fainted. Even Flo herself (Addie's stage name) in 1922 reminisced that she must have fainted, since she was the "delicate, fragile sister," whereas May was always "husky and robust." Reporters were adamant about this latter version, one writer even contending that "I do not believe May Irwin could faint if she tried!"[31] As Irwin's fame and reputation grew and she became the sister seen as more of a natural for the stage, the latter version may have seemed a more positive one for her to promulgate.

In any event, the Campbell sisters were a big hit in Buffalo, and after their six weeks Shelby sent them a contract and an invitation to return to Rochester. Upon their return, the girls could not find their names on the billboard.

Shelby had changed their billing from Georgia and Addie Campbell to May and Flora (later shortened to Flo) Irwin.

In 1876 the Irwin sisters began a vaudeville tour of the Midwest—earning up to thirty dollars per week for their work. Touring was not easy for them. Financial necessity meant that both children performed during illnesses. (In subsequent years, May would recall a bout of smallpox that left her so weak that she had to be helped onstage when she began performing too soon after her recovery.)[32]

In the summer of 1877, in Detroit during a vaudeville tour, Flo and May got their big break when Tony Pastor saw the girls in a matinee and offered them a contract to open in New York. Their debut would be September 13, 1877. To the sisters, it was a dream come true: "It was a great thing for us, for Pastor's was the Mecca of all ambitious variety performers—it was like heaven to the pious. Just to get to Tony Pastor's and be happy was in the mind of every struggling artist the length and breadth of the land."[33] This story, underlined by Irwin's mother's testimony, contradicts the fact that the sisters are elsewhere listed as making their New York debut several months earlier at Henry Miner's Bowery variety theater house, the London, in January 1877. Perhaps playing at a house that had so recently been raided for serving alcohol to its patrons at that late date did not match the Irwin sisters' idea of a respectable venue.[34]

Flo and May toured with Tony Pastor for several years, specializing in duets and short comic skits with titles like "A Rural Stroll," "The Idol of My Heart," and "On Board the *Mary Jane*." They offered their performances alongside clog dancers, seriocomics, jugglers, and animal acts (such as Professor Parker and his dogs). The sisters worked together and solo, sometimes appearing in musical reviews and parodies, at other times constituting part of the olio entertainment following one of Pastor's comedies. Billed as "the beautiful and accomplished lady character duettists and sketch vocalists," May and Flo together received between sixty and eighty dollars for a week's performances. May Irwin recalled this period as one during which her skills grew enormously: "In addition to my turn with Flo, I used to do the leads in the burlesque which always wound up the evening, and those burlesques were not written out, you know. I used just to get instructions, so to speak, and go on and carry them out. It's great training, throws you on your own resources so. Why, I played everything from babes in arms—fact—to decrepit old women."[35]

Such an apprenticeship with Pastor was the early training of many stars. He was certainly responsible for much of the success of two other stars often linked with May Irwin in precipitating vaudeville's early movements toward welcoming women as respected and well-paid performers: Lottie Gilson and Lillian Russell. Lottie Gilson was contracted by Tony Pastor in the late 1880s as a singer, and, because of her charm, he gave her the nickname "the Little Magnet."[36] Unfortunately, her personal life was marred by a succession of unsuccessful marriages, bankruptcy, and early death. Lillian Russell, born Nellie Leonard, came to New York from the Midwest after her parents' divorce. She auditioned for Tony Pastor in 1880 (in some versions, without her mother's approval), and he immediately hired her, introducing her to his audiences as an "English ballad singer." She gained fame as Pastor began to produce full-length travesties, that is, affectionate mockeries, of light operas. The hugely popular Gilbert and Sullivan operetta *The HMS Pinafore* opened at the Boston Museum in 1878 and then ran for several months in New York in 1879. Pastor's spoof opened in February 1879, right in the middle of the "Pinafore craze."[37] (Indeed, the craze was so widespread that a story from this period claimed that when Arthur Sullivan was visiting the "Wild West," a rowdy cowboy offered to buy him a drink when he discovered that he was the composer of *The HMS Pinafore.*)

Rewriting Gilbert and Sullivan in what could be termed a "travesty of a travesty"—that is, a spoof of a work already brimming with parodies of the English ruling class and the conventions of serious opera—may seem like overkill, but it was a common practice of the time (and has continued in cinema and onstage, from 1945's *Hollywood Pinafore* to the popular *Pirates of Penzance* takeoffs of the 1970s). Although cultural differences between America and England that lessen comic effects are often the reasons for these parodies, the failure of Gilbert and Sullivan to secure adequate copyright protection in America during the 1880s was also behind the vast proliferation of these pieces during the late nineteenth century.[38]

Just as the word *variety* had more than one meaning in the nineteenth century, *burlesque* referred to more than one type of entertainment. In addition to its application to a wide variety of parodies of everything from grand opera to Shakespeare,[39] burlesque became associated with the tableaux vivants featuring nude (in flesh-colored tights, that is) figures arranged to create a "picture" and accompanied with live music. The initiation of *tableaux vivants* in America was connected with the immense popularity of actress Adah Isaacs Menken, who appeared, in 1861, "nude" as Mazeppah, strapped to the back of a horse, and the subsequent "girlie shows," such as Lydia Thompson and her British Blondes. Burlesque also became connected with the honkytonks and dance halls of the West.[40]

In any event, Pastor's burlesques were the vehicles through which May and Flo found national attention. They had begun working with Lillian Russell as chorus girls in *Our School Girls,* but in 1881 May appeared in the role of Freddy ("an indentured prowler" in this version) opposite Russell's Mabel in Pastor's next burlesque, *The Pie-Rats of Penn-Yan.*[41] Then, in 1883, May played Angela when Russell took the lead in Pastor's version of *Patience.* Russell herself fondly recalled her first days with Pastor: "May and Flo were on the bill when I opened at Tony Pastor's and May gave me my first lesson in theatrical make-up. Queer make-up it was in those days, too, as judged by the modern practice."[42]

Many stars began their work with Tony Pastor and then moved on, often with his blessing and assistance. After suffering the death of her first child and the end of her first marriage, Lillian Russell left Pastor to become one of America's top comic opera stars, returning again to vaudeville in 1905.[43] May chose another route. She and her sister had grown into young women under Pastor's tutelage, and both married in the late 1870s. Flo wed actor John Morris. May soon acquired a full family and attendant responsibilities, marrying German-born Frederick Keller in St. Louis in 1878 and giving birth to two boys shortly thereafter—Walter in 1880 and Harry the following year. Then, in 1883, Irwin seized a chance to work in the legitimate theater with the renowned Augustin Daly. Her decision to take the offer broke up the successful sister act: "Oh, I was ambitious, . . . and in an ambitious person's career all advances seem like heavens—like the Buddhists, you see, we have a series of heavens."[44] Years after May and Flo split up, they would be remembered as "the best sister team then appearing on the vaudeville stage."[45]

Initially, Irwin's time with Daly was far from heavenly. At Pastor's she had been allowed to follow her own instincts, but at Daly's she entered an altogether different atmosphere, one where she was expected to listen carefully to the director's criticism. Irwin remembered an early rehearsal as a complete disaster:

> The Guv'nor [the company's nickname for Daly] was sitting down in the auditorium, and his solemn voice informed me, "Not in the least like it!" "Well, I'll try again," and I did. Then up to me came the remark, "I wonder where you have left your intelligence this morning." It was the last straw. I had never been spoken to like that in my life. And before all the company! I tried to take a brace, but I could not, so I broke down and blubbered. It was the first time I ever did such a thing.
>
> "Go on," said the inexorable voice, but I could only sob, "Well, now, I guess you'll have to wait for me!" "Very well; skip that and go on," and I retired to

> a dark corner and cried as if my heart were broken. Pretty soon Daly hunted me up. "Come, come," said he, "you mustn't do this. I treat all my people alike. If you don't do well, you as well as I, will be criticized. It is for your sake as much as for mine." And that was the last encounter of that kind that we ever had.[46]

Augustin Daly was perhaps the first—and certainly the most renowned—of a new breed of manager-director who did not begin as an actor. After several years as a drama critic, he opened his first theater in 1869. Although he also wrote and directed his own original scripts, he achieved fame through his adaptations of French and German plays. By the time May Irwin joined, Daly's was the most esteemed company of legitimate comedy in America. As actor-playwright Otis Skinner recalled:

> When Augustin Daly fixed his name to a three-year contract for my services I felt like a spent swimmer to whom a lifesaver has been thrown. Five years before I had gone to him to ask for a hearing, and the word he returned to the agent who had furnished my credentials was that *I would not do.* Now he had come to me, but I needed him far more than he needed me. If any man was capable of beating the tricks of exaggeration out of me, it was Daly. His company was composed of expert comedians; his theatre was one of popularity and of fashion and his productions the most talked of in New York. . . . First nights at Daly's were such sought after events that he could select his audience from the representative names from town.[47]

Daly's success rested on strict control over every aspect of his productions, with a special emphasis on what he considered a natural acting style and attention to ensemble work. Younger members of the troupe had to learn the hard way Daly's disapproval of "breaking curtain" or "the fourth wall." As a minor player recalled, Daly approached her one day:

> "I am told that you were in the front of the house last night, although you appear in the fourth act."
>
> "Yes, Mr. Daly, I was," I replied, rather surprised, and wondering why anyone should take enough interest in the trifling fact to report it to him. "But," I hastened to assure him, "I got around to my dressing room and was ready long before it was time to go on."
>
> Then he informed me, greatly to my astonishment, that I had committed a grievous fault; no one in any kind of reputable theatre, he said, ever was seen in front during a performance in which he or she appeared; such an act was against all theatrical rules, and usually met with a fine or some sort of discipline.[48]

Later, the same actress committed another grave error:

> We were all highly flattered at [an audience member's] evident admiration, and I guess all of us smiled at him in a pleasant sort of way, just to show him that we thought he was very nice; but, my gracious, what a wigging we got from "the Governor" the minute the curtain was down on that act! He left Mr. Wallack in the box and came flying downstairs after us, called us from our dressing-rooms, and told us that we must *never,* under any conditions, notice any living creatures on the other side of the footlights; they must be to us as if they did not exist.[49]

In forbidding this young actress to appear outside of the stage frame during a show or to make direct eye contact with an audience member, Daly was following some of the tenets of the new style of realism in the legitimate theater. The famous Meiningen players from Germany toured widely in the last quarter of the nineteenth century, bringing fresh ideas to Europe and America about theater production. Sets and costumes were finished in great detail with a new focus on historical accuracy. The troupe discouraged stardom, and all players rotated from major to minor roles. Perhaps the most stunning success of the players was in their ensemble acting, with attention given to all members of crowd scenes. In keeping with the new needs for more naturalistic stagecraft, which required that players perform within the scenic frame and interiors instead of in front of scenery, proscenium boxes moved to the auditorium, and the forestage, which had previously extended in front of the proscenium arch, became much smaller.[50] The separation between audience and actors was becoming Richard Wagner's "mystic chasm"—a border not to be bridged.

Of course, the realism practiced by both Daly and the Meiningen players was one emphasizing production and not drama. Often labeled romantic realism, it did not adhere to the strict rules of true realism, which included the use of only contemporary plays treating contemporary problems—such as Henrik Ibsen's oft-censored social dramas.

The rigors of Daly's company brought discipline to Irwin's work. His notes on a performance of *Nancy and Co.,* a play in which Irwin was a hit in her role as servant, gives a clear picture of his demands:

> The performances of Nancy & Co. are drifting away from the true spirit of the piece—& from the condition desirable in a perfect representation.
>
> Some have grown listless—some slothful—some so by rote as to get their words and sentences tangled—gigglings and suppressed laughter are frequent and ill-disguised—some have become *so easy* as to give no *force* to their voice

> & their words do not carry half the distance of the house—others have grown to make unnecessary pauses and breaks—others hurry and talk through their laughs, altogether there is a lack of that freshness & alertness which I want to see at every performance.
>
> The spirit which can permit such a condition of affairs is unworthy of the members of my company. Out of it grows grumblings and mutiny—a spirit natural to the Rabble, and not to the Ladies and Gentlemen who are treated with the extreme consideration with which I treat my company.[51]

Rehearsals under Daly were long and demanding. One of Irwin's favorite, and oft-retold, stories concerned Daly's many attempts to teach her that onstage, sometimes an action must be elongated to be clarified. Once Daly told Irwin to enter a room in which she was supposed to smell burned fish. He instructed her to "sniff, look around and sniff harder. 'I at once objected right out loud. 'Why, no,' I said, 'that would be absurd. I should never look around a moment. I should go straight to the fireplace where the smell came from, of course."[52] Irwin said that it didn't take her long to realize that Daly knew more about stage business than she did. Thus, she learned what Denis Diderot famously called "the Paradox of the Actor": in order to look "natural," the actor must often be artificial.

Soon, however, the usually serious Daly warmed to Irwin, and the other actors delighted in the presence of someone who was "altogether a new species to the decorous Daly company." Otis Skinner, as her fellow actor in the company, noticed that "if, during a rehearsal, a little group was seen in a remote corner giving out smothered peals of laughter, it was pretty sure to be May Irwin, all curves and plumpness, entertaining her hearers with her Negro songs, an imitation or a bit of drollery."[53]

It is not a matter of small significance that Irwin was able to elicit warmth from Augustin Daly. He was a much-feared autocratic director, demanding, tireless, and impatient, labeled by writer Charles B. Davis as "a most crusty, dictatorial party."[54] Yet a certain childlike forthrightness that marked much of Irwin's behavior seemed to catch the stern taskmaster by surprise. She didn't treat Daly with the respect he required from other actors and was quick to "speak her mind straight out" to him, especially when she felt she had been miscast. But while Daly "managed to maintain his aloof attitude with the others," cast members noted that "Irwin could get away with anything." Her youthful displays of temperament were met with smiles and laughter and attributed to her innocence.[55]

Under Daly's direction, May worked with a distinguished company of players. John Drew Jr. (the uncle of John, Lionel, and Ethel Barrymore and great-great-uncle of Drew Barrymore) and Ada Rehan were Daly's leading players. Usually coupled as romantic lovers, they "wooed and quarreled and fenced and fondled, and danced, adored, and spat their way through many a comedy, old and new."[56] John Drew was known as a warm and generous actor who reached perfection in light comedy under Daly's direction and later achieved greater stardom on his own. Ada Rehan excelled in Shakespeare as well as in Richard Brinsley Sheridan's comedies and was thought to be Daly's mistress as well as his favorite actress.[57] Indeed, after Daly's death, she was "helpless. . . . [A]cting was no longer a pleasure; it was an obligation."[58]

During her years with Daly, Irwin succeeded in a number of small roles, most often portraying a series of clever maids, including the amusing Lucy in *The Recruiting Officer,* the jealous Popham in *The Magistrate* (who tries to win her man with her wonderful cooking skills), the awkward Irish servant Betsy in *Nancy and Co.,* and the emotional Susan in *A Night Off,* perhaps her most successful role at Daly's. As Susan, Irwin received acclaim in New York, Paris, and London for a scene in which she had a hysterical sobbing fit after attending the debut of her master's tragedy in the theater. (Irwin traveled to Europe with the company for two tours—one in 1884 and another in 1886.) She soon became the "most striking and vivacious soubrette of Daly's theatre."[59] However, although Irwin longed for a comic role in a Shakespearean play, Daly would not hear of it. When Irwin complained to him about his choice of actress Edith Kingston for a role she felt she should play in *The Merry Wives of Windsor,* he retorted, "My Dear, you are much too modern for old comedy."[60] (Years later, Irwin upheld Daly's decision concerning Shakespeare, suggesting that she could even turn the tragedies into comedies. She said she would like to portray Juliet and have a nice Manhattan cocktail for her sleep potion and change the end of Shakespeare's tragedy so Juliet could collect Romeo's life insurance and have a good time after his demise.)[61]

Many of Daly's contemporaries praised him on his adaptations of German farces reset in the urban America of the time. These were the productions that Irwin shone in: comedies such as *Love on Crutches, A Night Off,* and *Nancy and Co.* As critic George C. Odell summed up the general opinion, "Daly's adaptations from the German were usually so transfigured that characters and episodes seemed wholly of the American scene."[62]

Consequently, Daly was advised by his assistant William Terry not to take Irwin along on tours to England because of her "modern" style. Terry maintained that "her kind of humor is peculiarly American and would not be understood over there." To his credit, Daly ignored this advice, and Irwin's humor "proved universal. . . . [She had] a real spirit of comedy in her . . . [with] silences as fun as her speeches."[63]

In 1884 her "modern" performance as the cheeky Caroline in *Needles and Pins* won particular praise as an apt imitation of "a maid servant of the period and a solemn warning to all future eras." By the 1886 tour, the ensemble work of the company was so tight and disciplined that London critics maintained that *A Night Off* was a "piece so full of humour [and] so well-acted [that its equal has not] been seen in London in many years." Even writers who were ambivalent in their reaction—such as one who noticed during a performance of *Nancy and Co.* that in the audience, "many people would not begin to smile until someone else smiled and settled the point as to whether it was really very funny or only silly"—had to admire the technical skill of the actors. During the 1886 tour, the troupe also played in Germany, Italy, and France, where Irwin was supposedly singled out by critic Francisque Sarcey as a comic of particular genius.[64]

Her unique comic timing would become one of the essential elements of Irwin's style. Years later, she would reiterate her gratitude to Daly for teaching her the value of a well-placed pause: "One thing [that Daly taught me] was the pause before speaking the line that makes the point. For instance, in my present play [*Mrs. Black Is Back,* in 1905], Miss Burby says to me: 'Didn't you ever lie to your first husband?' I wait a full minute for the audience to get the embarrassing import of that question to me. Then I answer hesitatingly, 'N-n-o.' In that scene every line gets a laugh, and I ascribe it in part to our pauses to prepare the audience for the next point."[65]

In fact, the combined years of training from both Pastor and Daly may have given Irwin just the edge she needed to catapult to major stardom. Irwin herself claimed that she learned "self-reliance" at Tony Pastor's while performing in a variety of sketches and afterpieces. Pastor encouraged Irwin's quick pace of speaking, which served her well in vaudeville. Here, her natural abilities were allowed to run rampant, for Pastor seldom corrected her and she was "quite spoiled." Working for Augustin Daly, Irwin learned to harness her instinctive talents by speaking more deliberately, alternating the pace of her speech, and ending more sentences with an upward inflection. Thus, Pastor allowed Irwin to show her natural ability, and Daly helped her to add skill to it. In Irwin's view, the combination of natural ability and stage skills creates the most effective comic style: "Some are funny naturally, and some understand the knack or art of being funny without being naturally so; but the best humorist of all is the one who, in addition to a natural humorous perception, has developed the knowledge of how best to apply it."[66]

During her employment with Daly, Irwin experienced increasing difficulties in her home life. Her husband contracted tuberculosis and became seriously ill. She was now responsible for his welfare as well as the welfare of her mother and her two small sons. Her hectic life in New York included rushing back and forth from the stage to her home across town: "She would put on her costume at her apartment and then, with a duster covering the stage clothes, would ride by streetcar to the theater, arriving a few minutes before curtain call. While she was absent from home, an Irish nursemaid whom Miss Irwin had engaged would take care of Walter and Harry C. Miss Irwin would hasten back to the apartment at the conclusion of her act to be with the children."[67]

In 1886 Frederick Keller died, leaving Irwin a widow with two small children. She felt deeply the weight of her financial responsibilities. And she wrote to Daly, explaining that she could not pay for costumes out of pocket:

> Forgot to tell you my dress and hat will be here this afternoon about four. Dress is $87.00. Hat is $18 or $20—they could not just say—I would have paid myself—as always and sent them to you later but I did not have the money to spare,
>
> Yours Respectfully,
> May Irwin[68]

At this time Irwin was making forty-five dollars weekly, with a contract that stipulated periodic raises. By 1887 she was receiving sixty dollars weekly with a promise of an increase to sixty-five dollars in 1888. Although at this salary Irwin was earning two and a half to four times as much as minor players, she still brought home less than half the wages of major stars such as John Drew and Jane Levin. Irwin certainly showed her shrewd nature in her additions to her contracts—such as the right to keep all of her clothes and to expect fair adjustments in salary for the extensions of runs. (Only one other actress added a similar request—and that was to keep half of her clothes!) In the spring of 1887, Irwin asked Daly's permission to accept other engagements and demanded that he inform her immediately what his plans were for her: "Now do not misconstrue my way of putting it for impertinence—I only mean to be honest. I have too much responsibility resting on me to be content to wait for your decision for a few weeks—(you must know that without my telling it)."[69]

But Irwin's time to move on was approaching. Armed with what she had learned about variety from Tony Pastor and about acting in legitimate theater from Augustin Daly, she decided to return to vaudeville. In the end, it was money that convinced her to return: "When an offer of three times my Daly salary came, just to do a single turn with the Boston Howard Athenaeum Star Specialty Company—well, I couldn't resist it."[70]

So in 1887, only four years after joining Daly's company, May decided to leave. She once again teamed up with her sister, Flo, working predominantly at Howard Athenaeum, based in Boston. They appeared in vaudeville shows, such as *City Directory,* which were often big hits in New York as well as Boston. They also performed together in olios and benefits from 1887 to 1890. During the summer of 1888, May took time off from Howard's to tour the West Coast in *Jed Prouty. Jed Prouty* became a star vehicle for actor and adapter of the story Richard Golden, who played the role more than two thousand times during his life.[71] Much like critics of Irwin's later productions, reviewers found the play a weak, "farcical representation of a New England village," while admitting that Golden's superior performance skills "brought out remarkably well" the "Scotch-like dryness" of the character.[72]

During the tour with Golden, on the advice of a friend, Irwin began investing in mining shares—at one dollar each.[73] This lifelong habit of wisely investing money would serve her well. By 1901 she had acquired an island in the St. Lawrence River, a house and lot in Canada, an automobile, a steam yacht, and several properties in New York City, including a house at 165 West Forty-Fifth Street, houses at 142 and 144 West Twenty-Eighth Street, and a house and lot on Lexington Avenue and Fifty-Fourth Street.[74]

The real estate that would become most important to May in future years was her island in the St. Lawrence River, among the beautiful Thousand Islands near Clayton, New York—where the United States and Canada meet. Irwin never tired of retelling the story of how she first purchased land in the region. She said that she fell in love with the area when she was only a girl touring with Tony Pastor's company and she and the company were treated to a dawn boat ride in the Thousand Islands. Irwin declared that when she saw the glorious sunrise on the St. Lawrence River, "[I] made up my mind . . . that someday, if ever I had money enough to buy a home, I was going to own an island."[75]

Irwin's chance came in 1891. She and her sister, Flo, had a six-week hiatus between seasons. Flo was now suffering from tuberculosis, and May decided to take her to the Thousand Islands region for a rest. After paying for her children's summer schooling and for her mother's expenses, May left for Clayton on the train. There she rented a boat and filled it with provisions and, after a rocky night sleeping in a boathouse, managed to row to Club Island and find assistance. Club Island seemed to Irwin to be the place she had always dreamed of buying. After discovering that the owner of the eastern half of the island wanted to sell, she took all the money she had (two hundred dollars) and offered it as a down payment. It took Irwin two years to pay the remaining eighteen hundred dollars, but on September 19, 1893, the deed was transferred to her.[76]

Club Island is the southernmost of a little cluster of islands at the head of which lies the much larger Grindstone Island. In the first few decades of the twentieth century, Grindstone Island boasted a thriving community of farms and stores as well as its own post office and the Grindstone Methodist Church. Irwin shared Club Island with Mrs. Frederic Pruyn, a landscape architect from New York City who also happened to be the daughter of banking magnate William Fellowes Morgan. Nearby islands included Watch Island, belonging to a wool merchant from Boston; Whiskey Island, the home of Bernard Carter, who was head of a Paris bank owned by Morgan; and Papoose Island, bought as a wedding present in 1884 by Morgan for his betrothed. This elite group, called "the coterie at the head of the island," came to the Thousand Islands to spend their summers. According to local historian Stanley Norcom, Irwin and her fellow property owners "differed from other residents of the island in the fact that they had not come to Grindstone to farm or to cut granite or otherwise make their living there. They brought their incomes with them from the eastern cities . . . incomes that were not subject to the ups and downs of the internal economy of the island."[77] Before Irwin settled in as part of this "coterie," she had to nurse her sister back to health and return with her to tour in *Boys and Girls,* by John McNally. The two were now under Charles Frohman's management.

The 1890s witnessed major changes in basic theatrical organization. Just as Irwin left both Pastor and Daly, so had the general culture of entertainment in America left those giants behind. Theater entered the world of big business and monopoly. In 1896 Charles Frohman, along with other businessmen such as Marc Klaw and Abraham Erlinger, organized the Theatrical Syndicate, which was to operate a monopoly of the best touring productions by controlling a large group of theaters throughout America. Its headquarters was in New York City, by this time the uncontested capital of theater in America.[78]

Mirroring the theatrical syndicate, two New Englanders, both former circus workers, Benjamin Franklin Keith (1846–1914) and Edward Franklin Albee (1857–1930), worked together to consolidate strict control of vaudeville with a "quadruple circuit" operated through a single United Booking Office. To suit the modern pace of life, they instituted the new idea of the "continuous"—a revolving series of acts that never drew curtain (also called the "Ferris" system, after George Ferris's remarkable wheel, first unveiled at the 1893 World's Fair in Chicago).[79] The day of the small theater and the individual manager was gone.

By the mid-1890s, Pastor's management style had become anachronistic. He represented the fading tradition of independent theater owners who operated only one venue at a time and fitted in with neighborhood businesses. Compared to Pastor, Keith and Albee aspired to build a large circuit by owning or leasing many theaters in the East. Pastor was known as the actors' friend; he often loaned them money, cared for them during ill health, and sometimes paid for their funerals. Keith and Albee, by contrast, rarely associated with vaudevillians and preferred to let the local resident manager judge a show. Pastor personally disliked the ruthless methods of the new breed of vaudeville impresarios, and he was unable to adjust to the new commercial methods of the big time. He continued to lose topflight performers to Keith and other chains as they signed contracts that prevented them from entertaining at his and other opposition theaters. Unable to pay larger salaries, Pastor relied increasingly on new acts or old-timers. By 1900 the Union Square had supplanted Pastor's New Fourteenth Street as the number-one theater in the area. Keith and Albee had successfully "upstaged" the Impresario of Fourteenth Street.[80]

Independent theater owners like Pastor had suffered greatly during the panic of 1893, which was even more devastating in effect than its predecessor twenty years earlier. Beginning with the bankruptcy of leading railroads, this depression moved rapidly through American society: "Within six months, more than 8,000 businesses, 156 railroads, and 400 banks failed. Already low agricultural prices tumbled further. Up to 1 million workers, 20 percent of the labor force, lost their jobs—the highest level of unemployment in American history up to that point, a level comparable to that of the Great Depression of the 1930s."[81] Matched with Keith and Albee's ruthlessness were their puritanical beliefs. Keith's "prudish temperament" supported his declared objective of ridding the vaudeville stage of all "profanity and vulgarity."[82] For his part, Albee opened many performances with a speech to the audience, lecturing them on proper behavior.[83]

And so vaudeville entered an increasingly urbanized, fast-paced, consumer-based world. Along with these changes, Pastor's call for "clean variety" followed by Keith and Albee's vows of moral superiority conformed closely with a new spirit of cultural elevation in other aspects of society while also becoming intertwined with a literal cleanliness. "The White City" as an ideal urban center constructed especially for the 1893 World's Fair in

Chicago served as a model for future architecture.[84] New mass advertising promoted mass consumption by suggesting "that purity and physical well-being were essential components of the modern lifestyle, and that clean, modern, standardized goods were the way to avoid infections and corruption of the self."[85] (This emphasis on cleanliness was certainly connected to the growing resentment toward new immigrants from southern and eastern Europe—populations deemed "less white" than earlier immigrants. Organizations like the American Protective Association, which boasted a membership of nearly a half million in 1894, were devoted to stopping immigration completely. The more moderate Immigration Restriction League simply wanted to separate the "desirable" from the "undesirable.")[86]

The consumer culture and spread of advertising in the 1890s led to greater development of the star system. Of course, the star performer had been present in America at least since British actor George Frederick Cooke toured the country in 1810.[87] But the rise in combination companies in the 1870s and 1880s hastened the importance of stars in attracting crowds. (Combination companies featured one play for a long run, usually on tour, and sometimes filling in the cast with local talent.) Popular actors began to take their own vehicles on tour, and their public came to see the star—not the play in which he or she was headlining. There was more and more coverage of the lives of actors in the press, and in the 1890s a new profession emerged to guarantee even greater publicity: the press agent. Among the new breed were Charles Emerson Cook, who managed David Belasco, and Channing Pollack, who worked for Florenz Ziegfeld.[88]

It was in this new world that May Irwin's personal star rose to greater heights. In 1892 May opened in *Poets and Puppets,* Charles Brookfield's burlesque of Oscar Wilde's *Lady Windemere's Fan.* She managed to persuade Frohman to allow her to include a new tune by Charles Harris and to allow her character, Ophelia, to sing it. The story was that Irwin, while entertaining a party of friends, overheard a musician strumming a tune on his guitar. May was so taken with the music that she copied the tune and wrote down the words. It was a sentimental number—not at all comic—and Frohman was reluctant to allow May to sing it. But she prevailed, and it became one of her best-known numbers—and one of the few still sung today:

FIRST VERSE
A little maiden climbed an old man's knee,
Begged for a story, "Do, Uncle, please . . .
Why are you single, why live alone?

Have you no babies, have you no home?"
"I had a sweetheart, years years ago
Where she is now, pet, you soon will know
List to the story, I'll tell it all;
I believed her faithless, after the ball"

CHORUS
After the ball is over,
After the break of dawn;
After the dancers' leaving,
After the stars are gone,
Many a heart is aching,
If you could read them all;
Many the hopes that have vanished,
After the ball.[89]

From this point on, May began to work on her own in the farces that were to bring her status as a major star. In 1893 she appeared in both *A Straight Tip* and *A Country Sport,* by John McNally. In the latter piece, which played through 1894, she and her leading man delighted audiences with their "impromptu" dance with dressers' dummies.

Now May was truly leaving Flo behind. Certainly, Flo's stage career had continually been overshadowed by May's success. When she performed with May (they last performed together in 1892), she was known as the "shapely figure of the duo" and a "tall and rather stately beauty" who often "appeared in male attire." Flo supposedly "furnished the good looks of the partnership, while the other supplied the bulk of the talent."[90] She succeeded May for a time in productions of *The Widow Jones.* Inevitably, comparisons were made between the performing styles of the two sisters: "Where May is sometimes merrily boisterous Flo is oftener quietly cynical. May bubbles but Flo crackles. [Flo] sings with plenty of liveliness and humor, especially the Negro ballads, and in her dancing she has an advantage over her sister in that she weighs considerably less."[91]

The two differed in their "public" management of their private affairs as well. After her marriage to John Morris foundered,[92] Flo wed U.S. senator Thomas F. Grady, a marriage that lasted from 1887 until 1898 and ended in divorce. After the divorce, Flo was involved in a scandal with another woman's husband: she was accused of carrying on an affair during secret meetings at the Hotel Minot on Eighth Avenue in New York City.[93] Because May's first marriage ended in death and not divorce, she was exempt from that taint, but she also managed to avoid scandal when her marriage to actor Hugo Toland was announced in 1891. (Both denied the wedding, and although there was a hint of more than a "passing relationship"—bolstered by the actor's unnecessary appearance in Chicago during May's work there and his close attendance of May during a run of *A Straight Tip* in New York—the *San Francisco Chronicle* printed their denial under the heading "Only Good Friends," and the matter was quickly dropped.)[94]

May's ability to retain a "pure" image was an essential ingredient of her success. Popular prejudice against actors *did* lessen in 1890s America. In fact, as representatives of new popular culture, many actors became "objects of pride and envy." Nevertheless, old puritanical notions about the immorality of actors still existed in the late nineteenth century. English critic Clement Scott maintained that it was only the rare female actor who could survive with her purity intact. (Although Scott targeted actresses in general, Irwin responded personally: "Rats, I shan't lose sleep over what a donkey says behind my back.")[95]

May's flip answer notwithstanding, the public still nursed conflicting feelings concerning the morals of theater folk. Critic Benjamin McArthur has noted that although surveys of church members indicated their widespread attendance of theater productions, many conservative churches redoubled their efforts to discourage these activities in the 1890s, going as far as forbidding members' attendance at all theater events.[96] (Interestingly, when full-length films began to gain currency, the purity of the lives of film stars was compared favorably to the lives of stage personalities, who "slept and ate at irregular hours and travelled in close contact with members of the opposite sex.")[97] In the early decades of the twentieth century, however, there was enough of a change in attitude that when socialite Mrs. Stuyvesant Fish invited Marie Dressler to her house for dinner, "the actress told Mrs. Fish that she would boast to her mother of having dined with the noted socialite, [and] Mrs. Fish rejoined that she would be 'proud to tell my children that Marie Dressler dined with me.'"[98] Naturally, this compliment is undercut by its subtext, the implication of noblesse oblige; Mrs. Fish was being gracious in according a major star equal status.

May's greater success in personal relationships and in public acclaim played a part in a lifelong troubled relationship with Flo. Although she may have been Flo's savior during her illness in 1891, by 1903 the sisters were celebrating a reconciliation after reportedly refusing to speak to each other for nine years. Notably, May insisted there never had been "any serious quarrel."[99] But in 1900, Flo and May had argued over whether Flo should be allowed to take *The Swell Miss Fitzwell* on the road.[100] In 1908 and 1909, the Irwin sisters began another dispute—this time over whether Flo should be allowed to produce George Ade's one-act play *Mrs. Peckham's Carouse* and appear in the title role. Apparently, May refused to allow her sister to produce the show, which George Ade had sold outright to May for a sum of two hundred dollars. When Flo opened, instead, in *Mrs. Mix Mixes,* which was essentially the same play with a different title, May exploded. She said that she would have allowed Flo to play the sketch when she herself was not doing it, but Flo's present "bodily appropriation" of the material hurt her deeply and she was upset with her sister's "base ingratitude."[101]

In 1912 Flo told a reporter who mentioned May that she viewed her sister as "a millstone around my neck." She maintained that she hadn't seen her sister in five years and then impatiently asked the journalist, "Could we not talk about her for three minutes?"[102]

Flo was evidently determined to perform in *Mrs. Peckham's Carouse,* with or without her sister's permission, even if she had to leave the country to do it. In the summer of 1913, she played the lead role with her own company at the London Pavilion in England.[103]

The disagreement over *Mrs. Peckham's Carouse* was raging again as late as 1927, when George Ade wrote a letter to Flo, explaining that he had sold the sketch to May long ago and "never wept over the fact that I might have collected thousands of dollars in royalty. When May bought the play, I was an unknown, at least as a playwright. She took a gamble on a little story I had and won out and I was very pleased when the play made good. I am sorry now that she is not disposed to let you use the piece but I haven't any pull with her or the husband." Three years later, Flo and May were to have their last reconciliation and planned a reunion for Christmas, in Los Angeles, where Flo was then living. However, Flo died on December 20, 1930, at the age of seventy-one of a heart attack, which reporters speculated had been "brought on by excitement incidental to her sister's promised visit," and May traveled west to retrieve her body for burial in the family grave in Valhalla, New York.[104]

But these tribulations lay far in the future for May in 1895, when she opened in McNally's *The Widow Jones* as the title character, Beatrice Byke. In the *Widow Jones,* the "widow" escapes a band of gold-digging suitors by going to Maine and pretending to be the widow of a man who supposedly drowned the year before she arrived in the state. Instead, the formidable Miss Byke ends up with the man's daughter, his debts, and, finally, him. The play was an enormous success, and the response in New York so moved Irwin that she was unable to give a final thank-you note to the audience without bursting into tears.[105]

John C. Rice was Irwin's leading man, and in the show, when he courted Miss Byke, cooing that "I should like to put my arms about your waist," she quipped, "I don't believe you could." After joking about the size of her waist, Irwin added a comment about the size of another part of her anatomy, as Rice leaned in for a kiss: "The great advantage of having a big mouth is that, while you are kissing, you can go on talking."[106] This flirtation between Irwin and Rice became famous (infamous in a few circles) when it was captured in one of the first films released in this country. In 1896 *The Kiss,* as it was titled, re-created in Vitascope fifteen seconds from the play, providing one of the few chances that remain today to see Irwin in action.

Even more instrumental in giving her rising star a major boost was the song "The Bully," which Irwin sang in *The Widow Jones.* Like many of the songs in Irwin's vehicles, "The Bully" had little, if anything, to do with the play. Although this was a common practice at the time, it nevertheless disturbed some reviewers, who noted that Irwin "introduces vocalizations singularly inopportune with reference to the continuity of the play's action."[107]

According to Irwin, when the play moved from Brockton, Massachusetts, to New York, critics decided that the singer was getting a little too fond of her interpretation of "The Bully," so they decided to test her resilience by a cool reaction to the number: "Miss Irwin sang the first verse and the chorus and the rows of press critics in front slouched down in apparent indifference and disgust. The comedienne, noting this, began to anger. She clenched her hands encased in white kid gloves tightly and sang with more spirit than ever. Just below her sat 'Diamond Jim' Brady with a sour expression on his face. Looking directly at him Miss Irwin whirled through the verses and the choruses and then marched off the stage. As she finished it was Diamond Jim who led the thunderous applause."[108] May Irwin would rarely have to do without that "thunderous applause" for many years to come. She was now New York's reigning "Queen of Comedy."

2

Stardom

97 requests for free tickets
63 authors trying to sell new songs
47 requests for photographs
20 requests for autographs
12 proposals for new plays
12 suggestions for charity
1 request for endorsement of a business college
1 request to use her name for a new cafe
1 offer for her to purchase a trotting horse
37 solicitations to try toilet preparations
23 inquiries on home life
12 queries if Irwin is her real name
1 request for a picture of her as a child
3 requests for her to form a link in a prayer chain.

Sun, November 26, 1906

In the early 1900s, May Irwin's celebrity had grown to such an extent that she would be besieged on a weekly basis by a range of requests such as those listed above. Her rise from a favored soubrette and singer to a major star began in the years following the opening of *The Widow Jones,* which also featured what was to become her most famous number, "The Bully." (I will examine "The Bully" in depth in chapter 4.) By the turn of the century, critics viewed her as the "personification of humor," "the one distinctively funny woman on the American stage," and—because of the presumed scarcity of comic ability in women—"a person of enormous consequence in comparison with the male of her species" as well as "her sex's pride and joy in the matter of humor."[1]

Irwin's fame spread further with the distribution of *The Kiss* to "kinetoscope parlors," where individual patrons could view it by gazing into a coin-operated machine. (The original public showing on Vitascope used one of the first motion picture projectors, affording audiences the first "moving" close-up.) Again, *The Kiss* was about fifteen seconds, taken from the last act of

The Widow Jones, and featured May Irwin and John C. Rice in a conversation carried on through the corners of their mouths pressed tightly together and followed by a theatrically large kiss. It is an iconic film analyzed in a number of articles even to this day[2] and strong testimony to the popularity of *The Widow Jones.* Contemporary film critic Jonathan Auerbach has described it as "well-rehearsed and well-known to its viewers."[3] The film is viewable on a number of sites and accessible as of this writing from the Library of Congress website at https:www.loc/gov/item/006943.

Whether audiences thought the piece of film "scandalous," as is often reported in basic film overviews, is a matter of debate. After all, the same kiss in the context of the play was considered perfectly acceptable. Of course, there is a big difference between watching a kiss onstage and seeing that kiss enlarged several times! As one critic observed in 1896, "Magnified to gargantuan proportions three times over, [*The Kiss*] is absolutely disgusting."[4] However, it doesn't seem likely that *The Kiss* stirred up too much controversy, except in the most conservative corners. After all, even in prudish Boston, a reviewer noted with approval that *The Widow Jones* was the only place a man could go and see a gin fizz being mixed. In any event, widely respected film historian Charles Musser has noted, "*The May Irwin Kiss* became the most popular Edison film of the year [1896]."[5]

From her debut in *The Widow Jones* in 1895 to her success in *Mrs. Peckham's Carouse* in 1907, Irwin appeared in a number of comic farces, almost all of which were adapted with her in mind. These were the years of her greatest popularity and the years during which she reduced audience members of every description to helpless laughter. Indeed, when Irwin performed, "plump matrons grew purple-faced with glee," "young girls shrieked with voices that took all kinds of queer inflections," and "a bachelor in the balcony bumped his head on the railing doubling up." During these years, May's fortunes skyrocketed. By 1905, according to the New York census figures, she was living with and supporting her two sons, Walter and Harry; two servants, Lillian Cavenour and Sarah Victor; and Sarah's three children. Sarah would remain May's cook and close companion for many years.[6]

Irwin starred in the kinds of farces that—coupled with the popular London Gaiety musical—were the precursors of American musical comedy. The English and American farce-comedies of the 1890s enjoyed wide appeal on the American stage. They dealt with ordinary modern men and women and soon included samples of the new ragtime songs that would become closely identified with Irwin.[7] *The Widow Jones* was particularly popular—it ran from 1895 to 1897, was revived in 1901, and then went on tour in 1902.[8]

At first, Irwin seemed content to work under her manager, William Harris, completing a long run of *The Widow Jones* and opening in another hit, *Courted into Court,* also penned by John McNally. Irwin's character, Dottie Dimple, changes her mind about divorce proceedings from her jealous husband, Worthington Best Jr., but can't get the judge (who has fallen in love with her) to drop the case. Such was Irwin's stature by 1897 that she decided to break out on her own, forming her own company under her own management and leasing the Bijou Theatre. Now new plays would be created solely as vehicles for May.

Naturally, Harris was unhappy about the breakup, but already had backup plans in place, as he told a reporter (with thinly veiled ire):

> Miss Irwin severs her business connection with me at the end of this season, and both *The Widow Jones* and *Courted into Court* are controlled by me. . . . [N]ext to her, I know of no one who can play *Widow Jones* so well as her sister Flo. May has had better luck, and I do not think that half the good material in Flo has been brought out. . . . Yesterday, I also engaged Marie Dressler. She will become a member of the farce-comedy stock company, which I shall organize next year, and which will include . . . all the other members of May Irwin's present company. . . . *[T]he same contract holds good with all the principals in Irwin's company, and I shall hold each and every one of them. I prepared that contract to fit just such a contingency as this. . . . No: none of my companies will appear at the Bijou hereafter.* As for Miss Irwin, I wish her every success in her new venture. I know she will wish her sister every success in *The Widow Jones.*[9]

As a theater manager, Irwin stood on the shoulders of notable women managers who worked earlier in the century, from Charlotte Cushman and Laura Keene to a significant number of lesser-known but successful entrepreneurs.[10] With her business acumen and her training as both a vaudevillian *and* a legitimate actor, she had charisma and acting talent on her side and reached the height of her fame in a string of hits: *The Swell Miss Fitzwell,* by Henry du Souchet; *Sister Mary, The Belle of Bridgeport,* and *Kate Kip, Buyer,* by Glen McDonough; and *Madge Smith, Attorney,* by Ramsay Morris. She also managed to steal actor Nicholas Sparks from his "ironclad" contract with William Harris's company to play opposite her in *Kate Kip, Buyer* and successfully negotiated to star in revivals of *The Widow Jones.* This frenetic pace, however, took its toll, and in 1902, during the last revival of *The Widow Jones,* Irwin collapsed from overwork. Of course, actors and actresses have been "collapsing from overwork" for centuries and being sent to rest or rehabilitate. Irwin herself claimed that she was simply suffering from a "bunch of jumping nerves"—nothing to warrant "hysterics."[11]

Irwin recovered in a "rest home" in England, where she claimed to have spent a lot of time teaching her landlords how to cook, thus undercutting the nineteenth-century idea of strict rest for the overwrought female. Soon after her return, she published a cookbook complete with recipes, jokes, and illustrations. Irwin later joked darkly about her English resting home, where the walls were decorated with portraits of the former proprietor—freshly deceased and photographed in his coffin.[12]

In 1904 Irwin returned to the stage and to celebrity. She began to use a new manager, Kurt Eisfeldt, who had worked formerly for a variety of circuses—including Ringling Brothers—as her press agent. Irwin's first venture was in the highly popular *Mrs. Black Is Back,* which opened in 1904 and ran for two years—including a performance in Washington, D.C., for President Theodore Roosevelt. By 1906 Irwin was starring in another vehicle, *Mrs. Wilson, That's All* (later changed to *Mrs. Wilson-Andrews*), by George Hobart, with the addition of the curtain raiser *Mrs. Peckham's Carouse,* the little piece that would cause so much strife between May and her sister.

This was also a successful period for Irwin in terms of her personal life. On May 26, 1907, she married Kurt Eisfeldt in Thousand Islands, New York. The ceremony was informal and private—only Irwin's two sons and a minister from Clayton, New York, were present—and it took place in the unfinished home that Irwin was having built on her island property. The newspapers enjoyed pointing out that the bride wore a "yachting cap" and her sons wore "rubber boots" and "sweater[s] of several years' service."[13] Newspapers also underlined the age difference between Irwin and Eisfeldt. At the time of the marriage, May was forty-five, and his age was variously reported to be between twenty-nine and thirty-nine. (He was thirty-four.) Some reporters labeled the marriage part of a contemporary "craze for youthful husbands," but others contended that, in this particular instance at least, "love and respect weigh heavier than age."[14] Irwin once said of her Austrian-born husband, "Kurt . . . was a fine press agent and a fine manager. And he's as good on a dairy farm as he was on Broadway. Straight shooter, that's what he is. Only two words are needed to describe my marriage with Kurt—'big success.'"[15]

Kurt was surely a shrewd manager, with a long background as a horse trainer and business manager for the Ringling Brothers Circus. Born in Vienna, he moved to Wisconsin when he was very young and fell in love with the circus when it came to his town. He joined the Ringling Brothers, five brothers who had decided at a very tender age to start their own circus. Unlike some of their rivals, the Ringling Brothers tried to keep circus life blemish free in deference to their Lutheran grandmother.[16] Nevertheless, it was a rough life and may help explain Kurt's later reputation as a formidable stepfather. Rumors were that May's children did not care for Kurt's stern and uncompromising nature. May's great-grandson Scott Irwin maintains that his father told him that one of the brothers actually tried to dunk Kurt into the St. Lawrence River![17] But perhaps as a former circus manager, he knew how to advertise May's star quality. After all, circus advertising was so aggressive that the cry for more publicity during May's day was "sell it like a circus!"[18]

Irwin's honeymoon in the Thousand Islands was a short one. By June 1907, she had returned to vaudeville to work under Keith and Proctor. For May, this tour proved to be her most profitable ever: "If May Irwin, who is about to return to vaudeville after many years' absence, . . . elects to work only twenty weeks in the year, her salary will equal that of the President of the United States. Her salary for two weeks equals that paid a congressman for a whole year. In other words, Miss Irwin will receive $2,500 a week for appearing on the stage for twenty minutes twice a day."[19]

But Irwin did not stay on tour for long. Instead, she broke her contract on March 7, 1908, and went to Europe with her husband and one of her sons. During the next several years, Irwin began to cancel performances frequently and to announce her imminent retirement to her home in the Thousand Islands. Sometimes her cancellations were because of illness. For example, in 1908 she contracted pneumonia and spent time recovering in Arkansas and Florida.[20] Then in 1914, she had to cancel performances because of a chill caught when her train was delayed in cold weather. (For this incident, Irwin unsuccessfully sued Southern Pacific railroad for fifty thousand dollars!)[21] At other times, Irwin canceled performances in order to spend more time with her family, to attend to her duties in the Thousand Islands, or to assist in charitable undertakings. Once she ended a tour two weeks early in order to attend a meeting of the American Jersey Cattle Club.[22] In the same year, she suddenly canceled an engagement during the Christmas season to go home and spend time with her sons.[23] And in 1914, she decided to close a show in order to pass out dolls to poor children for the holiday season.[24]

Despite her cancellations, Irwin scored a number of hits between 1908 and 1915. In 1910 and 1911, while still threatening her impending retirement, Irwin toured in *Getting a Polish* (initially titled *Mrs. Jim*), written by Booth Tarkington and Harry Leon Wilson. Tarkington's comments on Irwin's performance revealed that she was in top form, indulging in her usual improvisations: "In writing this play, Mr. Wilson and I have merely played the part of jewellers endeavoring to furnish the setting in which a jewel of matchless luster would sparkle to the best advantage. When the Almighty bottled up half the fun in the world in the person of May Irwin, he made the generous provision that the surplus should at all times be leaking from every pore, for the benefit of others. I would be a villain did I seek to plug the leaks."[25]

Among Irwin's other successes during these years were *Widow by Proxy,* which opened at the George M. Cohan Theatre in New York in 1913 and toured as far west as San Francisco, and *33 Washington Square,* which in 1915 included a command performance in Washington, D.C., for President Woodrow Wilson. Irwin also filmed a version of *Mrs. Black Is Back* that was released by Paramount on November 30, 1914, and hailed as "four reels of clean, wholesome, sidesplitting comedy," in which Irwin made "her personality felt throughout."[26]

While the plays built around her reflected Irwin's star status, they were certainly not notable in themselves. A review of *33 Washington Square* asserted that "in all her years as a star May Irwin has seldom, if ever, had a really good play." *Mrs. Black Is Back* was pronounced "not very promising material out of which a play may be made," *Madge Smith, Attorney* was "a very poor specimen of its own poor kind," and *Kate Kip, Buyer* was called "inexpressibly stupid."[27] In fact, most reviews of Irwin's comedies remarked on the inadequacy of the plays themselves.

In spite of the quality of the material, however, May dazzled. A review of *The Belle of Bridgeport,* generally conceded to be one of Irwin's least successful ventures, praised Irwin while condemning the play: "May Irwin's Personal Humor and Vivacity Save a Stupid Farce." Other reviews were similar in their focus: "May Irwin Makes Thin Play Almost Plump," "So Much May Irwin, So Little Farce," and "May Irwin Very Pleasing in Very Poor Farce." Critics of the period often bemoaned the poor writing with questions such as "Did May Irwin make John J. McNally, or did John J. McNally make May Irwin?"[28] The answer was inevitably "yes" to the former.

Often critics would make fun of Irwin's vehicles by quoting bits of dialogue they considered particularly "stale." For example, in a review of *Madge Smith, Attorney,* the journalist cited lines like these:

> "I'll take a chair."
> "Don't take it too far."
> "Your conduct shall be checked."
> "You ought to be checked in the coat room."
> "I have a sudden palpitation of the Heart."
> "Take some whisky" [*sic*].
> "No, I'm used to it."
> "I know, but it will do good."[29]

Just as Irwin was credited with "separat[ing] the gold from the dross" in these plays, her stardom dominated the choice of plays and their production.[30] Other actors had little opportunity to shine. Irwin was "on the stage nearly the entire time" and "did not dare to leave it." Her fellow performers were merely "feeders."[31] *Mrs. Wilson, That's All* was essentially "a monologue by May Irwin with songs by May Irwin interspersed." Critics sometimes commented on this phenomenon with a trace of asperity: "It must be sad to be in May Irwin's company. If you are a woman, you must be very tall and slim and silent and stand about admiring the exploits of the 'big chief.' If you are a man you have to feed the star with cues and let her get all the laughs."[32] "[Irwin] talks a quart, smiles a yard, sings a tureen-full and is a hostess in herself. . . . [Her supporters are] lay figures, like the dummies that the ventriloquist uses. If Miss Irwin could ventriloquize, she would probably insist on having real dummies."[33]

The force of personality and star power wielded by Irwin during these years reflected what scholars have described as a movement from "a culture of character to a cult of personality." In the theater, this transformation links to what might be called a triumph of style over substance, charisma over skill. The self-advertisement of actresses grew in what Susan Glenn has analyzed as "the Bernhardt Effect." Glenn maintains that the "divine" Sarah Bernhardt "took the revolutionary step of encouraging audiences to believe that what they saw on stage was not an actress playing a character, but a woman using that character to reveal herself to the specatator."[34]

Irwin certainly had technical skill, but, as was the case for many of the stars of the "personality school," every role she undertook was essentially the same. Audiences came to see her, not the characters she portrayed. This style was especially common in comedy, in which the old "character comedians" who had performed in a large repertoire of comedies, from Shakespearean to Restoration to contemporary, were being replaced by new comedians who relied more on their personal comic appeal and usually appeared in long runs of modern comedies.[35] Certainly, most stars who shared billing with Irwin were of the same ilk. For example, Peter F. Dailey, who appeared in *A Country Sport* and *The Widow Jones* with May, was described, rather caustically, by Lewis C. Strang as "a great actor in the extremely popular character of Peter F. Dailey, a part that he has played successfully, under various guises and amid diverse environments, for many seasons."[36]

Star power was aided by the dissolution of top stock companies—which had formed the backbone of American theater throughout most of the nineteenth century—and the growth of popular-priced minor stock companies (including the new summer-stock organizations) and touring companies. (Even the renowned Augustin Daly's theater was unable to survive its founder's death and closed its doors in 1898.) As noted in chapter 1, combination companies led to the replacement of the repertory system with the long run. Now a company could stage and open one play in a large center, such as New York or Chicago, and then take the same play for a long run on a predetermined tour of the country. Simultaneously, powerful new producers, such as Charles and Daniel Frohman, began to organize touring companies and to "sell" stars and plays to the general public.[37]

Many female stars became the centerpieces of musical comedies during these years, but most shared the stage more equally with fellow performers than May Irwin did. Marie Dressler was often paired with a young and beautiful star of equal billing (for example, with Bessie Clayton in 1900 in *Miss Prinn*), as was Faye Templeton (with Lillian Russell in 1900 in *Fiddle-dee-dee*). Trixie Friganza and Marie Dressler even appeared together in *Higgledy-Piggledy* in 1904.[38] But at least between 1895 to 1910, these stars did not have the advantage of having the control Irwin was able to exercise over her roles.

Because of her immense star power and appeal, Irwin was able to entertain her audiences not only onstage but also through the many articles she wrote for *Green Book, Woman's Home Companion,* and *Cosmopolitan,* as well as the interviews granted and articles written for all of the major newspapers. For the many contributions she made to journalism, she was elected a member of the Northern New York State Editors' Association in 1913.[39]

In interviews Irwin's intrepid nature sprang from an irrepressible spirit that seemed to make a comic impression on all who came in contact with her. Often this personal magnetism was overwhelming. When a businessman whom she had never met came in during an interview, she swept to her feet with "Aren't you Mr.——? I just thought you were. I've heard so much of you that I'm not going to wait for an introduction. Nobody would introduce us anyway. They're trying to keep us apart, that's what they're trying to do." One interviewer wrote of an encounter with Irwin: "Silence seemed to be the best policy for me to follow and I did not interrupt. The sentences were emphasized by sharp slaps on her knees, and bobs of the hand. A clear blue eye would pierce me at intervals, and leave me fearful, lest I had betrayed a grin."[40]

Undeniably, Irwin's fame and charisma allowed her to choose her own star vehicles. She chose farces that differed from the standard fare in several respects. All of her productions had contemporary settings in America (with some "traveling" to European capitals, such as Paris). She eschewed the Middle Eastern settings favored in many late-nineteenth-century musicals, such as *The Sphinx* and *The Wizard of the Nile,* popular 1895 productions alongside Irwin's opening in *The Widow Jones.* Nor did she follow another common formula: a combination of contemporary issues—such as feminist "agitation"—with fantasy and imaginary locales. For example, in *Santa Maria,* a fairy tale of a lost child, a gypsy, and the king of a mythical "Holland," an all-female jury was presented as a ludicrous possibility. In the opera *Ollamus,* "Miss Jones, an unsuccessful candidate for the U.S. Presidency, lands in Utopiana and attempts to overthrow the king."[41]

In the 1890s, the theaters were also overrun with a series of "girl" musicals, in keeping with the new American symbols of purity and progress in "girl" types (particularly the Gibson Girl and the Fischer Girl).[42] Sample productions were titled *The Shop Girl, The Bathing Girl, The School Girl, The Telephone Girl,* and *The Bicycle Girl.* Irwin's plays, however, do not have generic titles. Often the name of the lead character *is* the title.

The craze for "girl" shows during this period went hand in hand with the proliferation of images of young, beautiful, and seemingly "pure" types in the new field of advertising. These images of women became synonymous with America itself and, in an age of change, both supported and contained women's newfound freedoms. As Martha Banta has shown, powerful women championing for rights were often photographed with what she calls "roses at the breasts" to accentuate their femininity. And strong female athletes were often depicted reclining as dainty "nymph[s] by the sea." Banta includes a photograph of the phenomenal swimmer Annette Kellerman in this pose, an uncomfortable expression on her face.[43]

In contrast to the "girl"-themed shows, May's characters were distinct individuals, and as she grew older she openly expressed her disdain at the increasing pressure on women performers to appear forever young: "Who wants to be without a wrinkle? They're the marks of experience, thought, and character. I mistrust anyone over forty without a mark!"[44] May had a predilection for playing widows—of a particular sort:

> Now, there are widows and widows. Sometimes that word implies characteristics which are not altogether complimentary. For example, there is the widow who may have become such by the clever usage of potash or salts of lemon. Such a widow is not desirable. May Irwin could never appear in such a role. The widows she invariably creates are dear, good-natured ones, of the plump-and-forty-or-nearly type, who are addicted to tears and rich pastry.
>
> . . . And the rest of their characteristics are always according to the May Irwin standard of widows. A pleasant intermingling of tears and titters, some coquetry and a great deal of tact.[45]

If May's character was not a widow (or pretending to be one), she was invariably about to seek a divorce from an unruly husband (although she often made up with him by play's end). As I have previously described, in *The Widow Jones* the wealthy Beatrice Byke tries to escape money-hungry suitors by running off to Maine and pretending to be the widow of a man who had drowned the year before. Mrs. Peckham, of *Mrs. Peckham's Carouse,* intends to divorce her husband over his drinking habits. In *Getting a Polish,* Mrs. Jim is a widow who runs a boardinghouse but gets to go to Paris when a strike is made in her husband's mining claim. Mrs. Wilson of *Mrs. Wilson, That's All* waits for seven years after her husband has deserted her to have him legally declared dead. Dottie Dimple of *Courted into Court* is seeking a divorce when the judge falls in love with her. The simple premise of *Mrs. Black Is Back* is based on a widow's lie to her beloved—she has fibbed about her age and now must pretend that her grown son is a toddler. And in *Widow by Proxy,* Gloria Grey has to impersonate the young widow she has been helping rejuvenate.

The majority of Irwin's characters earn their own living, and they do so in a variety of ways. When she began performing in full-length farces, May had evidently had enough of the clever maids that had won her so much acclaim in Daly's company. Only with Matilda, of *33 Washington Square,* did she return to the role of housekeeper. Instead, she opted for actress (*Courted into Court* and *On the Hiring Line*), music teacher (*Widow by Proxy*), shopkeeper (*The Swell Miss Fitzwell*), lawyer (*Madge Smith, Attorney*), purchasing agent (*Kate Kip, Buyer*), and author (*Sister Mary*). These "working women" were connected to Irwin's strong feelings that women must be able to earn their own living. She once told a reporter from the *Toledo (Ohio) Blade* that she learned early in life that money was an absolute necessity for happiness.[46]

The plots of Irwin's scripts reveal the usual situations and subjects of farce—physical humor, lovers' quarrels, misunderstandings, and mistaken identities. Particularly prevalent in Irwin's comedies was the use of disguises, ethnic humor, and scenes of intoxication and petty vices, the latter commonly used to ridicule the reactions and behavior of proper society.

Irwin's farces often required her character to mask her true identity in order to pursue a worthy goal for herself or a friend. In *Widow by Proxy,* for example, the kindly Gloria Grey takes on the identity of a young widow in order to assist her in inheriting an estate. To maintain domestic tranquillity, author Alicia Penn, in *Sister Mary,* pretends that she did not write a book on marital advice. Matilda, in *33 Washington Square,* disguises herself as her mistress in order to help the latter escape from creditors. And in *Kate*

Kip, Buyer the heroine impersonates not only the daughter of two different senators but also the husband of another in order to ensure that the seat of government in an unnamed western state remains on her family's land.

Irwin's portrayal of ethnic stereotypes in her farces was confined to her performances of "coon songs," an essential comic element in virtually all of her performances. These songs usually had very little, if anything, to do with the material of the play. Other ethnic stereotypes were usually played by male actors; typical characters were the smooth and devious Count Adolfo De La Nocheburma in *She Knows Better Now* (given to exclamations of "Ay, caramba!" and "Dio mío!") and Pierre, the affected French messenger for Mrs. Wilson's dressmaker in *Mrs. Wilson, That's All.*

In Irwin's vehicles, the prudes and well-bred people of society are often distressed by the petty vices and misdemeanors of the common folk, with whom Irwin's character usually aligns herself. For example, in *Widow by Proxy,* Irwin shocks an exceptionally proper group of New England relatives by remarking that the nicest people she knows are in jail. In her plays and written articles alike, Irwin was particularly interested in deflating anyone who felt too self-important: "I can't bear pretence. Perhaps that is why so much of the fun in my plays arises out of the puncturing of self-deceptions with jabs of common-sense laughter." The object of her laughter was sometimes the individual too foolish to understand the real meaning of his or her own words. For example, she quoted the theater manager who, when consoled because of the small size of his audience, retorted, "Oh, well, it is not very good now but you ought to have seen it when the curtain went up for the first act. We had a big house then." Similarly, she joked about people who failed to understand the real meaning of others' words. For example, in one joke, the boor Chumley proudly relates a friend's comments on his speech: "'How was your speech received at the club?' asked one of Chumley's friends. 'Why, they congratulated me very heartily. In fact, one of the members came to me and told me that when I sat down he had said to himself it was the best thing I had ever done.'" (The use of the name "Chumley" may also indicate a class critique of the type Gillian Rodger examines in her discussion of "swell songs.")[47]

Irwin's tendency to poke fun at the pompous male, both in print and in her plays, sometimes extended comedy based in popular styles and subjects into less acceptable territory. The humor of the time typically celebrated the "average white male and his point of view" and consistently depicted women as the butt of jokes. In gag books of the period, as Brooks McNamara has noted in his study "The Literature of American Popular Entertainment," "All women were presented negatively . . . as blatant sex objects, physical grotesques, shrewish wives, termagant mothers-in-law, and sinister gold-diggers." Irwin, however, made fun of the average white male, even blithely ridiculing male political figures, thus transgressing what Linda Martin and Kerry Segrave describe as a "proscription . . . [having the] the force of [an] 'ancient taboo.'" She extended this tactic even further in ignoring the fourth wall of the theater and directing much of her comedy directly to the women in the audience. As feminist scholars have pointed out, sometimes "the threat to male dominance isn't women laughing *at* men; the threat is women laughing *with* women."[48] In a later chapter, I'll consider how this strengthened Irwin's work on behalf of women's suffrage.

However, Irwin was careful to satirize female characters who went too far in their disapproval of what she regarded as harmless entertainment. In her plays, humorous situations frequently occur when characters attempt to hide vices, such as drinking and card playing, from those who disapprove of them. Thus, in *The Swell Miss Fitzwell,* a bottle of liquor is hidden in a dress-maker's model at Miss Fitzwell's shop. Mrs. Wilson of *Mrs. Wilson, That's All* pretends she is holding a suffrage meeting instead of playing a game of whist with some friends when her aunt Libbie (an ardent feminist *and* temperance leader) makes an unexpected call:

> (Omnes hide cards quickly and Mrs. W. rises and begins to talk as tho she'd been making a speech)
>
> (Enter Aunt Libbie just as Mrs. W. starts her speech. Aunt Libbie listens with approval)
>
> MRS. W.: I repeat, woman's suffrage is my theme!—woman's suffrage, the solution of every problem!
>
> AUNT LIBBIE: Quite right, my dear!
>
> MRS. W.: How do you do, Aunt Libbie! Sit down! (Aunt Libby sits . . . listening intently)
>
> MRS. W.: Whyo, [*sic*] I ask you, are the real rulers of the world today? The women! Without women what would this world be? Nothing but one continual political meeting on its way to a saloon![49]

Such card games were plentiful in Irwin's plays and often served as opportunities for Irwin to entertain the audience with songs.

But the petty vice of intoxication provided Irwin with her best-known scenes of comedy. These scenes inevitably featured a woman having her first encounter with "demon alcohol," either deliberately or otherwise. In this scene from *She Knows Better Now,* the timid Mrs. Thompkins allows her friend Angelica to seduce her into trying a spot of whiskey for courage:

MRS. T: I feel so weak. You see, I didn't eat any breakfast. I was so upset. [Drinking, choking and coughing.] Oh, it's wretched stuff!!

MRS. S: Drink it—every drop!

MRS. T: [Again attacking whiskey] Oh, Angelica, you are a wonderful woman! You could make anybody do anything. [. . . regarding herself in the mirror] You know nothing but a complete state of intoxication would make me feel comfortable in this wrap, Angelica. [Shaking glass.] This isn't so bad when you get used to it. [Laughs happily.] My knees are beginning to stiffen already. It gives you sort of a cozy feeling, doesn't it?[50]

In *Mrs. Peckham's Carouse,* Irwin portrayed Mrs. Peckham, a militant temperance crusader who is given rye whiskey when she faints; she enjoys the effects immeasurably. She decides then and there that it would be better if she delayed her afternoon's speech to the "Daughters of Total Abstinence."

In *Sister Mary*, an aunt, who is described as a "specialist in temperance and other people's business," mistakenly gives the title character brandy in the belief that it is a nerve cure.[51] Irwin's performance of this intoxication scene was given particularly favorable notices:

> A drunken leer, which grows broader as the effect of the dose deepens, a few awkward gestures and the sticking of some quill pens in her hair are almost the only means she employs in this scene. But she keeps the audience convulsed with laughter.[52]

> Miss Irwin takes a large glass of whiskey under the impression that it is nerve-tonic. First comes the physical pain, broadly, but artistically burlesqued. Then her face expresses a sort of surprise, mixed with stupefaction and vagueness. Gradually this darkens into fixed, earnest contemplation. That look of honest solemnity, which so often colors the face into which alcohol has freely passed, is given on the actress's mobile and radiant countenance. She just sits there and looks, and looks, calmly. Then she pulls herself together and makes a desperate determination to write something. One quill won't work, and goes into her hair. Another follows. The inkwiper gets her face into trouble, and thus the broader and more familiar stage effects follow, well done.[53]

Of course, much of the humor in Irwin's intoxication scenes came from the contrast between the physical manifestations of drunkenness and the character's continued mental obliviousness. Mrs. Thompkins of *She Knows Better Now* is unaware of how drunk she is becoming; neither Mrs. Peckham nor Sister Mary seems aware they are even drinking.

Reflecting the temperance movement of the time, Irwin did receive letters from fans who questioned the propriety of a mother with two children ridiculing so "serious a problem as liquor." Irwin replied that she was always careful to keep her portrayals of drunkenness within the bounds of good taste and always knew when to stop.[54]

In choosing intoxication as a comic subject, Irwin certainly tapped into the humor of the times (perhaps of all times). In a manual designed as part of a home correspondence course to assist hopeful writers in devising sketches, Brett Page listed "drink" as one of the comic themes of "universal interest" and included George M. Cohan's note that "intoxication in almost any form" is good for a "sure-fire laugh." As indicated, Irwin's portrayals of characters such as Mrs. Peckham and Sister Mary featured inebriation as the center of a comic turn. Cohan adds the qualification that intoxication "must never be revolting."[55] Irwin's depictions of drunkenness were praised for their subtlety and lack of vulgarity.

In her excellent study on the films of Marie Dressler, Victoria Sturtevant discusses Dressler's remarkable use of an overweight but athletic body in her depictions of drunkenness. In so doing, Sturtevant draws from the rich store of research connected to Mikhail Bakhtin's definition of the "carnavalesque." Bakhtin's work *Rabelais and His World* looks at the early celebrations allowed by the medieval Catholic Church, similar to the early Feast of Fools, which turned hierarchical structure and normal codes of decent behavior upside down. Anarchy reigned and found expression in overindulgence in eating, drinking, dancing, and sexuality. As the development of comedy in Western drama has been connected to Dionysian ritual, so has it been related to this connected idea of "Carnival." Carnival is a temporary break from a normative social structure, but one that Frances Gray has questioned, especially as concerns its liberating value for women, since during "the last three thousand and one half years, sexuality has meant male sexuality."[56] When a woman takes too many liberties, even in the tradition of Carnival, it can be a risky business. Here Sturtevant describes Dressler's style:

> Her urge to dance, the physical freedom and exuberance of drunkenness, as Bakhtin celebrates it, shows the enormity of her flesh and emphasizes unassailably the life of the body. Her drunk routine is precisely an expression of carnival excess, a body temporarily, dangerously, and pleasurably out of control. Although many male comic stars were known for their drunk specialties, most obviously Chaplin and W. C. Fields, it would seem to be a measure of exactly how dangerous the whole prospect of a drunk woman could be that I find no other female comedienne [in film] who did a regular drunken "bit."[57]

Although May Irwin regularly used a "drunken bit" onstage before 1900, her performances rarely provoked the critical wrath Dressler's sometimes did. As I have suggested, the reasons for this are manifold. Irwin's portrait was not perceived as being as "masculinized" as Dressler's. She was round and could certainly move and dance, but she was much shorter and softer than Dressler, her hair often in curls. Her drunks were (not always, but often) unaware of their inebriation. Her style was of an entirely different order.

But just as important, Irwin was much more adept than Dressler at the game of playing "both sides of the fence." For example, both Dressler and Irwin were champions of women's rights, but Irwin used scenes of intoxication (as in *Mrs. Wilson, That's All*) alongside scenes concerning suffrage. By doing this, she was, in part, severing her solidarity with domestic feminists, dissociating from the temperance movement, and aligning herself with the mainstream outlook of the American male. Thus, she avoided the taint of the "thin-lipped and humorless prude averse to any form of spontaneity, life, or joy."[58]

Avoiding this "taint" could have cost her support among women. Membership in the Women's Christian Temperance Union (WCTU), formed in 1874, grew rapidly in the 1880s and 1890s. By 1892 the organization had expanded to 150,000 members (by contrast, the dues-paying members of the National American Woman Suffrage Association were approximately 13,000 at that time). Indeed, the first "gender gap" in political issues was recorded in Illinois in 1919, when a poll showed that women were twice as likely to support Prohibition as men were.[59]

But even as Irwin distanced herself from temperance views, she used the platform of the stage to bring supporters of woman suffrage closer to her, while teasing them a bit about their ardor. (In his sketch manual, Brett Page also listed "woman suffrage" as a theme of general appeal, and monologues with titles like "Suffragette Susie" are common in collections of vaudeville routines.)[60] Irwin not only used fake suffrage speeches as comic satire within such farces as *Mrs. Wilson, That's All,* but could also make friends with suffrage supporters. She recalled how she once launched into an impromptu speech for women's votes because she was having trouble eliciting laughs and remembered that a suffrage convention was being held in town. During her performance, she managed not only to win her audience's laughter but also to gain support from the local women's suffrage club, which was occupying the front row of the theater. In an observation that simultaneously makes fun of the suffragists while aligning herself with their cause, Irwin said, "They rose up like a battalion of soldiers to meet me. Each one wore a grim smile and black kid gloves . . . [and] begged me to set a date for a lecture on women's suffrage."[61] I will consider Irwin's involvement with the suffrage movement in greater detail in a later chapter, but her description of suffragists in the front row of her audience gives a clue to the composition of that audience.

Despite her occasional return to vaudeville, May Irwin spent her years of greatest stardom appearing in some of the most important theaters in New York and on tour, attracting a largely middle-class crowd. Although there are few quantitative records of audience composition from this period, a 1911 study from the well-known Russell Sage Foundation provides the following estimates. For higher-priced New York theaters (which cost between one and a half and two dollars per seat), the study estimated that 51 percent of the audiences were of the leisure class, 47 percent of the middle class, and 2 percent of the working class. Gender division is reckoned at 50 percent men and 45 percent women (and 5 percent children under eighteen years of age).[62] In contrast, audiences of vaudeville houses were 60 percent working class and 36 percent middle class. Care must be taken in using these figures, as it is not clear how "class" membership was determined. In some surveys, young working-class women listed theater attendance as their favorite leisure-time activity.[63] Of course, vaudeville—at ten cents to one dollar per seat—was much more affordable than legitimate theater. A two-dollar ticket would require months of saving for a working-class individual—an entire family would have had to save a great deal. The price of even vaudeville admission would prevent weekly visits for many members of the working class. Of course, ethnic theaters drew crowds at low prices, and free passes were sometimes available.

Nevertheless, a large portion of Irwin's audience was middle class, and the suffrage movement from the 1890s to the 1920s included large numbers in that class. Although May's audience might have included fewer temperance supporters during this period, the effect was likely even further minimized once the suffrage and temperance movements began to diverge. By the 1890s, as Ruth Bordin explains, "brewers and other liquor interests began to see prohibition as a possible result of the woman's ballot. They began to oppose suffrage with all their considerable money and influence and the suffrage forces grew afraid that any alliance with temperance groups would defeat their own cause. . . . Temperance was seen as too great a danger to the woman's ballot to command active support from suffragists."[64]

The success of a performer's work, however, often has more to do with style than content of material (although the two are undeniably intertwined). This was doubly true in Irwin's case, given the weakness and predictability of these farces. Certainly, a sense of her inimitable timing can be gleaned from the descriptions of the intoxication scene in *Sister Mary.* Unfortunately, opportunities to see and hear recordings of Irwin in performance are scant: the aforementioned Vitascope piece *The Kiss* and six recorded songs are all that are known to remain.[65] Paramount Pictures turned *Mrs. Black Is Back* into a film—but all copies have been lost. Irwin did leave a set of home movies made in the Thousand Islands and kept in the museum in Clayton, New York.[66] This valuable footage includes brief reenactments of performances—with friends holding up placards with titles such as *Mrs. Black Is Back, She Rolls Her Own,* and *Give the Little Lady a Hand.* The film is particularly telling, as it reveals some of the most distinguishing elements of her style—elements that, through repetition over the years, have become indelibly etched in her physical bearing. As in her plays, the joys of inebriation are underlined in Irwin's home movies, in which she is filmed drinking, kissing her drink, and then luring her husband, Kurt, into a tent to drink and kiss. In the next scene, entitled *Then Came the Dawn,* the two lovers stumble out of the tent, obviously suffering from a severe hangover. (Notably, unlike what would certainly be true in Dressler's case, the man *willingly* goes after the drunken bait!)

There are also clues to Irwin's style in the critiques and newspaper reviews and in the scripts themselves. These scripts are not readily available, but a number do exist on microfilm in the Library of Congress. They reveal several keys to Irwin's style that account for her comic success. Most notable is Irwin's ability to tease every bit of comedy from her plays through verbal virtuosity, a sure sense of timing, and a spontaneity and directness that helped her to establish a close relationship with her audience.

For content, Irwin's verbal skills relied both on word play and on contrasts in subject matter. Sometimes she used malapropisms or nonsense language, as in an amusing German lesson in *She Knows Better Now,* or the description of her first automobile driving session in *Mrs. Black Is Back:* "He said to me he could teach me in one lesson. Just grab the wheel in front of you with both hands, put one foot on the accelerator and the other on the rheostat and let the left elbow gently rest on the deoderizer, then keep the galvanized wire connecting with the automatic fog whistle closely between the teeth, let the elbow be in touch with the quadruplex, while the apex of the left instep is pressed over the spark coil and the right works with the condenser."[67]

More often, however, Irwin depended on a rapid-fire change of subject matter. Here, for example, is Mrs. Wilson's suffrage speech, which moves quickly from suffrage to shoes: "I repeat, ladies, since time immemorial down-trodden women have suffered under the iron heel of man. And speaking of heels who makes our shoes—men! And with what fiendish ingenuity do they fashion our shoes so that they pinch and bruise our tender feet. It is a well-established fact that every woman in the world, with possibly three exceptions, has small feet and should wear a size 2-A."[68]

Irwin's use of shifting subjects and verbal pyrotechnics echoed a very familiar comic technique in vaudeville. The confused speech in *Mrs. Black Is Back* about automobile lessons recalls a well-known monologue of the time, malaprop-riddled "German Senator," by Aaron Hoffman: "My dear friends and falling citizens: My heart fills up with vaccination to be disabled to come out here before such an intelligence massage of people and have the chance to undress such a large conglomerated aggravation."[69] As the monologue continues, the senator shifts through a remarkable chain of subjects, much like Irwin did in Mrs. Wilson's imitation suffrage speech.

These shifts in subject matter gave Irwin ample opportunity to employ what she called the "most essential quality of a comedy line—surprise: You feint with your right and deliver a short jab with your left."[70] Thus, in *Widow by Proxy,* impostor Gloria Grey moves suddenly from panic to complete self-assuredness:

> How do I look? Widowy? (Fusses with hat, veil, train, etc.)
>
> Help! I'm getting panicky! (Then forgetting her notes) I'm forgetting my lines. When were we married? When did our husband die? Dolores—I mean, Gloria, I am getting weak in the knees—and water on the brain—and aphasia—(Groans) Oh, if I live through this day—(Different tone, now vanity) Is my veil on straight? (Strikes haughty, superior attitude).[71]

This brief excerpt shows how Irwin was able to succeed comically on a number of levels: the rapid contrast of the two competing emotions with no transition; the scatterbrained panic coupled with the misplaced self-importance of the character, which gives the audience a feeling of superiority; and the comment about "forgetting" lines—slyly referring not only to the lines her character needed to know for her impersonation but also to the lines in the farce itself.

When dealing with journalists, Irwin also spoke in the rapid patter of many of her characters, coupling this with a tendency either to direct a comment to a listener without allowing him or her to answer or to respond quickly to her own hypothetical question. For instance, in an interview in which she told the story of her first appearance on the stage, she interjected asides to her interviewer: "Well, I was born—I had to submit to that; there is no royal road to life anymore than there is to learning—I was born a baby—a tiny little bit of a thing—only so long (12 inches) and so wide (half a yard) and—oh, don't be afraid to speak up, I have stayed that shape ever since."[72]

Because of the number of songs interspersed in Irwin's productions, these subject shifts could be useful ways for her to work her way into a song. How often she employed this technique can only be surmised, since much of this work was improvised and the songs are not included in the scripts. One of her own typed monologues gives an indication of the format she may have followed:

> (After song: "Home Sweet Home".)
> Home sweet home, same little fireside, same little parlor and the same little land lord waiting for the rent. The old fashioned homes were the real homes. They were so roomy. Now-a-days they haven't even any room for furniture. I know a friend who used her Victrola all last summer for an ice chest. Everything is different now. Everything! Even our one dollar bills look like twos, two dollar bills look like tens, they look like them but they don't spend like them. A fellow with a bunch of new money rings up his girl and says "Meet me in front of Rector's dearie." Then he takes another good look at his bankroll, meets her in front of Rector's and takes her to Child's. The only thing that time hasn't changed are "Married Men"—they're still husbands. Very still when they come home in the morning, they still take their shoes off in the hall and they still put on the same old Alibis.
> [song: "Alibis"].[73]

Irwin's rapid shifts in subject matter drew comic strength from her particular sense of timing, one of the essential elements of her style. She skillfully put to work the lessons she learned about pace from Tony Pastor and Augustin Daly—contrasting an accelerated pace with silence to great comic effect.

This sense of timing is also noticeable in Irwin's coon shouting. In her recording of "The Bully," Irwin contrasts an up-tempo "lookin' for dat bully and he must be found" with judicious rests after "round" and "found." Similarly, in the "Frog Song," she replaces the "well" in the following lyrics with a silence: "He stubbed his toe and in he fell / And de niggahs all said he went to—well." (To our ears, the coyness about uttering the word *hell* after using the racial epithet is particularly jarring.)

The contrast between an accelerated pace and silence also found expression in Irwin's physical timing. Her depiction of Sister Mary's alcoholic stupor, for example, was lauded for its juxtaposition of broad "familiar stage effects" with a "perfect spiritual absence which rests on Miss Irwin's face in the early stages."[74]

In the same way, the comic effects of stillness contrasted with movement can be seen in *The Kiss,* which opens with Irwin's face and John C. Rice's face pressed tightly together. They are initially perfectly still except for their mouths, from the corners of which they are chatting animatedly. Likewise, in her home movies, Irwin appears in a close-up in which the stillness of her face and calmness of expression contrast with a very deliberate but quickly executed wink.

As evidenced in the example of her "impromptu suffrage rant," Irwin often "improvised" entire speeches that were tailored to particular audiences. Reviewers marveled at another of Irwin's onstage qualities, her "imitation spontaneity which passes as improvised fun." She "utters witticisms as if she had never for a moment thought them out," so much so that "one can hardly imagine that she learns her part by rote."[75]

According to some reviewers and herself, Irwin's "irresistible naturalness and spontaneity" may not have always been feigned. In previews she sometimes forgot her lines but recovered quickly: "Although Miss Irwin was not always entirely sure of her lines, she fished for them so ingeniously that the house enjoyed her performance better than if she had been letter-perfect." Irwin herself said, "I don't suppose there is ever a performance where I keep to my lines," and she complained that it was difficult to teach company members to play along with her: "I go ahead and have fun with myself, but I always lead back to them and give them their cues. It's the rarest thing imaginable to find someone who will enter into my mood and play up to me. . . . It's too funny to see the faces of the others on stage when I introduce something new."[76]

During her time, Irwin had few equals on the stage in her ability to use improvisation and ad libs. It seems doubtful that a woman of Irwin's acting background would often forget her lines during a long run (although aging usually increases that likelihood, even for the best actors!). More likely, she made free use of her scripts, for Irwin had the habit of buying an entire play and rewriting sections of it to fit her own comic abilities, leaving ample room for improvisation. She wrote to one hopeful playwright, maintaining that she did not need a new play at the time, but might consider buying an existing script outright and revising it herself: "I don't consider the last two acts as good as the first. I would have to put a lot of thought and energy [into it] . . . as I have always done with every new piece I played no matter who wrote it . . . and I have never consented to giving me any credit for a line or situation."[77]

It is also true that a mistake in performance creates humor and a connection with the audience, and then the mistake is intentionally repeated in subsequent performances until its "spontaneity" wears out. In two very different ways, the advertisement of Irwin's "improvisations" was an excellent public relations strategy. Audiences are attracted to performances during which they can see or "own" some wonderful mistake that was cleverly covered or an improvisation that seems meant for them alone ("Did you see the performance when——happened?"). Indeed, Irwin's ad libs were sometimes noted in the newspaper, as in this special sent to the *New York Times* when Irwin made a pointed joke about William Jennings Bryan (known as the "Boy Orator," he ran for president three times but is probably now best known for his part as prosecutor in the famous Scopes trial on evolution): "May Irwin, in 'The Widow Jones' last night, when her adopted husband, John James Jones, was tearing his hair and declaiming in a vain effort to mollify her, turned to the audience, and, with a sly wink, said 'The Boy Orator.' The house yelled, and President Cleveland, who occupied a box, laughed himself red in the face."[78]

On one level, improvisation and the idea that Irwin's "witticisms" were perhaps not "thought out" render her a "wild untutored phoenix," a woman whose comic ability really has nothing to do with her own effort. This makes her comedy less threatening and more acceptable when drawn from feminine impulses that lie beyond the realm of masculine logic and language. As Irwin's contemporary Kate Sanborn maintained: "The wit of women is like the airy froth of champagne, or the witching iridescence of the soap-bubble, blown for a moment's sport. . . . [U]nlike men, women do not write out their impromptus before-hand and carefully hoard them for the publisher—and posterity."[79]

Adding to her appeal, Irwin's improvisational skills were used not only with her fellow actors but also with her audience. In fact, her delight in taking cues from the audience was an important component of her style. She was said to be "in cahoots" with them, indulging in a "habit of frankly and emphatically taking her audience into her confidence." She reveled in working with her fans: "The audience and myself must first sort of 'get together' and when we are on good terms I find that I can hold them to my heart's content." Unlike other performers, she even asked that the theaters she played in be kept a bit brighter than usual to enhance this getting together: "I like to have a little light in the house, so that there may be more of a unity between the players and the audience."[80]

Irwin's need for light in the audience—harking back to much earlier days in theater—as well as the descriptions of audience members "shrieking" and "doubling up" with laughter seem to contradict new ideas about spectatorship in the last quarter of the nineteenth century that served to dampen audience response. Many books of manners from the period dispensed the advice of James Smiley's *Modern Manners and Social Forms* of 1889: "Perfect quiet should be maintained during the performance, and the attention should be fixed on the stage. To whisper or do anything during the entertainment to disturb or distract the attention of others is rude in the extreme. It is proper to applaud, when pleased, as that encourages and gratifies the performer, but do not stamp with the feet. . . . During the intermission it is in order to converse in a low tone, but loud talk or laughter . . . is always in bad taste in any public place." Critics have maintained that these "new rules," which were applied to both vaudeville and the legitimate theater, were an attempt to control the working class. As such they acted as "a kind of gag rule that reduced [the working class's] role in a powerful arena of cultural expression to their relatively weak economic standing at the box office."[81]

May Irwin's performances offered permission for greater audience reaction and interaction, which, while not condoning the rougher tenor of the antebellum audiences, fostered a greater bond with all classes in her audience. Though tactics such as these did strengthen Irwin's connection with her audience, they also distanced her from both the character and the play. This confirmed critical opinion that Irwin really played only herself: "There is only one character, so far as I can remember, that May Irwin has ever performed—and that is her adorably humorous self." She tended to agree with reviewers in this respect: "No, I'm not an actress, although I've been a good many years in that profession, I couldn't act to save my life. I'm myself, and without conceit, I suppose I may say the public seems to like, or have liked me."[82]

It was conceded that Irwin's magnetic personality, even had she performed in a masterpiece, would outshine the material. As Alan Dale put it, Irwin "could play Juliet and there would be more Irwin than Shakespeare" in the production. Critic Alan Dale may have helped Irwin's success in that he was a new kind of powerful critic who disliked artificiality and spoke plainly—going as far as naming the actress Clara Morris the "Queen of Spasms." He was not fond of Shakespeare and said he felt that his duty was to the audience rather than to the profession. Although he was not a great fan of comic farce in general, he was an important supporter of Irwin and her inimitable style.[83]

Even if it was disingenuous of Irwin, a well-trained actress, to deny her skill, she had indeed discarded Daly's rigid adherence to the "fourth wall." By downplaying her real acting ability, she put herself on a plane equal with her public; her contention that she played only her "natural self" gave her an authenticity that added to her appeal in an age of mechanization and alienation. In a true sense, Irwin was popular because her immense magnetism and comic talent combined with the embodiment of American success in the late nineteenth century. First, Irwin was reflective of the new, restless spirit of urban America. She was an ambitious woman who kept moving upward, never letting her background prevent her success. Even if she was "too modern for [the] old [Shakespearean] comed[ies]" that were a staple of Augustin Daly's theater, she could still compete with the best actors in his company. Yet she invited the audience into her world; she did not think of herself as separate from and above them. If a poor girl like Irwin could achieve success, then why not any member of her audience?

If the character Irwin presented to her public was that of her own natural self, that self included a physique and face that were an integral part of her style. Her wide lips, large chin, and expressive eyes carried her personal magnetism across the footlights. Caricaturist Kate Carew even made up a set of "Irwinesque mouths" for the *New York Times*, published with the caption "Miss Irwin's mouth is more necessary to New York than the Statue of Liberty."[84]

Irwin was very effective in using these physical characteristics, especially her large mouth and her weight, for comic effect. (As I pointed out in chapter 1, one of New York critic Alan Dale's favorite lines was in *The Widow Jones*, when Irwin remarked, while presumably demonstrating, "The great advantage of having a big mouth is that, while you are kissing, you can go on talking.")

In particular, Irwin used her physical appearance and generous girth to shape two other important aspects of her performance: a childlike attitude combined with a motherly maturity. Irwin's persona of a mother-child was well summed up by Alan Dale: "Everyone knows that she has a mischievious [*sic*] eye, an ingratiating mouth, and a way of saying a thing which is an odd mixture of infantile precocity and matronly suavity."[85]

This mixture of the infantile and the matronly was sustained in Irwin's songs, as, for example, in the oft-reprinted photograph of her rendition of "The Bully," which emphasized a childlike pout with hands balled into little fists on her hips. In *The Widow Jones*, she sang "The Shadow Song," a piece about the terrors a small child faces in the darkness of the night. A reviewer noted the combination of identification with the child and the "adult appreciative of the troubles of children."[86] In *Sister Mary*, she offered a song, "My Bed Is Like a Little Boat" (verses by Robert Louis Stevenson), in the persona of a small child. Praised as "the daintiest little air in town," it included stanzas such as these:

My bed is like a little boat,
Nurse helps me in when I embark;
She girds me in my sailor coat,
And starts me in the dark

And sometimes things to bed I take,
As prudent sailors have to do—
Perhaps a slice of wedding cake,
Perhaps a toy or two.[87]

Critic Harold Wynne went so far as to link Irwin's essential appeal directly to her childlike quality:

May Irwin, it is true you're stout and in your teens no longer.
'Tis true your charms are opulent and mellow;
One can't deny your healthy voice is just a trifle stronger
Than that which cheers the average sort of fellow.

And yet I do protest you win my honest admiration
The cause of which effect's extremely simple
You make me think of some plump baby crowing in elation
That beams jocundity from every dimple.[88]

Of course, not everyone was as kindly disposed to the childlike behavior of Irwin's characters:

> Fie! Fie! Fie! Giddy! Giddy! Have you seen those kittenish new photos of May Irwin? They are a scream. When an obese elderly lady, who hasn't seen her shoe tips in years, drops her double chin on her capacious bosom and looks upward with a coy and coquettish smirk, the shock is as rude and abrupt as if you had caught your grandmother flirting with the elevator boy. There was a time when May could with propriety indulge these photographic eccentricities, but it was way back in about 1872. Things are not the same now that they were in the last century shortly after the close of the Civil War.[89]

Irwin's childlike quality was often captured both in photographs and in caricatures of the period, and she had no intention of paying attention to a few naysayers. Two of her favorite poses for photographs were hands clasped in front; head tilted with a shy, broad smile; and arms crossed and one hand up to her lips. A caricature from *Sister Mary* even includes the caption "The expression on the face recalls that of the small boy watching his big sister with her 'steady.'"[90]

Irwin's childlike poses are repeated in her home films. In one scene, titled *Mrs. Black Is Back,* she poses with head coyly tilted to one side and her hands in front. When someone next to Irwin straightens her head, Irwin holds the pose for only a second before returning to her previous position. Later, in a section entitled *She Rolls Her Own,* which begins with Irwin rolling up her stockings, she exhibits mock distress over a man's preoccupation with two other women by pulling away from the group, wildly thrusting both hands to her head, and then placing both hands to her lips in a pouting position reminiscent of many of her earlier photographs.

Irwin's few recordings of coon songs also reveal the persona of the mother-child. A childlike, light delivery marked Irwin's singing on these recordings. Even when one takes into account the raised pitch of early recordings, it is clear that Irwin's vocal quality was not that of a heavy chest belt, but one that mixed an earthy quality with clear head tones. She also added, in recording, syllables to the sheet music to make cute internal rhymes. For instance, in "May Irwin's Frog Song," her frog from Yankety Yank doesn't jump from "bank to bank" but from "bankety to bank." The syncopation throughout the songs is emphasized with little slides that anticipate the delivery of Shirley Temple.

In an essential way, Irwin balanced her strong and independent characters and her capable maternal figure with her technique of playing the child—either in her delivery or physicality or in her songs sung from the child's point of view. In her use of a child's perspective, she was related to other female comics of the time, such as the celebrated Lotta Crabtree and the diminutive Isabel d'Armond. Crabtree, however, depended almost exclusively on her "kid character," which she coupled with an innocent sexuality. D'Armond played characters who were always unaware of the audience's laughter, portraying them with an "air of droll seriousness [and] something of the intentness of a child at play." In combining child with adult, Irwin portrayed characters who were at once naive and bold, confused and capable. As in the review of "The Shadow Song," critics noted that her renditions of children's songs seemed to portray equally the protective mother and the small child. In a sense, she was both the mother of the audience—gently pointing out the foibles of all children—and the child owned by the public. She was one of the "song and dance artists" who approached a vaudeville audience "with the direct, familiar appeal of . . . [a] child of its own creation."[91]

What was the nature of this "child" in the context of the times? Women playing children—onstage and in life—have been seen as a restraint of female appetite (for food and sex), especially during times of progress in women's emancipation. The late Victorian Age *was* such a time of change and one during which the idea of dieting was first introduced to the middle-class public of America and new images of impossibly small-waisted women with narrow shoulders began to appear in fashion. Critic Susan Bordo observes that during such times, "dominant constructions of the female body become sylphlike—unlike the body of a fully developed woman, more like that of an adolescent or boy (images that might be called female desire unborn)."[92] Additionally, the image of a grown woman playing a child can titillate and attract an audience in its tension between sexuality and innocence.[93] Certainly that *may* be true when a diminutive comic performs a "kid" character in costume. In Irwin's case, she is likened to a baby—with round, soft flesh and a mouth that could be seen as a chick's desire or need to be fed (with applause!).

But Irwin didn't hide her motherly figure or girth. The switching back and forth between May the capable mother and May the coy and helpless baby is more complex in its effect than is initially apparent. The audience longs and gains pleasure in *identifying with* and *controlling both* images. In this sense, both the child and the mother can serve as wish fulfillment for an audience living in a time of deep cultural conflicts; between a still predominantly fleshy, maternal female figure and a newer, sleeker image; and between what Jackson Lears has termed the "fantasies of pre-Oedipal wholeness" as well as "a need to be up and doing, dominating the world of *mater* and matter."[94]

In both her mother and her child personae, Irwin continually received praise for the self-deprecatory nature of her comic style. As one reviewer put it, Irwin was one of "the very few persons capable of making fun of themselves at all." Others may have lampooned her, but "the much-caricatured May Irwin also makes fun of herself." Viewers observed of Irwin that "before we have time to laugh at her, she laughs at herself."[95]

Offstage as well as on-, Irwin followed her own advice that "without a sense of humor a person is deprived of the power of self-criticism." She made fun of her personal thriftiness by advising home owners to cook with coal and to obtain it for free by "liv[ing] near a railroad and making faces at engineers."[96] When Irwin told and retold stories about Augustin Daly's attempts to correct her comic acting, she made fun of her own career. She joked about the fleeting nature of fame with a story of the number of songs she had to sing to a clerk in Oswego, Canada, before he was convinced that she was indeed May Irwin and cashed her thirty-dollar check. She showed humility when she opened an address to a group of businessmen in Watertown, New York, by declaring her inadequacy in speaking to the illustrious group, comparing herself to the bridegroom who, when called on to talk at his own wedding, "put his hand on his bride's shoulder and said 'This thing has been thrust upon me.'"[97]

But the largest body of self-critical material that Irwin used was about her weight (pun intended). She gave a Jersey cow as a present to comedian Fred Stone, noting that "she weighs about the same that I do." She worried that the future might be difficult for her, because her "air-taxi" would need to be "very strong." And she enjoyed relating the discomfort of others when they expressed concern about her ability to fit in a normal-size space, as when her maid returned from inspecting a hotel room with "De room's all right, suah, but Miss May, de doah suah am narrow." In public speaking, laughter greeted her demonstration of the physical awkwardness of a fat woman camping on an island, "trying to prepare and cook the lamb chops and get . . . supper ready, with a lantern held up in one hand, like this."[98]

Weight might bear the humor of an article as well as a joke. The piece "May Irwin in the 'Legitimate'" was a spoof in which Irwin told an interviewer that she intended to play Juliet in Shakespeare's tragedy in the upcoming season:

> The public seems to want Juliets . . . and all the girls are getting into the ga— that is, all the leading actresses are putting on Juliet. . . . Why not a heavy weight Juliet? I could go on at the weight with less than three weeks' training and put up a Juliet that would make a lot of them quit. You know it has long been my ambition to close my stage career in the legitimate and I think Juliet is a part that is just fitted to me. I have given the character much study and, though the part is heavier than my past work, so am I.[99]

The article included the subtitle "Her Appearance Marks a New Era in Stage Construction" and an illustration of the balcony scene, which would require the use of sturdy supports and a net.

Of course, for her part, Irwin was simply doing what many comics of her day and any day have done, mining the comic gold of her ample girth for every ounce. And she often did this by inviting the older women of the audience to laugh with her at the ravages of time. One of her most popular recitations, "A Painful Memory!," lamented her growing stoutness and mourned a dress from the past:

> I take it out of its hiding place,
> My friend of the bygone years,
> And I gaze upon it with an aching heart,
> And my eyes are filled with tears;

I smooth out each crease with a trembling hand,
And hold it up to the light—how old and worn it is,
The fabric now that was once so fresh and bright!
It shimmers there in the waning light,
My old silk dress so brown.
And with beating heart I try it on,
My dear old faded gown!
Over my shoulders I throw the dress,
And it tumbles down to my feet!!!!
But the hooks and eyes that once were friends,
Never again shall meet!!!!
I clasp it closer and closer still
With throbs of exquisite pain,
But the hooks and eyes that once were friends
Never will meet again!
Then I sit me down in mute despair,
For the struggle is all in vain.
And I know full well, as I place it back
In its hiding place once more,
That only in dreams those hooks and eyes
Will meet as in days of yore;
And I long with a passionate longing
For that meeting that never can be,
For the slender waist of a day that is gone
Will never come back to me.[100]

Irwin earned so much laughter and applause for this piece that she repeated it in *She Knows Better Now.* She also used this recitation in her act when she returned to vaudeville for a time in 1907 and again when she replaced Emma Calvé at the Palace in 1915. Her act in 1907 included so many jokes about her size that one reviewer remarked that it should have been titled "Me and My Adipose."[101] In May's farces, plot details use Irwin's plumpness for comedy. *Mrs. Black Is Back* features an amusing subplot in which a physical fitness instructor tries to help Mrs. Black lose weight. The determined Mrs. Black somehow ends up putting on more poundage under his tutelage. In the "smuggling" scene in *She Knows Better Now,* Irwin extracted jewelry from her abundant sleeves and "shed several frocks from her plump and perspiring form—to shrieks of laughter" from the audience.[102] (Trixie Friganza was also known to wear multiple layers of clothing and then "discard . . . them one by one throughout the course of her act.")[103] Joking about girth also recurs in Irwin's home movies: in a section called *Give the Little Girl a Hand,* a friend tries vainly and comically to heave Irwin's chubby frame up into a tree house.

Critics admired Irwin's ability to select roles that highlighted her heaviness: "May Irwin is the only woman of the stage who has thus far come forward with sufficient assurance of her hold upon the affections of the public as to warrant her in joking about her own embonpoint. Circumference is the bugaboo of other actresses. May, however, makes it a staple source of fun."[104] Despite this critic's claims, there *were* many actresses on the scene during this period who made their "circumference . . . a staple source of fun." The "bull-dog miened" Marie Dressler amused audiences with costumes decorated in "upholstery fabric" and accentuated her size (and athletic ability) by dancing with tall, very thin partners and manhandling them.[105] Trixie Friganza often wore a large, clown-like outfit while she strummed a tiny ukulele, singing one of her signature songs, such as "Won't Someone Kindly Stake Me to a Man?"[106]

Irwin's use of self-denigrating humor, common among women comics, not only served to lower her personal status and assure the audience that she was no better than anyone else (and indeed perhaps more foolish than many), but also served to transform her foibles, through laughter, into assets. This technique has been well-summarized elsewhere: "Laughing at one's shortcomings is not only a way of diminishing their importance and potentially overcoming them but also a technique for cleansing them of pejorative connotations imposed by the dominant culture and, thereby, turning them into strengths."[107]

Like Dressler, Friganza, and others, Irwin did not attempt to hide her plumpness. Unlike her stout contemporaries, however, she preferred to accentuate her rotundity by wearing beautiful gowns meant to be attractive. She did not portray an asexual and overly raucous fat woman, as did Marie Dressler. In fact, an early critic noted that Marie Dressler had a lot of talent and might put one in mind of May Irwin, "if it were not for an unfortunate coarseness which frequently mars [Dressler's] best work and awakens repugnance instead of amusement in her auditors." Nor did Irwin exhibit laughable man-chasing sexiness like Sophie Tucker or Trixie Friganza. She did not depict an aggressive woman hungry for male companionship. All of her characters, from Kate Kip to Mrs. Black to Matilda the maid, were eagerly sought out by eligible men. And she was often accompanied in her offstage joking, as in her comic article "Seats Too Small for May Irwin," by

Eisfeldt, her younger and attractive second husband. Unlike Dressler, or May Robeson—who often wore a partially bald wig—Irwin did not "sacrifice her good looks for the supposed demands of humor." She was plump *and* pretty. Even though she broke with the traditional styles deemed suitable for stout ladies, her beautiful costumes often made the viewer forget her girth: "[Irwin wears] a bodice so broken in line by insertions of cream-toned lace, that one almost forgets that the underarm width is twice that of the average figure." She insisted that men liked size in a woman and that "a woman judges her attractiveness by a purely fictitious idea of what men like." Irwin also stated adamantly that, although she was admittedly large, she felt free to wear "any color or stripes desired" in choosing her wardrobe: "Colors? Yes, I believe there ought to be chiefly light colors in comedy. I choose all the colors for the women's gowns in my company. And people seem to think that stout people can't wear light colors, but I always wear them, sometimes pink and blue, but often white."[108]

Onstage as well as off-, Irwin seldom appeared in black, the color often recommended for overweight people. Widow Mrs. Black favored "pink chiffons and point laces and diamonds," and as the belle of Bridgeport Irwin wore an abundance of ribbons and bows. Sister Mary appeared in horizontal stripes of "peach-colored cloth." In *Mrs. Wilson, That's All,* she was described as "wearing white chiffon over white silk" and "cream net built over white satin," and other characters displayed themselves in an array of fine embroidery and bosom-enhancing décolletage.[109] Additionally, Irwin's plays afforded her many chances to dress in evening wear. For example, in *Madge Smith, Attorney,* Irwin's character must give a fancy breakfast in formal attire to pay up on a bet. In *The Swell Miss Fitzwell,* the title character moves to Paris and dons a series of dazzling gowns; Mrs. Thompkins in *She Knows Better Now* visits Paris to procure beautiful gowns.

Irwin's interviews, as well as the reviews of her critics, emphasized the agreement others often had about her attractiveness, despite her rotundity. When Adolph Klauber of the *New York Times* interviewed Irwin on a number of subjects during a run of *Mrs. Black Is Back,* he made a point of adding an aside in which he disagreed with Irwin about the brilliance of the writing in her productions (but pretended to agree during the interview!). Later, she showed him a picture of herself dressed in a way that she thought might not be a good idea for a stout woman: "'But I decided to be in the picture, flowers, full skirt, round neck, and all. My friends tell me they are not unbecoming, what do you think?' Here it was a pleasure—and a truth, fortunately—to be able to agree with Miss Irwin's friends."[110]

Onstage, Irwin moved gracefully and daintily in her evening gowns, despite her girth. Critics noted that although she was "as large and apparently as unwieldy as ever," she seemed to be able "with a few movements of her body [to] . . . suggest any sort of gait whatever." Her dancing was praised for its "nimbleness"; when she danced, she seemed "to lose 100 pounds of her weight." Indeed, she is still graceful in later years on home film—at one point, she hikes up her skirt and strikes a surprisingly dainty ballet pose. Irwin made no apologies for her size—she reveled in it, prophesying a future in which fat would be the preferred condition. Soon, instead of "clever little Miss Annie Russell" or "winsome little Maud Adams," critics would be cooing about "charming, big May Irwin" and "wonderful, enormous Fanny Davenport."[111]

Irwin's immense popularity had many facets and worked on many levels. What makes her stand out among those who came before and after her is the manner in which she was able to orchestrate these dimensions to create a complex and highly marketable persona. Scholars have noted that the power of a female comedic personality depends on a combination of three elements: comedic talent (simply the ability to elicit laughter), sexual appeal or attractiveness, and personal competence (as the audience perceives it) in areas such as artistic talent, intelligence, and economic power: "These three elements . . . [must] work together to create a balance of power. When the performer strikes the proper balance . . . the audience will find her funny, appealing, fascinating, and non-threatening."[112]

The successful appeal of a female comic typically ranges from the gentle to the raucous and is closely connected to her perceived competence. The "proper balance" of sex appeal and personal competence often means that one trait cancels out another. That is, a beautiful, sexy comic often portrays a naive or stupid character; a clever or boisterous comic is often unattractive or overweight. (Contemporary critics have noted that this situation has changed somewhat in that a female comic *can* be both pretty and smart—indeed, sometimes is expected to be so.)[113] But most of Irwin's contemporaries fitted comfortably into these categories. Demure comediennes, like Irene Franklin or Lotta Crabtree, played naive children, and Eve Sully and the better-known Gracie Allen teamed with their husbands to play adorable nitwits. Sophie Tucker, Marie Dressler, and Trixie Friganza, on the other hand, played fat, undesirable women whose humor was often derived from their inability to trap a man.

However, Irwin was able to achieve a distinctive blend of sexual appeal and personal competence, unlike any of her contemporaries. She did this not by negating traits in any area but by creating an internal balance *within* each trait. For instance, Irwin played characters who were both fat *and* sexually attractive. She did make self-denigrating jokes about her weight, but she coupled these jokes with a sense of pride and glory in her rotundity. She was meant to be appealing and attractive to the opposite sex in her fancy costumes, complete with bows and lace in pastel colors. The characters she portrayed were eagerly sought out by members of the opposite sex, not for their money or powerful connections but because of their feminine appeal. She balanced the mental quickness of her characters' use of a pun or a double entendre with a scatterbrained quality shown by an inability to focus on one subject at a time. And although she achieved great success in portraying women in states of inebriation of which they were totally unaware, she also prospered in roles in which she shared with the audience a disguise or trick played on other characters.

Her characters were both *apart from* and *at one with* her audience. She was a highly competent star who was just "one of the common folk." Of course, these traits are not exclusive of May Irwin—they are recognizable in all sorts of celebrities of today and yesterday. What is remarkable is how successfully she maintained them in so many areas of her professional and, at least to her public's knowledge, personal life.

Again, Irwin's special appeal had to do with balance—not only between the old and the new but within a variety of contradictory styles and content. In maintaining this equilibrium, Irwin was careful to balance her comic traits, never to completely allow one to overwhelm another. In other words, she did not maintain popularity by playing a positive trait against a negative one (as a beautiful, dumb comedienne might or as an aggressive or intelligent but unattractive comedienne might); instead, she revealed just enough of the underside of her positive traits to remain nonthreatening to her public.

In sum, Irwin was irresistibly funny in performance. Onstage, her magnetic personality overshadowed both the inferior scripts of the farces she starred in and the abilities of her fellow actors. Once she moved from her early vaudeville beginnings and her work as a series of comic servants in Augustin Daly's company, she could choose her own roles—a variety of independent widows and professional women. In her major farces, Irwin relied on popular contemporary strategies for humor—including situations that required her to take on false identities, humor based on ethnic stereotypes, and satire at the expense of straitlaced people from polite society who disdained vices such as drinking and card playing.

Irwin enhanced the commonplace material in her plays with her considerable verbal virtuosity, her inimitable timing, and her spontaneity and direct contact with her audiences. Her style combined the childlike with the maternal. Her self-deprecatory humor, which often focused on her weight, had another side to it that was self-affirming—she was heavy but beautifully clothed; she was rotund but graceful.

Irwin blended these skills like no other to create a compelling persona that defined her success for more than a generation. When James L. Ford wrote "The Coming Queens of Comedy," he quoted an old theater manager on the two requisite skills of great comediennes: "[They] could make you laugh whether you wanted to or not, and each had the gift—almost as rare in women as that of creative humor—of being able to reach out across the footlights and take an entire audience . . . into her confidence." This manager cited May Irwin as one of the greatest ascending comic stars, one who practically "took the audience into her lap and talked to them like a big sister."[114]

Both on- and offstage, then, Irwin created a powerful persona and an array of conflicting characters. She was both a character *and* herself, inviting her audience to laugh *with* her (May Irwin) and *at* her (the character). Thus, critics were able to state with equal truth that Irwin "casts her inferiority in our faces," and "the beauty of it all is that while we think we are laughing at her expense, she is really laughing at ours." Irwin exhibited the masterful ability to make fun of both others and herself—and to let the audience see themselves in her and laugh at themselves as well. Laughter was the goal she was most committed to. "Sometimes I feel a certain regret that perhaps my name will go down in history, if it even trundles along that far, as 'the woman who sang coon songs,' more than the woman who made the public laugh. The latter would be the height of my ambition."[115]

In truth, May Irwin has been relegated to the dustheap for years because of the racist "coon songs." Yet as I'll explore in the next chapters, they were probably responsible for her greatest success, both in comedy and in the creation of her image.

May Irwin's childhood home. Courtesy of Whitby Archives, photograph 17-123-002, Whitby, Ontario, Canada.

The Irwin sisters, Flo and May, with Tony Pastor, ca. 1885–87. TCS2, Houghton Library, Harvard University, Cambridge, Mass.

Undated photograph of young May Irwin. Courtesy of the author.

FORTY FOURTH REGULAR SEASON

BOSTON MUSEUM

ESTABLISHED 1841

MR. R. M. FIELD, Manager.

SIXTH ANNUAL VISIT,

AND

ENGAGEMENT FOR TWO WEEKS ONLY,

OF

Mr. Augustin Daly's Company of Comedians,

FROM DALY'S THEATRE, NEW YORK,

Comprising this year the following Favorite Artists and New Candidates for Favor:—

Miss Ada Rehan,
Mrs. G. H. Gilbert, Miss Virginia Dreher,
Miss Edith Kingdon, Miss May Irwin,
Miss Jean Gordon, Miss Agnes Perring,
Mr. James Lewis,
Mr. John Drew, Mr. Otis Skinner,
Mr. Charles Leclercq, Mr. Wm. Gilbert,
Mr. Frederick Bond, Mr. E. P. Wilks,
Mr. Charles Fisher,

AND COMMENCING

Monday Evening, May 4, 1885,

WITH THE PRODUCTION,

FOR ONE WEEK ONLY,

Evenings at 8, Wednesday and Saturday Afternoons at 2,

of the Most Successful of all the FAMOUS COMEDY SUCCESSES OF DALY'S THEATRE, an Entirely Novel Comedy (from the German of *Stobitzer*), by Mr. Augustin Daly, entitled,

LOVE ON CRUTCHES

THE ORIGINAL CAST.

Sydney Austin, a gentleman of leisure, who has written something, ... Mr. John Drew
Guy Roverly, a gentleman of leisure, who has seen something, ... Mr. Otis Skinner
Dr. Epenetus Quattles, Love's postman..... Mr. James Lewis
Mr. Bitteredge, "interviewer"..... Mr. William Gilbert
Podd, a valet in place..... Mr. F. Bond
Bells..... Mr. J. Stapleton
Annis Austin, an ideal of the misunderstood..... Miss Ada Rehan
Eudoxia Quattles, posing for martyrdom..... Mrs. G. H. Gilbert
Mrs. Margery Gwynn, inclined to tempt Fate a second time, ... Miss Edith Kingdon
Berta, Mrs. Gwynn's maid..... Miss Jean Gordon
Netty, maid to Mrs. Austin..... Miss May Irwin

Guests, Etc.

TIME—The Present. PLACE—New York.

ACT I. passes at Austin's. The Summer Breakfast Room on the Piazza.
ACTS II. and III. in Mrs. Gwynn's Parlors and Conservatory.

ACT FIRST.—"Who is Marius?"
ACT SECOND.—A Bottomless Treasure.
ACT THIRD.—The Bubbles are Blown.

The New Scenery from..... ROBERT'S MODELS
New Incidental Music by..... HENRY WIDMER

Every performance will be, as heretofore, under the personal direction of

Mr. AUGUSTIN DALY.

Stage Manager..... } For Mr. DALY, { ..... Mr JOHN MOORE
Musical Director..... } { ..... Mr. H. J. WIDMER
Business Manager..... } { ..... Mr. RICHARD DORNEY

THE ORCHESTRA, under the direction of MR. GEORGE PURDY, will play the following selections:

1. Overture—"King of Diamonds" . . . . . Lavalee
2. Waltz—"Sea Shells" . . . . . Waterson
Cornet Solo, Mons. E. N. Lafricain.
3. Medley Selection . . . . . Geo. Purdy
4. March—"In the Ranks" . . . . . Warren

Monday Next, May 11th,

LAST WEEK of MR. AUGUSTIN DALY'S COMPANY,

and Production, for SEVEN PERFORMANCES ONLY, of

A NIGHT OFF

The Very Latest Success of Daly's Theatre, New York,

written by MR. AUGUSTIN DALY upon a subject suggested by the German, and pronounced by press and public of New York as the

Most Amusing and Laughable Comedy

produced in many seasons.

Saturday Evening, May 16th,

FAREWELL OF MR. DALY'S COMPANY

SPECIAL NIGHT and SPECIAL PRODUCTION,

by General Request, of

SHE WOULD AND SHE WOULD NOT

For the RETURN of the

BOSTON MUSEUM COMPANY,

AND

CLOSE OF 44th DRAMATIC SEASON,

Two of Augustin Daly's Most Laughable Comedies,

SEVEN PERFORMANCES EACH! SEVEN PERFORMANCES EACH!

Monday, May 18th,

Augustin Daly's Comedy of

BIG BONANZA

Monday, May 25th,

Augustin Daly's Comedy of

LEMONS

being the first production in nine years of these mirth-provoking plays. Each will be cast to the strength of the Museum Company, and constitute a fitting close to a

BRILLIANT AND SUCCESSFUL SEASON.

THE PIANOS used are from..... MESSRS. CHICKERING & SONS
CABINET ORGANS from..... NEW ENGLAND ORGAN COMPANY

STAGE MANAGER

Playbill for Augustin Daly's plays *Love on Crutches* and *A Night Off*. Courtesy of Karen Killian's private collection.

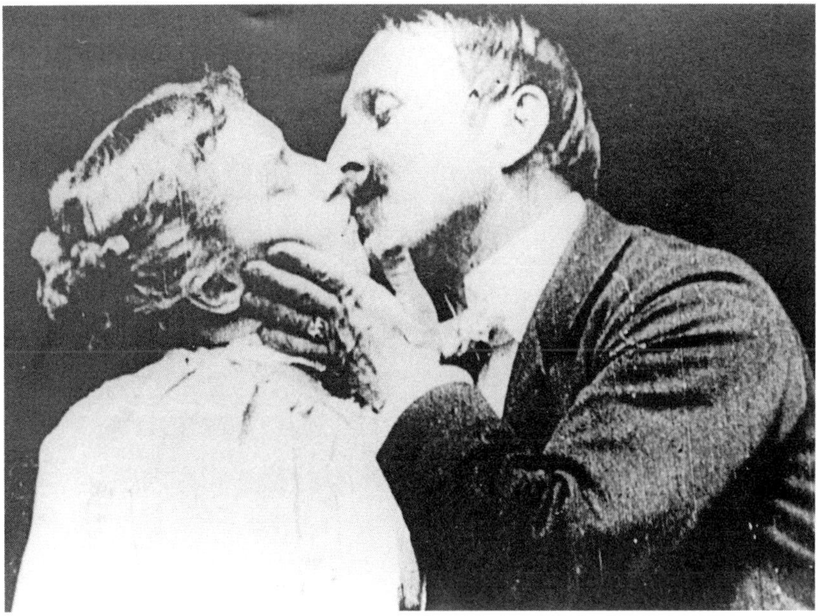

The Kiss (1896) on Vitascope. Courtesy of Whitby Archives, photograph 34-000-017, Whitby, Ontario, Canada.

May Irwin in *Mrs. Peckham's Carouse*, ca. 1907. Courtesy of Whitby Archives, photograph 34-000-014, Whitby, Ontario, Canada.

Flo Irwin in *Widow Jones*. Courtesy of the Harry Ransom Center, University of Texas, Austin.

May Irwin in *Widow by Proxy,* 1913. Courtesy of Karen Killian's private collection.

May Irwin in *Getting a Polish,* ca. 1910. Courtesy of Karen Killian's private collection.

3

The Profoundly Troubling History of the Coon Song

Coon shouting took Negro stereotyping to levels of hateful, grinning crudity that even the worst minstrel shows had rarely achieved.

—John Strausbaugh, *Black Like You: Blackface, Whiteface, Insult and Imitation in American Popular Culture*

If it were possible to measure vulgarity in music, the coon song would certainly represent the nadir.

—Sam Dennison, *Scandalize My Name: Black Imagery in America Popular Music*

Irwin's fears that she would be remembered only for her coon songs may have been well founded. Indeed, in her obituary, the *New York Times* noted that the plays Irwin starred in were already mostly forgotten, "but the ditties she nursed into popularity are still the stand-bys of the old song books." In the longer run, however, May Irwin may have been, to paraphrase one of her own tunes, "laid on the shelf" because of the racism of these numbers. These songs are representative of a large collection of undeniably heinous racist music and memorabilia that have only in recent generations been widely viewed and acknowledged as such. Unfortunately, the failure to confront an embarrassing past can only promote racism by denying its existence. In this respect, archivists such as David Pilgrim of the Jim Crow Museum of Racist Memorabilia at Ferris State University have done an admirable job of preserving artifacts that serve what Pilgrim describes as a "powerful remembrance of America's racist past."[1]

It is simply not possible to write about May Irwin without delving into this subject, for if coon songs were indeed the "nadir" of "vulgarity in music," then May Irwin was their most prominent purveyor throughout the period of their peak popularity—from the 1890s until World War I. Her success as a coon shouter warrants a careful analysis of the layers of meaning in these songs, considering the context of the times and the skill with which Irwin manipulated these meanings—consciously or unconsciously.

What were coon songs? Simply put, they were ragtime melodies coupled with lyrics purported to be representative of contemporary African American life. As such, they included wildly exaggerated themes, lyrics written in "Negro dialect," and references to various objects supposedly making up racist caricatures of black life—for example, alcohol, razors, chickens, watermelon, dice, guns, pork and beans, and rabbits' feet.[2]

In her excellent thesis comparing white and black composers of the coon song, Leah Cathleen Cothern notes that the term *coon* has been used to refer to different subjects in American slang—from rural backwoodsmen to members of the Whig Party—before becoming, during Reconstruction, a derogatory term for blacks. She surmises that, in addition to being associated with the supposed dietary preferences of black people, the word's application to Whigs and then Republicans may have become a descriptor of African Americans through its connection with the "old Coon" Abraham Lincoln, who bore responsibility for freeing the slaves.[3]

Coon songs did not only use "coon" as a moniker for African Americans. Their lyrics were also replete with the epithet "nigger." The word itself came from the Latin name for black (*niger*). But it has been seen as a derogatory term for African Americans at least as early as 1619, when the first black slaves came to Jamestown. During the Revolutionary War, British soldiers used the term to denigrate the antiroyalist colonists.[4]

Like most popular songs of late-nineteenth- and early-twentieth-century America, coon songs were closely connected to the birth of instrumental ragtime music. Ragtime, a style connected with white minstrelsy, black jazz, and white march music, consists of melodic lines with syncopation over a bass in four-square march style. The important element in ragtime is the syncopation—which is fitted to the older forms of marches, two-steps (actually a type of march in 6/8 time), and similar duple or quadruple-meter dances. Instrumental rags follow traditional forms used in the older music but add a variety of styles of syncopation in the right-hand melody. The syncopation, coupled with the use of dance music, renders ragtime music catchy and lively.[5]

Ragtime songs borrowed some of these new syncopations and combined them with simple melodies of two-part verse and choral structure. An example of the syncopation a ragtime tune might use is illustrated in the following number, in which a simple syncopation is repeated in the bass line mimicking the melody line:

"Never Raise a Razor" (1906), by John Lowitz (popularized by May Irwin).

Another type of syncopation, often referred to as "ragging," set the syncopated melody line against an unsyncopated bass line (as in instrumental ragtime) in a pattern of three notes over two:

Irwin's "LuLu Song" (1896), by Summit L. Hecht.

Coon songs, then, were ragtime songs whose lyrics were usually in black dialect and whose themes relied heavily on popular and appallingly unflattering stereotypes of black life and folk. May Irwin's repertoire of coon songs was replete with such stereotypes

Of course, the stock characters of coon songs did not spring up overnight. From a minor character in American plays, "the Negro" of the eighteenth century (often nameless but later possessing monikers like "Sambo") blossomed with the well-known Thomas Dartmouth Rice, who created "Jim Crow" in 1828. His model was supposedly a crippled, shabby stable boy. "Daddy" Rice put on blackface and sang:

> W'eel about and turn about
> And do just so,
> Eb'ry time I w'eel about
> I jump Jim Crow.

This stereotype was soon imitated and joined by another character created by blackfaced actor George Washington Dixon, who performed as "Zip Coon." Zip Coon was the city black—lording it over his country cousins with his convoluted, error-filled "knowledge." The song "Zip Coon" dates from 1834 and repeats the phrase "Old Zip Coon is a very learn-ed school-r," followed by the nonsense chorus, "Zip a du-den day, O zip a du-den du-den du-den du-den du-den day."[6] The idea that everyone had to learn Old Zip Coon's song led to other songs commenting on its ubiquity. In fact, my father used to sing this song to me when I was a little girl and had no idea who or what Zip Coon was:

> Oh, there was a man with a double chin
> Who performed with skill on the violin
> And he played in time and he played in tune,
> But he couldn't play anything but Old Zip Coon

In the version I heard, the violinist had to be sent far away to find a place where people had never heard of that song!

The black characters of the early minstrel shows were the pathetic but basically benevolent progenitors of the coon-song types that I will come back to later in this chapter. They are featured prominently in the songs of Stephen Foster and the lesser-known black composer James A. Bland, who wrote "Carry Me Back to Old Virginny" in 1878, "a masterpiece of ballad writing that was immediately compared to Foster's best."[7]

The popularity of the coon song is hard to overestimate. In the 1890s alone, at least six hundred coon songs were published in sheet-music form, and many of the popular numbers sold in the millions.[8] A majority of the credited composers of such songs were white. Kentucky-born, red-haired Ben Harney, who wrote such songs as "Mr. Johnson, Turn Me Loose" (Johnson was slang for policeman) and "You've Been a Good Old Wagon, but You Done Broke Down," dubbed himself the "inventor of ragtime" and performed with a black partner as his "servant, Strap Hill."[9] Charles E. Trevathan, a sportswriter and horse-racing judge, was credited with composing two of Irwin's most famous numbers, "The Bully" and "The Frog Song." George M. Cohan, at the tender age of seventeen, wrote "Hot Tamale Alley," and Theodore Metz claimed composition credit for "A Hot Time in the Old Town" (although, as in the case of many of these numbers, the original source was rumored to be a black singer).[10]

But there were many coon songs written by and attributed to black composers as well. In fact, one of the most notorious coon songs of the era, "All Coons Look Alike to Me," was written by the popular singer and composer

Ernest Hogan, who perhaps drew on a tune by a black male singer overheard in Chicago's red-light district, "All Pimps Look Alike to Me."[11] Called "the model for many subsequent songs on the black male-female relationship,"[12] Hogan's song moves from the male voice of the jilted lover complaining about his lady, Lucy Janey Stubbles, who has left him, to the black female's voice of the chorus:

> All coons look alike to me,
> I've got another beau, you see,
> And he's just as good to me as you, nig! ever tried to be,
> He spends his money free,
> I know we can't agree,
> So I don't like you no how,
> All coons look alike to me.

Black composers also wrote songs that featured portraits of idealized love, as represented in "Louisiana Lize" and "Ma Mississippi Belle," both written by the team of Bob Cole and the Johnson brothers (J. Rosamund and James Weldon). These airs were considered more refined than other coon songs, and the writers were defined as "nurture[rs of] the hybrid of coon song and sentimental ballad."[13] The famous black comedy team of Bert Williams and George Williams Walker was also responsible for a number of coon songs, including "Mama, Does You Love Your Honey?" and "Mammy's Pickaninny Boy."

Importantly, the black composers of coon songs were among the first of their race to earn any real money in musical theater. In 1897–99, Bob Cole was responsible for *A Trip to Coontown.* Cole left the Troubadors, a black group headed by white managers, when he was refused a raise even though his compositions and his own performances had been extremely successful. His partner, Billy Johnson, soon joined him, and they created *A Trip to Coontown,* on a very limited budget, with an all-black cast and producers. It took a few years of lean times, but the production opened on Broadway in 1899.[14]

The comedy team of Williams and Walker—as mentioned above—had an even more successful production in *In Dahomey* with an all-black team. The show featured Williams and Walker and opened on Broadway in February 1903, after a very brief tryout period. Walker always played the slick, dandified con man. The highly paid Bert Williams, perhaps the most famous black entertainer of his time, specialized in caricatures of the slow-witted, hard-luck "coon" much decried by later critics. Like many light-skinned Negroes, he performed in blackface. The tale of *In Dahomey* is a clever satire of the back-to-Africa movement of the time. Williams and Walker con a group of blacks from Georgia to follow them to "Dahomey," supposedly a lush area of Africa. Walker declares himself king and Williams his prime minister. The show attracted huge crowds of African Americans, relegated to different seating than the white audience, but dressed in tuxedos and ball gowns—as splendid as any garments featured in the white section. After a six-week run, the production went to London's Shaftesbury Theatre for two hundred performances. They even gave a special performance for King Edward at Buckingham Palace.[15]

Both black males and females sang coon songs. Charles Wright, or "C. W. Bebee, the coon shouter," sang "When a Coon Sits in the Presidential Chair," one of a group of coon songs that revealed the "ludicrous" state of affairs that would result with blacks in any power position. W. L. McMullen accompanied his coon singing with sophisticated guitar playing and was lauded in the black newspaper of Indianapolis, the *Freeman*. Bessie Gilman, with Wright's Colored Comedy Company, sang "Mammy's Little Pumpkin Colored Coon." Carrie Hall voiced hits like "What You Gonna Do When the Rent Comes Due" and "The Game of Goo-Goo Eyes." Belle Davis and Bessie Hamilton also made their mark singing coon songs. There were white male coon shouters as well. For example, both Arthur Collins in 1902 and Len Spencer in 1903 made recordings and a lot of money on the popular "That's the Way to Spell Chicken," for which the African American composer, Sydney Perrin, received a total of fifteen dollars.[16]

But the most popular coon shouters were white women. A large proportion of white female vaudevillians tried their hand at coon shouting—Marie Dressler, Eva Tanguay, Nora Bayes, and Trixie Friganza all joined in the fad. Jewish comediennes, notably Stella Mayhew and Sophie Tucker, blacked up and sang coon songs that contemporary critics have noted "found currency in and capitalized on the suppressed identity of these Jewish performers."[17] Both Tucker and Mayhew were known for their "Mammy" characters. Other white women, such as Josephine Gassman and Mayme Remington, led "pickaninny acts," singing songs like "Mammy's Carolina Twins" with a band of dancing black children (usually all boys).[18] The "refined" Clarice Vance was known for her delicate renditions of numbers such as "Don't Forget to Bring Your Money Home" and "If Anybody Wants to Meet a Jonah, Shake Hands with Me." On the other extreme of the continuum was Artie Hall, the "Georgia coon shouter," who specialized in raucous dancing, elaborate blackface makeup and wig, and songs like "I'm Living a Ragtime Life" and "I Don't Care What Happens to Me Now."[19]

In this amazing cultural stew of coon shouters, why, then, should May Irwin's work be singled out for analysis? The simplest answer is that May Irwin, who did not perform in blackface, was the performer most closely associated with the birth of the coon-song phenomenon. Whether Irwin was the *first* white coon shouter is not a question that can be answered conclusively, but she was certainly credited as such. One critic explained that, sometime in 1894, "May Irwin was coming East with a new tune she had picked up in a Pullman car from the guitar of Charles E. Trevathan [who] had brought it up from the South. The irrepressible May was so struck with the tune that she ordered a supply of words for it, and into *The Widow Jones* went the song. . . . 'The Bully' was a knockout overnight. Coon-shouting, as translated into Caucasian, was born."[20]

A much richer account is told by Ian Whitcomb in his book about ragtime. Of course, its truthfulness is questionable—but it certainly paints a picture of a much rougher ragtime society: "Charles Trevathan, a sportswriter and night bird, was travelling with Miss Irwin on the Chicago train and for a diversion he sang her a hilarious knockabout story about a murderous coon. 'Needs some polishing but it's a runner for the show, Charlie. Where'd you get the number, you're no writer? Same place you got that cough?' The sportsman admitted that he'd taken it down on his shirt cuff at Babe Connors's place in St. Louis. 'The girls dance on a mirror and they wear no drawers, see?'"[21]

Whichever version one may choose to believe, it's certainly true that "coon song" and "May Irwin" were indelibly linked. In 1893, "The white vaudevillian May Irwin was using this material [coon songs] in her act, and she became firmly identified with a series of 'coon songs' during their vogue." On the first page of *May Irwin's Songs,* it was noted that "no woman in America sings negro songs like May Irwin. . . . the popular mind has associated Miss Irwin so closely with the singing of these dialect songs . . . that one is prepared to believe that she has made a lifelong study of the subject."[22] Although earlier prototypes for the coon song may be plentiful, their introduction to the general public was connected to Irwin's performances of these songs on the stage. Review after review of Irwin's shows focused on her admirable handling of coon songs. Some examples include the following: "[Her] imitation of a 'coon' is extremely in advance of the real article and much more desirable"; "Nobody but May Irwin completely caught the characteristics of the American coon"; and "Her singing of 'coon' and other strongly accented songs was, as usual, a taking item of the bill of fare and of delicious if humble flavor. . . . [I]n her imitation of darkies . . . her assumption by turns of the easy style, the airy, the solemn, the surly, the contemptuous, the distrustful and the defiant, was masterly."[23] The association of Irwin with the coon song is so strong that *The New Grove Dictionary of American Music* offers a picture of May Irwin under the entry "coon song."[24]

Thus, May Irwin's close association with the coon song was significant, both in the development of her own popularity with audiences who saw her performances in New York or on tour and in disseminating the words and music of coon songs throughout America. As noted previously, the public's interest in the coon song seemed almost boundless: "At the peak of its popularity, the coon song was ubiquitous at every level of entertainment, and songwriters labored to supply the insatiable demand."[25]

The coon song's booming popularity coincided with the rapid expansion of the sheet-music business, fueled by new techniques in mass production, the creation of higher-quality paper, and more uniformly printed music. This explosion ensured that Americans all over the country would be inundated with these songs: "The music business itself underwent fundamental changes during the 1890s. It became an industry of no mean proportions. . . . Literally tons of music flowed from Tin Pan Alley—music that more than any other entertainment medium reflected the spirit of the times. The exuberant cocksuredness of expansionist America found its best expression in its songs during this period."[26]

Even a cursory study of the sheet-music covers of the time suggests a wealth of stereotypical images, featuring outrageous caricatures of black men and women with enormous lips, eyes, and wide nostrils. These characters are literally trapped in the visage of the coon. For example, on the cover of "Coon, Coon, Coon" the word *coon* encompasses the illustration of the black male, with the *C* enlarged to contain his face and the *o*'s becoming huge poppy eyes. Often, black characters of all ages are portrayed as children "playing" at being grown-ups, even when the song is ostensibly about adults, as in "I Couldn't Stand to See My Baby Lose" and "I Ain't Got Time to Be Your Baby."

In addition to the usual plethora of chickens, razors, dice, and watermelons, the covers of coon-song sheet music often display men and women overdressed in the latest fashions. Thus, "Hot Tamale Alley" features a picture of May Irwin standing beside a black couple dressed luxuriously, both with bright shining diamond stickpins and large hats. One cover of "All Coons Look Alike to Me" features a variety of coon "types," all dressed in different suits, with canes and diamond stickpins or top hats—but all similar in their exaggerated lips and kinky hair. In stark contrast was the way white society was displayed in popular ballad sheet music of the same time period. The cover of "After the Ball," for example, depicts a large group of sedate, graceful, and attractive white men and women in sophisticated, but understated, evening gowns. Although the 1880s and 1890s were the age of ragtime and coon songs, it was also a golden age of other popular songs that remain well known today. The early 1880s featured many "gang songs"—those that could be sung easily by groups of men and women—such as "Bring Back My Bonnie to Me," lilting ballads like "The Fountain in the Park" (known more by the first line, "While Strolling in the Park One Day"), tearjerkers like Paul Dresser's "The Letter That Never Came," and urban hits like "The Sidewalks of New York."[27]

While most current collections of songs from the "Gay Nineties" include hits like "After the Ball" and "Bring Back My Bonnie to Me," they do not include the equally popular coon songs. Nor are most people today aware that the nostalgic images of Currier and Ives, whose lithograph offices churned out "chromos"—new mass-produced copies of paintings and illustrations—and shipped them all across the United States for prices averaging two to three dollars,[28] also helped reinforce negative images of African Americans. Although Currier and Ives were known for their reproductions of paintings by John Audubon, Winslow Homer, and Rembrandt Peale, none of these replicas included African American painters. Instead, Currier and Ives produced, from the 1870s to the 1890s, a series known as the Darktown Comics. One need only compare the tender naturalism of African American painter Henry Ossama Tanner's 1893 *The Banjo Lesson* with the Currier and Ives print *Darktown Banjo Lesson* (1886) to see the stark caricature in the latter, which is inscribed with an added caption supplied by white writers: "Thumb it, Darkies . . . oh how loose I feel!"[29]

At the same time that sheet music and chromos were flooding the country, the parlor organs of the 1870s were being replaced by pianos.[30] Because sheet music was arranged for voice and piano, this enabled families all over America not only to perform coon songs themselves but also to absorb the sheet music's iconography and its depiction of black life. In this way, Americans with little or no experience of African Americans began to form a warped mental picture of the environment and characteristics of the race. Thus, the ubiquity of sheet music during this period offered a medium for visual as well as aural stereotypes.

I have taken time here to describe the atmosphere and broad dissemination of these images in order to paint a clear picture of how powerful and pervasive they were in society. It is no wonder, then, that by 1900 a female comic could quip "I'm as popular as a safety razor at a colored picnic" anywhere north or south of the Mason-Dixon line and always get a laugh. Much has been made of the variety of ethnic humor that existed alongside the lampooning of blacks, where "blackfaced 'Ethiopians' rubbed elbows with various other brands of broadly played ethnic stereotypes and impersonations, for equally low laughs—the brawling Irish, wheedling Jews, oily Italians, thick-headed Germans, inscrutable Chinamen, gullible country rubes and so on."[31]

It is true that other ethnic groups not only suffered parody on the stage but also endured remarkable social prejudice—nineteenth-century advertisements for maids often included "No Irish need apply," and Jewish comedians as late and illustrious as Groucho Marx were barred from hotels and golf clubs. (Groucho's famous quip when he was refused admittance to a swimming pool was a request for his daughter to be allowed to go in up to her waist—since she was only half-Jewish.) Early Irish ethnic songs certainly mirrored the animosity toward the Irish, sometimes using stereotypes that were also applied to African Americans:

> Patty McFadden was lazy and fat
> And the hair of his head grew out of his hat
> He had but one son and he christened him Pat
> Mash whack Fadden, Fadden ni ah.[32]

During the 1890s, Maggie Cline ("the Irish Queen") gained fame singing "Throw Him Down, McCloskey," by John W. Kelly. Although this song has a celebratory air and featured the strong comic abilities of Cline, the lyrics paint an unflattering picture of the Irish temper, pointing to the composer's admission that he was "ready to fight at the drop of a hat":

> They fought like two hyenas till the forty-seventh round,
> They scattered blood enough around, by gosh, to paint the town,
> McCloskey got a mouthful of poor McCracken's jowl.
> McCracken hollered, "Murthur," and his seconds hollered, "Foul!"
> The friends of both the fighters that instant did begin
> To fight and at each other the whole party started in,
> You couldn't tell the difference in your fighters if you'd try,
> McCracken lost his upper lip, McCloskey lost an eye.[33]

Immigrants were also subject to acts of persecution and not even immune to the ultimate terror of lynching. For example, the White League in New Orleans was responsible, in 1891, for torturing and hanging eleven Italians accused of plotting to kill a policeman. Even the *New York Times* concurred with the action, comparing Italians to "rattlesnakes.[34] (Also outside the scope of this study are the tragic assimilation stories of Native Americans and Chinese.)

In this tangled web of meanings in the representation of race and ethnicity on the vaudeville stage, it may be true that, on one level, the humor "had a liberalizing effect on the public . . . [becoming] an instrument whereby new groups were introduced to the culture—initially demonized and ridiculed, later impersonated, then emulated and eventually appreciated and loved." But in the case of African Americans, this melting-pot theory contains serious flaws. That's because compounding the shame of slavery is the harsh backlash against the progress made by African Americans after the Civil War. Many excellent studies of this period have been published during the past decade, revealing the deeply troubling context of coon shouting.[35]

In the years leading up to the Civil War, the North certainly had its share of clashes between abolitionists and antiabolitionists. In New York, these forces were especially prevalent and often connected to nativist impulses (and to the performing arts). In 1834, in the weeks leading up to the Farren Riot over the supposed firing of an American actor by the English manager and stage manager of the Bowery Theater, abolitionists' stores were set on fire and blacks were beaten in the streets. On July 9, while American actor Edwin Forrest was starring in *Metamora,* a crowd of almost a thousand, which historians speculate was a splinter force from an antiabolitionist mob, broke down the doors of the theater and rushed the stage. On the same evening, the house of a well-known abolitionist—Lewis Tappan—was sacked. Rioting continued for two days.[36]

Financial panics in 1837 and 1857 increased the negative feelings of impoverished northern whites toward black freemen seeking equal footing in a shrinking economy. A particularly violent riot in New York, after the war draft in 1863, resulted in the deaths of more than one hundred people, almost all of whom were African American.[37]

The North's killing of fifty thousand civilians in the South has become what historian Jackson Lears has termed the "rationale for treating civilians as belligerents [which] foreshadowed contemporary excuses for 'collateral damage.'"[38] It also exacerbated poverty among southern whites and fueled their ill feelings toward former slaves.

The immediate aftermath of our nation's bloodiest war is well studied. After the Civil War and during the period known as Radical Reconstruction (1867–77), biracial government successfully existed in the South for a time. African Americans gained considerable political power and held important positions in government, churches, and educational institutions. The "black-and-tan" conventions during Reconstruction would be short-lived. The Compromise of 1877 effectively ended the promise of equality. In the election of 1876, the Republican candidate for president, Rutherford B. Hayes, lost the popular vote but gained the southern electoral vote and hence the presidency by promising "the withdrawal of federal troops from the South and the end of any sustained federal effort to protect black rights."[39] The suppression of the rights of the new African American citizenry would take a while to reach its full effect. As late as 1885, travelers to the South noted a frequent intermingling of the races. That year T. McCants Stewart, an African American journalist from Boston, ventured for the first time into the American South. He expected discrimination aboard the trains, especially when white passengers entered a full car in which he was seated. But no one asked him to move. He later declared: "I fairly foamed at the mouth, imagining that the conductor would order me to [move next to] a seat occupied by a colored lady so as to make room for the white passenger. [No such demand occurred] . . . and I feel I am as safe here [in the South] as I am in Providence, Rhode Island. I can ride in first-class cars on the railroads and in the streets. I can stop in and drink a glass of soda and be more politely waited upon than in some parts of New England."[40]

However, by the late 1880s, Jim Crow laws—which required separate public facilities for blacks and whites—began a serious curtailment of black rights. The first of these laws concerned train transportation. In 1887 Florida passed a law mandating separate cars for blacks and whites, and similar laws were soon passed in Alabama, Arkansas, Louisiana, and other southern states.[41] Black leaders in New Orleans began the fight against early Jim Crow laws, organizing black riders who refused to remain in separate accommodations and then taking their cases to court. At first the black defendants won, and the Louisiana Supreme Court declared that the Jim Crow law on separate transportation facilities was unconstitutional, at least when applied to travel between states. But in 1896, when the case arose in *Plessy v. Ferguson* and was taken all the way to the U.S. Supreme Court, the Court ruled for the constitutionality of separate but equal facilities for blacks and whites. Part of Justice John Marshall Harlan's lone dissent is often cited: "The arbitrary separation of citizens, on the basis of race, while they are on a public highway, is a badge of servitude wholly inconsistent with the civil freedom and the equality before the law established by the Constitution. It cannot be justified upon any legal grounds."[42]

Plessy v. Ferguson would not be overturned until 1954. The Court's earlier decision represented a pervasive social attitude. In 1900, for example, Dr. P. B. Barringer presented an address at the University of Virginia contending that "if you scratch a Negro, you will find a savage" and calling for the South to act "before another generation of Negroes is allowed to arise" and to "remove the Negro from politics—not, perhaps, forever—but certainly until the proper time." Dr. Barringer was a well-respected physician who studied heredity. The meeting was held by the Tri-State Medical Society—with an introduction that stressed the importance of open discussion about the "Negro problem." Pamphlets of the speech were disseminated throughout the South.[43]

If groups like the Ku Klux Klan were responsible during Reconstruction for "the most extensive example of home grown terrorism in American history," the unbridled venom these groups directed toward black citizens only grew in the years after the North's abandonment of the South ended Reconstruction.[44] Recent histories estimate that in the South alone between 1880 and 1890, there were *at least* thirty-two hundred black men lynched.[45] It was at the height of this ugly backlash that May Irwin became the most popular coon shouter in America. In her capable hands, she clearly underlined the growing belief that "a negro may have aspirations, but a coon has none."[46]

In this climate, even the most successful African American had little chance of being assimilated into the "melting pot." Meanwhile, marriages among members of different European immigrant groups newly arrived in America increased dramatically. Within only one generation of having relocated to America, nearly 50 percent of northern Italians and Irish immigrants, and even larger shares of Scandinavians and Germans, married outside of their own groups.[47] By contrast, intermarriage between African Americans and white immigrants of any ethnicity was not only socially risky but also illegal in many states. Antimiscegenation laws were introduced into the New World as early as 1661, and by 1924 thirty-eight states in America outlawed such unions.[48] Despite such laws, there was evidence everywhere of illicit congress between the races from our earliest history, and anyone with "one drop of Negro blood" was considered African American.

By the turn of the twentieth century, in this world of "separate but equal" facilities, black stage performers may have worked side by side with whites, but black theater patrons were strictly segregated from white patrons and were allowed seating only in upper balconies. Meanwhile, as popular-culture critic David Nasaw has observed, assimilation of virtually all European ethnic groups proceeded apace:

> "White" immigrants and ethnics who dressed appropriately, acted decently, and had the price of admission were welcomed inside the commercial amusement centers. As Henry James discovered in 1904 on his return to the United States after a twenty-year absence, the "aliens" were everywhere being rapidly Americanized or, as he put it, magically lifted to a new "level" "glazed . . . over

> . . . by a huge white-washing brush." Even the Italians, he found, had lost their "colour," which of all the European "races, they had appeared . . . most to have." James' use of metaphors of color to describe the Americanization of the "alien" was particularly apt. For what most distinguished the European Americans from the African Americans was the former's ability to lose their "colour."[49]

Even when Bert Williams and George Walker brought *In Dahomey,* the landmark musical written and performed by blacks, to Broadway in 1903, the audience segregation policy was strictly enforced. The house was packed, and black patrons argued at the ticket counter, offering to pay much more than the dollar charged for orchestra seats. The theater manager stood his ground; orchestra seats were for whites only.[50]

It was in these segregated Broadway houses that May Irwin gained her stardom. Her plays, as we have seen, were peppered with songs, the majority of which were coon songs that had very little to do with the script or her character. Of course, Irwin sang innumerable songs during her long career, and not all of them were coon songs. She sang songs early on in vaudeville skits with her sister, Flo, at Tony Pastor's, and she featured them in the plays that became her starring vehicles from the 1890s to the 1910s. She was often trying out new numbers night after night, and she sang her favorites again whenever she was pulled out of one of her many retirements from the stage to perform for special events or to embark on limited runs of shows. (Her most famous non–coon song was "After the Ball," mentioned above.)[51] Irwin sang many love ballads and comic songs, often with themes of domestic strife relating to white couples—sometimes of specific ethnic backgrounds. For example, her Irish love song "Honora Doolin" was popular, as was "The Kellys Are at It Again," which focused on a couple who were always disturbing their neighbors, either by calling each other baby names or later by their fighting.

It would be impossible to account for every musical number that Irwin performed in her life.[52] However, the variety and composition of her repertoire during her most active years as a performer (1890–1915) can be inferred from major sheet-music collections of the period, from reviews of her shows, and from her recordings. She performed well over one hundred songs, and at least two-thirds of these are clearly identifiable as coon songs. Additional songs in her repertoire, some unavailable in sheet music, have highly suggestive titles and were often written by composers associated with coon songs. For example, "I'se Laid Him on de' Shelf" has a title in strong dialect and was written by George Waugh Arnold, who was famous for creating coon songs during this period, such as the popular "Everything Is Lovely and the Goose

Hangs High." Coon songs also constitute most of the repertoire Irwin wrote herself—of the thirteen songs whose words or music are directly attributable to Irwin, eleven are coon songs.

The percentage of coon songs is even higher in the published collection *May Irwin's Songs.* All of the songs listed by title alone are coon songs. All but one of the songs printed with words and music are coon songs, as are three-quarters of the songs for which only lyrics are given.[53]

In 1907 May Irwin recorded six phonograph records under the Victor label. Two of these numbers, "Moses Andrew Jackson, Good-bye," and "Ma-tri-mo-ny," were not successful and dropped from the catalog in 1910. In 1908 the number "Don't Argify" was combined in a double record with "You Splash Me and I'll Splash You," sung by comedienne Alice Lloyd. In 1909 "The Bully" was combined with "When You Ain't Got No Money, Then You Needn't Come Around." These two double-sided recordings remained in the catalog until 1919. In 1913 "May Irwin's Frog Song" was changed to "The Frog Song" and joined with "Clarence" (the name should be Clarice) Vance's "I'm Wise" and remained in circulation until 1923. Of these six recorded numbers, all but "Ma-tri-mo-ny" are clearly coon songs.[54]

Some speculate that Irwin also recorded a number of songs on cylinders in 1898 under the name of Lady X. That is quite possibly accurate, since famous singers of the day often recorded on cylinders under pseudonyms, and many of the recordings listed under Lady X are numbers made famous by Irwin. Most of these numbers are coon songs.[55]

Anyone can hear May's Victor recordings online at a number of sites—the Library of Congress holds all of her Victor recordings (see note 65 in chapter 2). The Victor catalog issued monthly supplements, touting their new records: "Besides Irwin, only one other popular artist—Blanche Ring—another stage performer—was featured on any of the monthly Victor supplemental catalog covers between January 1906 and June 1910. These spots were reserved for the most commercially successful artists, indicating that Victor recognized and capitalized on Irwin's popularity."[56]

Having established the cultural context of the coon-song fad and May Irwin's central position in its propagations, I turn now to the point of view from which she sang her songs and the thematic material in the lyrics of her best-known numbers. In discussing the multiple meanings possible in both text and subtext, I bear in mind that, as one reviewer put it, "the words, disassociated from the music will create no clear picture in the mind of the reader of the effect [these songs have] when sung on the stage by a competent singer."[57] In Irwin's case, the catchy ragtime tunes with their repetitive choruses that seem to invite listeners to join in were usually accompanied by a bouncy march about the stage and sung with little slides from note to note in a mild dialect. Moreover, Irwin sang without blackface and usually in beautiful clothes reflective of the best fantasy wardrobes of white middle-class women.

The dozens of coon songs written or made popular by May Irwin can be divided into seven distinctive groups, according to the stereotypes featured. The stereotypes prevalent in coon songs have been discussed by critics such as Sam Dennison and James Dorman, although their studies are not organized by specific stereotypes alone. Dennison moves freely from traits depicted in coon songs (a desire to be white, a predilection to thievery, and so on) to specific stereotypes—such as the "Bully" and the "Jonah." Dorman concentrates on the similarities and differences between the Negro in older minstrel songs and in coon songs. My study adopts the stereotypes identified in previous studies along with combinations that fit the particular representations in May Irwin's songs. (For example, the "Pathetic Coon" is a combination of Dennison's "Jonah" character and "Buffoon" character.)[58] I have divided Irwin's numbers according to "voices" she used most often: the female voice of the "Female Victim" and the "Greedy Gal" and the male voice of the "Idealized Coon" and the "Pathetic Coon." In the next chapter, I will look at May's tunes that employ an outside narrator describing an alternative "Coontown" and the aggressive male voice of the "Dandy" and the "Bully."[59]

Female Voice: Female Victim and Greedy Gal

May Irwin gave voice mainly to two female characters—the Female Victim and the Greedy Gal—although a few of her numbers included an idealized female lover. The idealized female lover in these romantic songs is often shown as simple-minded, even when goodhearted. For example, "I Couldn't Stand to See My Baby Lose" pokes fun at a wife who first ruins her husband's card game by turning out the lights and then leaves him for a while just to worry him so he can lose enough weight to be a good jockey. Naturally, she does these things purely out of love. In "I Just Can't Help from Lovin' That Man," the singer praises her lover, who is gainfully employed in moving furniture and who gives her rides in the moving van. He's a good man who "has a heart that's just about a few yards wide," and when his love is ill he cures her with a chicken pie. Of course, to fulfill the racist stereotype, he never buys chickens but always steals them, cleaning out the "chicken coops for miles around."

Three of the songs using the Female Victim stereotype were written entirely or partially by Irwin herself. She wrote both words and music for "I Miss Dat Bread" and "'Tain't No Sense in Lovin' Dat Way" and the music for "Dan."

(Only a few lines of "I Miss Dat Bread" are available—it appears to be about a woman whose husband decided to quit providing for her.)

Perhaps the most sensational victims represented in this group are the singers of "I've Been HooDoo'd" and "A Pickaninny Flew in de Cabin Do'," neither of which was written by Irwin. In the former song, a woman has refused to marry her suitor, who, in turn, puts a spell on her. The spell causes innumerable ailments, including aching bones, chattering teeth, insomnia, anorexia, and, presumably, eventual death:

Went to a doctor and he couldn't tell the matter,
Says he, You're a gone coon, you've gone up the spout,
He looked at my head, and my hair fell out,
Nobody knows how funny I feel,
Even the husk fell off my heel.

In the latter number, a woman receives an extra baby from heaven, which her husband kills in a fit of rage when she burns the bread. (This number was unpublished, and whether Irwin ever actually performed it is uncertain; I found it hidden in the back of my collection of her well-known material.)

Two of the victim numbers are notable for the strength of the female characters portrayed. The first is "Dan," about a bigamous, "deceivin' man" from whom the female singer is seeking a divorce. The second number, "'Tain't No Sense in Lovin' Dat Way," is an unusual number about wife abuse that seems to take the black woman's part with considerable empathy. The refrain is certainly in keeping with Irwin's strongly expressed feelings of mutual responsibility in marriage:

Dere ain't no sense in lovin' dat way
I be the mummy and you have all to say
I'm full of affection and I'm willing to mind
But I wants to hear my voice sometime
If you say "no" that "no" is law
And if I opens my mouth I gets it in the jaw
You must either be mutual or say good day
'Cause 'taint no sense in lovin' dat way.

Significantly, "'Taint No Sense in Lovin' Dat Way" is the only number I've found that Irwin copyrighted herself. She did so in 1904 and then performed it the same year in her successful production *Mrs. Black Is Back*. Here she seems to break out of the normal coon-song mold for female characters.

In some of these numbers (as in the aforementioned "All Coons Look Alike to Me"), the female is the victim of her own fickleness. In one of her popular melodies, May moved from the black male's point of view in the verse (in which the male laments the loss of his "little Lou") to the black female's point of view in the chorus. This tune is aptly titled "I Don't Care to Be Your Lady Friend No More" and presents this sentiment: "I'm another nigger's baby and I'd like you better maybe, / If you'd go and let them shoot you in the war . . ."

About half of Irwin's songs in female voice are told entirely from the Greedy Gal's point of view. Typical are "Honey, Don't Sigh," in which the singer is attracted to a "high livin' coon who has a pearl-handled razor," and "The New Love's Come to Stay," in which the woman has dropped her old beau for a "copper-colored nigger." In "I've Got Him Dead," the female is in no hurry to give in to her suitor, because she knows she has him hooked—he's so in love that he'll spend any amount of money on her:

How happy I'm gwine to be,
When dis coon and me are wed
To know my man is livin'
And still I've got him "dead."

The dangerous Greedy Gal in "Miss Sampson Brown" may represent the most violent of this type. The singer here serves as narrator, warning all that Miss Sampson Brown is never seen without her razor and "is what you call a reglar carvin' Jennie."

Arguably, the most popular song of this type is "When You Ain't Got No Money, Then You Needn't Come Around," which Irwin recorded twice on the Victor label and which she featured in her show *Kate Kip, Buyer.* In this song, a loser at dice and horse races is rebuffed by his lover when he is broke. It begins in the black male's voice but shifts to the female's point of view in the chorus:

When you ain't got no money, well you needn't come around
Ef you is broke Mister Nigger I'll throw you down
De only coon dat I can see is de one dat blows his dough on me,
So when you bring de stuff Mister Nigger I'se to be found
But when you ain't got no money, then you needn't come around.

Male Voice: Idealized Coon and Pathetic Coon

It is songs in the male voice, however, in which Irwin performed the majority of her work. More than half of her numbers were sung in the persona of the Idealized Coon and the Pathetic Coon. The first stereotype, represented most frequently in her songs, falls into two general types. Songs of the first type, as in "On the Levee before the War," are sentimental, joyous numbers filled with nostalgia for the old South and descriptions of fun-filled religious meetings and dances. They feature mild dialect and a yearning for the antebellum South, complete with cotton, steamboats, happy slaves, and watermelon: "Don't that music a swellin' just hit your feet, like a watermelon sweet." The most famous number of this type, "A Hot Time in the Old Town Tonight," features the black male exhorting all of the females in town to accompany him:

> Come along get you ready wear your bran, bran new gown
> For dere's gwine to be a meeting in that good, good old town
> Where you knowded ev'rybody and dey all knowded you
> And you've got a rabbitsfoot to keep away de hoodo
> When you hear that the preaching does begin
> Bend down low for to drive away your sin
> And when you gets religion, you'll want to shout and sing
> There'll be a hot time in the old town tonight, my baby

Like most numbers of sentiment, "A Hot Time in the Old Town Tonight," sung more often by the lesser-known coon shouter Josephine Sabel, gazes with undisguised longing at the happy life of blacks. An exception to this tone may be seen in "Rollin' to de Sea," in which a black male, reminiscing about the beautiful river that flowed by his shack at old Massa's plantation in Mississippi, qualifies his longing by noting his present bettered state:

> Now I hab a little farm, wife and children of my own
> And I wouldn't swap my chances wid de king upon his throne,
> But of evenings when my banjo thrums, I'd sometimes like to be,
> Where I'd watch de ribber rollin', rollin', rollin' to de sea.

The second type of Idealized Coon song deals with romantic love. "Sence You Went Away" and "Ma Mississippi Belle," both from 1900, are from the pen of Cole and Johnson and are simple, sweet tunes in heavy dialect. The singer in "Sence You Went Away" laments that "Seems lak to me de stars don't shine so bright" since his lover has gone. The protagonist in "Ma Mississippi Belle" recounts the virtues of his lady love, introducing her as "a little gal I call ma Belle, how I love dat gal, no tongue can tell."

One of the romantic numbers concerns a black soldier and offers an interesting exception to the usual portrait of African Americans as cowardly. In Will Accooe's "Ma Dandy Soldier Coon," a soldier who is the "pride of de black platoon" returns with medals from the front. Although the lyrics do not betray any intended irony, and this "soldier coon" is portrayed as truly courageous, the black soldier is lampooned as a "dandy" for his supposed love of fancy dress.

Irwin herself wrote the words and music to two such songs. "Mamie, Come Kiss Your Honey Boy," a popular number from the play *A Country Sport,* praises marriage from the point of view of a young man anticipating his wedding day, and "Mandy" woos its title mistress with:

> Mandy, Mandy, I love you,
> As the lily loves the dew
> I ax yer is yer gwine to be true
> To yer sweetheart Andy?

The second most frequent stereotype in Irwin's repertoire was the Pathetic Coon. Related to the Idealized Coon, this character was pathetic either because of his complete laziness and shiftlessness (as the old Buffoon or plantation coon) or because of his hard luck (usually called the Jonah). Sometimes this stereotype might be both lazy *and* unlucky.

The lazy variant inhabits several of Irwin's songs, including her own composition "The Big Handout," about a black man looking for free help; "Don't Argify," which was a popular recording of Irwin's and featured a simple, catchy little tune about a lazy black who admonishes others to "amble, gamble, ramble, scramble, don't argify!"; and "I Ain't Gwine ter Work No Mo,'" in which the black male singer opines that the "best occupation is recreation." Likewise, "I've Got Troubles of My Own" plays on the idea that the African American is unable to recognize his duty to others. Billed as "a bit of coon philosophy," the song features a deacon complaining that he is tired of working on other folks' problems. Here, even a religious leader whose congregation looks up to him is incapable of empathizing with others or looking beyond his own selfish desires.

Perhaps Irwin's most popular Pathetic Coon, however, was the hard-luck coon portrayed in "Mr. Johnson, Turn Me Loose." This number may have been recorded twice by Irwin and is one of two songs added into Irwin's stage hit *Courted into Court,* which received the most recognition from audiences and critics. (The other was "All Coons Look Alike to Me.") "Mr. Johnson, Turn Me Loose" is mentioned in every one of Irwin's major obituaries, and it is commonly associated with the birth of ragtime songs, as Philip Furia notes in *The Poets of Tin Pan Alley:* "In Harney's 'Mister Johnson, Turn Me Loose' (1896), the first ragtime song to become a major hit, . . . listeners were delighted not only by the syncopated rhythm but by the idiomatic plea of the caricatured black to 'Mister Johnson' (slang for police)."[60]

The song focuses on a man caught gambling by "Mr. Johnson," whom he begs to "turn him loose," promising that he will "be good." In the second verse, this gambler turns thief and gets nervous when he is in the process of stealing chickens, because one of them "sneezes," and the sneeze reminds him of the time that another "big black coon" was stealing a chicken and, caught by Mr. Johnson, ended up getting shot:

> And now he's playin' seben eleben,
> Way up yonder in de nigger heabn,
> Oh! Mister Johnson made him good.

The moral of this story is that "the only good coon is a dead coon." Like the majority of the songs centered on the Pathetic character, "Mr. Johnson, Turn Me Loose" is written from the black male's point of view. Often, Pathetic Coons are coupled with Greedy Gals who either want more material goods than the put-upon lovers can provide or are simply too faithless for one man. In "Why Don't My Baby Write and Tell Me Why?" the hard-luck Eph Jackson laments that his best gal has left him and refuses to answer his letters (even though he has been to a voodoo specialist to seek assistance). In "My Baby I'll Go, Too," written by Irwin, a "nigger [who] lov'd a yaller gal" is rejected but follows her around continually, to the amused derision of crowds of his neighbors. And in "Keep Your Eye on Your Friend, Mr. Johnson," a cuckold follows his friends' advice and keeps his eye on someone he suspects of philandering with his wife. After securing "evidence," he sues for divorce but winds up paying alimony to both his ex-wife and her lover.

May's coon songs depicted several character types, ranging from the sentimental to the disreputable. These songs variously represent the female voice or the male voice—or sometimes both. Although all of these songs traffic in egregious and demeaning stereotypes, perhaps none is as flagrantly racist as "The Bully." Variously titled "The Bully," "May Irwin's Bully Song," and "The New Bully," this number became May's specialty. In chapter 4, I will look more closely at May's aggressive characters and explore the possible reasons behind her phenomenal success with this material.

4

The "Only One Boss Bully"

Have yo' heard about dat bully dat's just come to town?
He's round among de niggers a layin' their bodies down.
I'm a lookin' for dat bully and he must be found.
—"May Irwin's Bully Song" (1896)

Pathetic Coons and Greedy Gals were standard fodder for Irwin's song hits, but they were outlasted by her "Frog Song" and, especially, her "Bully" song, perhaps the most pernicious number in the entire coon-song repertoire. This chapter takes a closer look at these songs and considers how they were received and their possible implications.

Outside Voice: Coontown

If the Pathetic Coon appealed to Irwin's white audiences' sense of superiority, the songs she sang from an outsider's view made that appeal more blatantly. These numbers reveal a black society parallel to a white one. In these "coontowns," white conventions and social groups are parodied in an alternative, inferior universe. Here is a world where superstition runs rampant, all people enjoy watermelon and steal chickens, and simple preachers misread stories from the Bible—as in "Bible Stories," where the story of Noah's Ark becomes one in which Noah swipes the menagerie of animals he is entrusted with and sells them to Barnum's circus. "Live Humble," written by Irwin herself and reprinted in her cookbook, also features this interpretation of the creation of the world:

De world was made in six days,
Den dey made de sky;
Den dey hung it overhead
And lef' it dere to dry.
Den dey made the stars out of niggers' wenches eyes,

Just to give a little light
When de moon she doesn't rise.

"The Frog Song" takes a look at this alternate society and delivers a thinly veiled warning to the black member who might consider stepping out of his own neighborhood. The number is about a frog who went in the wrong pond, stubbed his toe, and drowned, all because he couldn't stay where he should have stayed:

An' jus' lots uv folks is like dis foolish frog uv mine,
A' runnin' into trouble jus' to pass de time,
An' de devil's allus loafin' 'round heah jus' to grab de' kind
Dat nevah hasn't nothin' else to do.

"The Frog Song" borrows the oft-repeated sentiment from another song, "Stay in Your Own Backyard." This well-known number gave typical advice to black children—they would be safe if they just remembered their place, "on dis side of de high boahd fence."[1] It also made the conflation, common at the time, of blacks and bullfrogs.[2] Although its advice is pointed, the song can be (and has been) revived in other versions in which the word *niggahs* is replaced by *neighbors*. It is perhaps through this sanitizing that "The Frog Song" has become one of Irwin's most enduring numbers. It remained in the Victor catalog until 1923, longer than any of her other songs, and it was probably the last song she sang in public—as part of a celebration of the one hundredth anniversary of Mark Twain's birth in May 1935, to a crowd of ten thousand in New York's Central Park.[3] Linked to "The Bully" in popularity, "The Frog Song" is mentioned in reviews of Irwin's vast repertoire as one of the two that became known throughout America.[4]

Male Voice: The Dandy and the Bully

"Coontowns" were often peopled with another stereotype, the "Dandy." The Dandy is an urban creature, far different from the raggedy Jim Crow figures who were prominent in sentimental and romantic tunes. The Dandy is a black male figure who dresses well and thinks highly of himself, often displaying an "uppityness" that reveals his supposedly outrageous self-image of being as good as a white man. Thus, in "Everything Is Lovely and the Goose Hangs High," the main character prefers the restaurant Delmonico's to possum eating and keeps an "ancestral castle on de River Rhine." Part of the humor, as in other Dandy numbers, is derived from the singer's insistence that he is from "real black high up folks," and not mulattos. That is, he's so purely black that he's white. He is as good as whites because he doesn't have a trace of white in him.

Although not a staple in Irwin's repertoire, many coon songs feature a Dandy who covets the white man's fortunes and wants all of the things a white man has—his automobile, his house, and, of course, his woman.[5] In songs such as "Dat's Just What 'Expotentisious' Means," the speaker in question has attended "Darktown College" and acquired a vocabulary full of malapropisms in his attempt to master the "white man's language." Of course, the use of malapropisms has been a constant fount of humor—from the original Mrs. Malaprop created by Richard Brinsley Sheridan in the late eighteenth century to the Wayans brothers' "educated" prisoner portrayed on the 1990s TV show *In Living Color.*

Such Dandies often fail miserably and instead revert to their counterpart—the Pathetic Coon. For example, in "I've Got a White Man Working for Me," the white employee turns on his black employer and buries him and all of his neighbors in a large hole, taunting them: "Remember, coons, . . . I'm far above you."[6] Perhaps the most well-known number of this type is "Coon, Coon, Coon," made famous by vaudevillian Lew Dockstader and including this refrain of a black man's unsuccessful longing to be white:

> Coon! Coon! Coon!
> I wish my color would fade;
> Coon! Coon! Coon!
> I'd like a different shade . . .
> Coon! Coon! Coon!
> Morning, night and noon,
> I wish I was a white man, 'Stead of
> Coon! Coon! Coon!

Irwin's Dandies, however, are of a stronger mettle. In "Syncopated Sandy," the title male is "a dead swell coon with stately tread" who is a typical "Darktown dandy." Sandy is related to his plantation brethren in his happy-go-lucky and "reckless life." He is a "happy and contented coon, without a care or strife." However, included with this number is another set of lyrics entitled a "'Coon Parody' on Syncopated Sandy." Here Sandy becomes a "bold bad nigger crook" who beats his wife and is "the meanest man who ever lived." The "'Coon Parody' on Syncopated Sandy" underlines the tendency of Irwin's Dandies to transform not into the Jonah type but into the Bully, which I discuss further below.

May Irwin did not sing many Dandy numbers, but three already mentioned were rather well known: "Everything Is Lovely and the Goose Hangs

High," "Syncopated Sandy," and "Hot Tamale Alley." "Syncopated Sandy" is told from an outsider's point of view, but both of the other numbers are told from the black male's point of view. "Hot Tamale Alley," one of Irwin's hits in 1896, is sung from the point of view of a Dandy who has a lover named Sally. (Irwin herself wrote the lyrics to accompany George M. Cohan's music.)

But May Irwin gained her greatest fame when she moved from the Dandy to the Bully stereotype. The Bully character could creep into songs that focused on other stereotypes. This even occurs in some of Irwin's most romantic numbers. So although "May Irwin's LuLu Song" is mainly a courting number in which the male singer is asking for the beautiful Miss LuLu's hand in marriage, the singer makes references to the jealous suitors he will chase off when he finally achieves his goal:

An' if yo' han' I wins fum you,
Dem jealous nigs doan' fear,
I'll say, an' squelch dem all, fo' sho'
She's mine, yo' coons; d'ye hear? Hear me, Niggers?

The pathetic hard-luck character who typically remains passive in the face of adversity can also transform into a Bully. In "All Coons Look Alike to Me," the female voice switches to the male, as he warns, before the second chorus:

For I'm worried, . . Yes I'm desp'rate,
I've been jonahed, . . and I'll get dangerous,
If these words she says to me . . .

Dandy songs may also merge into the Bully stereotype in their use of violent imagery—jealous men, razors, and guns. In "Hot Tamale Alley," Sally is such a "little lump of sweetness" that just to be seen with her makes the man of her choice the object of insane jealousy:

I'm her man, the whole coon clan, would carve me if they could;
Talk about your jealous niggers, how they'd like to pull the triggers,
Of the guns they carry, and a target make of me.

Such violent imagery fills the entire song when the Bully is the main character.

The Bully is often a cheater with a strong stripe of cowardice. In Irwin's "Crappy Dan," the singer "always rolls sevens, never threes," because he has loaded dice, and because of his tendency to get caught, "Crappy Dan has allus' his gun." In "Ain't Dat Scandalous," from 1911, Badland Bill and BeeBee Small mix it up over a lady friend, causing appalled onlookers dismay "to see such impropriety among de' best society." In "Never Raise a Razor 'Less You Want to Raise a Row," the normally mild-mannered Abram Jackson Smith ends up in a violent scuffle in which he "carves his initials on the other fellow's neck." The message of this song seems to be that any black male, no matter how peaceable, can be provoked to violence by the mere sight of a weapon of any sort (especially a razor).

Not only did Irwin not sing many Dandy songs, but she also did not sing many Bully songs, even though her most popular number of all was a Bully song. Titled "The Bully" (sometimes "The New Bully"), this was the hit song most closely identified with May Irwin. Irwin recorded it twice under Victor's label (as discussed previously), and its popularity was extolled in all of Irwin's obituaries. One retrospective of her life noted, "For years, 'Have You Heard May Irwin Sing The Bully?' was a catch phrase." Introduced in her show *The Widow Jones* in 1896, "The Bully" immediately became a favorite of audiences, so much so that the *New York Sun* could maintain, by the end of that same year, that "since she [May Irwin] made a hit in 'De New Bully,' setting every family piano and every family vocalist throughout the land to playing and singing it, her audiences demand Negro songs." Irwin's later songs were often compared to "The Bully," as in the review of *Kate Kip, Buyer,* in 1899, which admitted that her new songs were very good, but "none equal [to] 'The Bully,' which won her so much renown." Contemporary scholars often point to "The Bully" as "the unquestioned paragon of bully songs."[7]

As noted in chapter 3, a version of "The Bully" was supposedly played for Irwin when composer Charles Trevathan was traveling with her on a Chicago train, and she thought it could provide the needed hit for her new show, *The Widow Jones.*[8] (Warring stories of the origins of coon songs are rampant, and, in 1906, it was reported that Irwin actually learned the tune at the "Moulin Rouge of America" in San Francisco.)[9] The song has a bouncy, appealing rhythm (much of the humor in the number was derived from Irwin marching around to the chorus with a tuba accompaniment). But the story involves cold-blooded murder, featuring a dangerous Bully always looking for a fight, ready to use his omnipresent razor to cut up anyone who crosses his path. It was sung by Irwin in the persona of the black male, a "New Bully" who is looking for another "Bully" to kill, so he can remain the one and only "Bully":

> Have yo' heard about dat bully dat's just come to town?
> He's round among de niggers a layin' their bodies down.
> I'm a lookin' for dat bully and he must be found.
> I'm a Tennessee nigger and I don't allow,
> No red-eyed river roustabout with me to raise a row,
> I'm lookin' for dat bully and I'll make him bow.

CHORUS:
When I walk dat levee round, round, round, round,
When I walk dat levee round, round, round, round
When I walk dat levee round,
I'm a lookin' for dat bully an' he must be found.

A closer look at this most performed number of Irwin's reveals a plethora of negative images of blacks coupled with generally comic content designed to amuse audiences. The song tended to go on for six to eight verses when Irwin sang it, presumably because of audience demands. Some versions included even more supplementary verses about crap games and chicken theft. In all the use of alliteration and similar word play is meant to add to the comedy, as in "the red-eyed river roustabout" and "shake my sugar heel." The Bully uses as many slang synonyms as possible for razor—"steel," "ax," "trusty blade"—and the emphasis is on the importance of having that object on hand at all times. The New Bully is distracted in his mission by a dance at Parson Brown's, where he stops to "cut a shine" and "wing a reel" with "Miss Pansy Blossom." (Irwin was doubtlessly able to elicit a laugh with her temporary switch to Miss Blossom's trembling: "'Law, Mr. Johnsing, how high you make me feel!") He initially runs into problems when a "coon across his smeller swipes a watermelon rin'," but he eventually catches up with his nemesis and, comparing himself to a "sparrow hawk," a "black cloud," and a "cyclone," actually kills him:

When I got through with bully, a doctor and a nurse
Wa'n't no good to dat nigger, so they put him in a hearse.
A cyclone couldn't have tore him up much worse.
You don't hear 'bout dat nigger dat treated folks so free.
Go down upon the levee and his face you'll never see.
Dere's only one boss bully and dat one is me.
(Repeat chorus)

These harsh words contrast not only with the music of the piece, but also with Irwin's furious energy and the childlike demeanor she employed while performing the Bully. In the recording of the song, Irwin's coy, light delivery and lilting attack of each note contrast markedly with the song's crude imagery. Her singing was accompanied with a march about the stage, and reviewers noted that "the rendering of the song requires more work and energy than any other composition Miss Irwin ever sang. The business is very strenuous, and the Irwin expressions must be exercised in all their subtlety. The comedienne wore gloves when she sang 'The New Bully,' and so strenuously did she labor with her hands that the gloves were torn at every performance."[10]

A photograph identifiable as Irwin in her "Bully" stance appears on several of her sheet-music covers, including at least three songs that aren't Bully numbers: "I Ain't Gwine ter Work No Mo," "Magdalene, My Southern Queen," and "I Don't Care to Be Your Lady Friend No More."[11] (Of these, only the latter has *any* textual elements that might relate to Irwin's pose.) In the picture, a tightly corseted May stands with her arms akimbo, her hands in tight fists, and a full pout on her face.

A comparison of the sheet-music covers of coon songs from the period reveals that, in most numbers, May Irwin's iconography differs materially from others of the age. Irwin's version of "All Coons Look Alike to Me," for example, does not incorporate any caricatures whatsoever: it includes only her signed photograph. When caricatures do occur on Irwin's sheet music, they are usually off to the side of her picture or peeking from behind the frame. For example, in "I Just Can't Help from Lovin' Dat Man," a full-length portrait of a smiling May, her hand coyly covering part of her mouth, partially blocks the caricature of a black female who emerges with a wide, full-lipped grin, pointing to a horse-drawn moving van in the distance. Beyond the van stands the small figure of her irresistible man. In "I Ain't Gwine ter Work No Mo," the Bully photograph of May stands beside an illustration of a young black man leaning sleepily on a fence post, his woodcutting ax cast aside. Nailed to the fence post is a sign that reads, "For That Tired Feeling, See May Irwin."

In contrast, however, Irwin's sheet-music cover of the Bully does conform to the conventions of the age (an exception to the usual iconography for her numbers). One of the most widely circulated covers for the Bully consists of a large caricature with a note in the upper-left-hand corner, signed by May Irwin, stating that "this is the only correct publication of 'The Bully Song,' as sung by me, in 'The Widow Jones.'" The Bully is wearing loud striped trousers (in the original, in lurid colors) with rolled-up cuffs, an ill-fitting plaid jacket, and a huge polka-dot bow tie. He has enormous feet in spats—with the heel extending to the back from the leg almost as much as the rest of the foot extends forward—and a low-slung straw hat over his small and oddly shaped cranium. Huge poppy eyes, gargantuan lips, wide nostrils, and tiny ears complete his visage. In his right hand, he carries a large razor, open and ready for action. This razor is also prominent in another version of the sheet-music cover, in which the Bully holds up a picture of May, which partially covers him, but still allows the viewer to see that same polka-dot tie and lethal weapon.

The popularity of "The Bully" song was legendary for many years. In the 1920s, Charles S. Gilpin played the leading role in the first national tour of

Eugene O'Neill's *Emperor Jones* and was praised for his "remarkable performance, one soon not to be forgotten," full of "superb acting" with "barbaric" intensity. According to the *Boston Transcript,* when his character, Brutus Jones, "swaggers out of the palace," he is meant to be whistling. Gilpin chose to whistle a tune his audience would have recognized as appropriate to the African American turned king, "May Irwin's Bully Song."[12]

The New Bully even has the dubious distinction of being the first black character in a comic strip, a child posing as "the straight razor-wielding leader of a street corner gang, the New Bully represented the epitome of the stereotype of the dangerous predatory black."[13] (The strip's writer, Richard Outcault, did not find success with the character and soon replaced him with his new creation, Buster Brown.)

As late as 1925, Irwin "emerged from the dim past" to perform her sketch *Mrs. Peckham's Carouse* as part of a series of vaudeville acts at Keith's Theatre in Boston. The audience cheered and "demanded some of her older fare. . . . [They were] rewarded with a humorous piece about a dress that did not fit after being resurrected and also one of her best known songs of the bygone age, 'The New Bully.'"[14] "The Bully Song" was even available in new sheet music as late as 1941 in a sanitized version that replaced *niggers* with *neighbors* and *poor folk.*[15]

From the vantage point of the twenty-first century, the success of coon songs—particularly a number like "The Bully"—is difficult to understand. We can appreciate the physical humor that was inherent in Irwin's performance, and we can even understand the dark comedy, metaphorically, in the contrast between style and content. But before we consider the possible levels of meaning from a contemporary standpoint, a look at reactions from the time period is in order.

May Irwin herself did not come in for specific, pointed disapproval, at least publicly, by the black newspapers (except for the implication that only a "certain class" of theatergoer would appreciate her coon songs). Descriptions of the reaction of black audiences are rare, but her appearance at an "Old Colored Home" to an all-black audience garnered this review (from a white critic):

> May Irwin's jolly face beamed all over as she came to the front and met a storm of greetings. She began with "Crappy Dan." The colored listeners had their eyes riveted on her, and their lips followed her words while they swayed in time with the music and broke out hilariously at the familiar ideas she expressed. The men especially were interested and were caught when the actress came to the lines:

> "Dey wasn't no niggah dat ever frowed six But I knowed I had 'im beat."
>
> The men appeared chiefly uproarious, however, over the confidential information that "wid a little bit o' lead de dice allus comes seven."
>
> Miss Irwin was borne to the front again by most enthusiastic hurrahs. This time she sang "The New Bully." She had more than her usual abandon when she scowled and swung around as the invincible colored gentleman with an ax and razor. Each time she mentioned the razor and threw in the bravado the colored audience lost all control. When she reached that sentiment: "I'se gittin' so bad, I'se skeered o' myself," the demonstration lasted for three minutes.[16]

Here, Irwin reserves her most famous, most violent number as a special treat for her black audience, who seem to know the lyrics well enough to practically sing along. That all of their enthusiastic response is feigned for a white star does not seem likely—there is a sense in which she is accepted as *laughing with* her audience. (It is important to note that Irish songs and German songs, sung by other entertainers, were also on the evening's bill of fare.) The harshness of some of the menacing images of the bully was undercut by Irwin's sense of humor and playfulness. Of course, this condescending review is an outsider's interpretation of the audience's reactions. In this version of the song, the encore is included, which was added when the audience demanded it:

> When you see me comin,' h'ist your windows high.
> When you see me goin', hang your heads and cry.
> I'm lookin' for that bully and he must die.
> My madness keeps a-risin', and I'se not gwine to get left.
> I'm gettin' so bad dat I'm askeered of myself.
> I was lookin' for dat bully, now he's on a shelf.

Naturally, the three-minute "demonstration" following "I'm getting' so bad dat I'm askeered of myself" connects to the obvious paradox of a bully who is more vicious than he himself can handle! Along with Irwin's childlike demeanor, this also lends a ludicrous unreality to the entire performance. It is not clear whether Irwin had any children with her during this particular performance, but she did tend to bring small black children onstage with her when she performed this number, which would certainly add to the appeal of the number for both black and white audiences.[17] So close was Irwin's association with this practice that, at the last performance of *The Widow Jones,* the ushers brought in a present of what "appeared to be a barrel of food" until "out of it hopped two pickaninnies"—her closing-night gift.[18]

As noted earlier, Irwin's physicality as she marched about, doing her version of a cakewalk—the pseudosophistication of the Bully lent itself to cakewalking—gave Irwin the opportunity to clown. Drawings of Irwin's cakewalk emphasize her plump backside, wildly swinging arms, wide smile, and tendency to look as if she were about to pitch over backward.

Besides simply laughing at Irwin's rendition, black audiences may have also been laughing for another reason. The cakewalk may have had African origins and was performed at plantation parties where the prize for the best couple was a cake. Yet there is also plentiful evidence that, in creating the cakewalk, slaves were actually parodying the stiff and proper manner that whites had of dancing: "Blacks on the plantation had developed [cakewalking] as a satire of their White masters. Their backs stiffly arched, their butts held tight, their elbows out and their knees kicking high, they strutted, bowed, and twirled their canes in a blatant parody of the way tight-assed, stiff-necked White folks moved. White folks loved to see black dancers execute a fine cakewalk, and demanded to be taught how to do it, apparently unaware that they were being mocked." (David Krasner cites research that indicates whites sometimes *did* know they were being imitated, but may have mistakenly thought their slaves just didn't have the ability to execute the steps of the formal dance!)[19]

What did the black population in general think of coon songs during their greatest popularity? Black views were seldom expressed openly, but evidence suggests a complex range of reactions. The most frequently reported response was one of complete disdain, focused on the "lowbrow" quality of coon songs in particular and ragtime music in general. It is easy to see why middle-class blacks, anxious to move forward, usually tried to distance themselves from coon songs and cakewalks. Classical black musicians pronounced coon songs "the worst kind of rot," with "no real Negro character or sentiment in them." Black newspapers, following the ideas of W. E. B. DuBois, wanted, instead, to glorify old Negro spirituals as the true folk music of "the race" and to stress its importance and connection to high culture. The *Chicago Defender,* founded in 1905 and one of the most important black newspapers in the country, supported racial "uplift" through these folk songs and lamented the lack of audience they received: "Dvorak's symphony, 'From the New World,' as every one knows, utilized characteristic elements which he had discovered in the song of the Negroes which had come to his notice while he was a resident of New York. And since then some American musicians have based compositions on Negro folk-songs. But the results of these experiments and researches do not seep through to the consciousness of the general public, which is heir in all this musical domain and should not be deprived of its enjoyment and inspiration."[20]

As time went on, the cakewalk became particularly problematic for aspiring middle-class blacks, who were disturbed by the dance's "sexual overtones" that "risked implying harmful stereotypes that resulted from and even justified slavery." In turn, in an attempt to overturn this perception, African American dancers such as Aida Overton Walker were hiring themselves out to teach whites a proper, sophisticated style of cakewalking.[21]

Second, some black newspapers of the 1880s and 1890s decried coon songs because of the way white people had taken over the genre. These critics claimed that original coon songs were authentic, but the numbers became more and more ludicrous in the hands of white folks:

> The first coon songs sung on the stage were really coon or negro songs. The music and some of the words were composed by negroes and sung by them, not in parlors and theaters, but as these natural minstrels worked. Some smart song writers began adopting the lines sung by the negroes, and as many of the words as could be used in polite company. The success of the songs was instantaneous. May Irwin was made famous in a night by "Mr. Johnson, Turn me Loose," and she still retains a firm hold *on a certain class of the theater-going public* of the east by singing coon songs.[22]

Here the insult has to do with the way coon songs have been stolen from black singers and repackaged in unrecognizable form. For a third group of critics, however, coon songs, even when written and sung by the black man and full of negative stereotypes so loved by whites, fail to produce any real financial reward for the black musician—adding insult to injury: "The colored man writes the 'coon' song, the colored singer sings the 'coon' song, the colored race is compelled to stand for the belittling and ignominy of the 'coon' song, but the money from the 'coon' song flows with ceaseless activity into the white man's pockets."[23]

Finally, as middle-class blacks bemoaned the existence of the coon song and black musicians bemoaned its theft by whites, some black performers responded in kind, either parodying white coon shouters or rewriting the popular "All Coons Look Alike to Me" in varied ways: "All Chinks Look Alike to Me," "All White Folks Look Alike to Me," "All Spaniards Look Alike to Me," "All Coons Don't Look Alike to Me," and the oddly titled "All Colored Folks Look Like Little Black Gnats to Me."[24] These evidently received enthusiastic applause and laughter from both blacks and whites in the audiences.

Belle Davis, one of the most successful black coon shouters, chose to compete directly with May Irwin. Davis, as slender as May was chubby, thrust out her elbows, balled up her fists, and drew her lips into a sulky pout as she made sport of Irwin's singing. (Many beginning—and rival—performers imitated star performers. As a child, Elsie Janis was instructed by her mother to begin her vaudeville turn with a parody of May Irwin. The young Mae

West cut her teeth mimicking Eva Tanguay.)[25] Born of a white father and black mother, this "cream-colored chansonette" made the following mind-boggling statement to the newspapers:

> But, honest, I don't want to talk to paper men. I know paper men don't like to talk to me 'cause I'm black. One paper man said last week that I sang my songs in a way that would make May Irwin's hair turn yellow with envy. That's the whitest man I ever heard of. He spoke what he felt and didn't think whether he would offend anyone or not. I like that man. I think he's one of those that would *forget the color of my skin and just close his eyes and listen to my singing.*[26]

To be heard, Belle Davis needed to *not* be seen. To be seen, she tried to place herself in a different class of blacks than the "bad niggahs [who] disgrace themselves tryin' to be white." When asked by her interviewer which class of black she did belong to, she answered, "Me."[27] Yet even in her own "class," she earned money "tryin' to be" a white woman who was trying to be black. Like many of her peers, Belle moved to Europe to escape prejudice, performing widely with her team of "pickaninnies." Because of her light skin color and the very dark color of her charges, she was sometimes mistaken for a white woman.[28] In an odd way, then, she paralleled May Irwin's performance with a black toddler onstage. (In simplest terms, in a dazzling array of shifting identities, black performers like Belle Davis were imitating May Irwin's cakewalk, May Irwin was both satirizing her *own* cakewalking ability and mimicking black cakewalkers, and black cakewalkers were satirizing white dancers, who often mistook satire for poor imitation or else turned to black performers to teach them to execute a proper cakewalk!)

In Belle Davis's insistence that she did not want to be associated with "bad niggahs" in the minds of white people lay the fear of what this association might harbor. Black critics noted that no African American could "go to a theatre nor listen to a phonograph without being told that he is a 'coon.'" Even though this usage of the word *coon* "is only meant as an assumed name, just to amuse or cause laughter," danger lurked in its constant repetition, especially to children, who "are educated that a colored man is a 'coon.' What was meant as a jest is taken seriously."[29]

How much of the coon stereotype was accepted by the white audience as indicative of reality, and how much was perceived as fantasy? It may be that, in one sense, Irwin's representations were popular and palatable because they were *not* real. White reviewers continually remarked that her impersonations of "a wicked colored person of the streets" as a "fair complexioned woman in evening dress . . . without aid of make-up or accessories is startling . . . and [hence] gratifying." In fact, her performances were so exaggerated that they could jar a spectator—as they did this reviewer—who observed with horror that in one of her performances, at the end of Irwin's first verse, a back curtain parted, revealing "a genuine negro, in the most impossible conventional negro minstrel clothes . . . holding a large razor in his hand. The effect is dreadful. It dampens the enthusiasm of the audience immediately. The song is a bit fantastic, exaggerated burlesque, founded in no respect on fact, and quite without reality. So the apparition of the living negro introduces into the scene an element entirely at variance with the effect of Miss Irwin's song."[30] The reviewer's protestations to the contrary, this "dreadful" effect seems linked to his fear of the reality of African Americans with razors. (I'll return to this idea later in the chapter.)

How realistic were the fears of black critics that whites would take the "coon" of the coon song as a reflection of reality? If we begin with a look at the Greedy Gal stereotype, we can see why African Americans might be concerned about the sexuality it represented. Greedy Gals are often "Jezebels," the direct opposite of the virtuous mammy. As late as the 1940s, even writers sympathetic to the black woman's plight took the Jezebel figure as representative of an inbred trait: "Torn from the tribal restraints and taught an easy complaisance for commercial reasons, she was to be had for the taking."[31] Thus, white men were free to think of what was undoubtedly often rape as an act of mutual consent. Not only was the Greedy Gal "easy," but her very identity as a black woman was denied her. Utterly consumed by the white female image, she refused to have anything to do with male coons who "all looked alike" to her. As a cipher, she "wouldn't marry a nigger" and "wouldn't marry a white man what would marry a nigger."[32]

This invisibility even extended to the very concrete existence of the female coon shouter. In an odd twist, black female coon shouters were generally praised for their similarity to the "originals," who were invariably white. Thus, "Miss Ida Day belongs to the May Irwin class" and "Miss Ramonde is of the May Irwin style," just as Clara Smith was the "black Sophie Tucker" and black dancers' moves were in acts "of the Eva Tanguay order." If the prototypical coon shouter was white, there was little room for black women. (Some black singers tried to break out of this trap by singing unconventional numbers, as Ada Overton Walker did when she sang "Vassar Girl.")[33]

Furthermore and interestingly, one character not directly represented in Irwin's work was the sexless, good-hearted "Mammy," except in general references in songs idealizing the South. It is essential to understand this figure, however, because in an important sense Irwin, with her ample, motherly figure and with some of the publicity shots and stage appearances she made with a small black child in tow,[34] *was* a sort of "white mammy." In turning the mammy figure on its head, she rendered the black mammy voiceless and invisible, serving a similar function as the white mammy impersonators who traveled the Chautauqua circuits of the early twentieth century, bringing "stories of the old South and the crooning lullaby's [*sic*] of the old Negro mammies." Mammy impersonators, such as the well-regarded Mary E. Bell, were often hired by women's clubs to teach members the ways of the old southern Negro so they could learn to be mimics themselves for amateur shows and charity events. Like Irwin, they eschewed blackface and dressed beautifully; unlike Irwin, their stated purpose was not entertainment but education. Most white mammies claimed to have learned their remarkable prowess at imitation at the knee of their own colored mammies—back in "the good old days," when faithful servants knew their place and adored their white mistresses. This act not only reinforced their position as aristocrats who grew up in a genteel society with servants, but also stirred dreams of an imaginary past, marked by "white supremacist nostalgia for antebellum paternalism and supposedly faithful slaves; the glorification of white domesticity through a black maternal figure; claims of intimate and satisfying bodily contact between black women and white women in the private sphere of the white home."[35]

That May Irwin, a Canadian of humble origins, contributed to this romantic longing for the old South removed the fantasy even further from its source than did the likes of Mary E. Bell—in this respect, real mammies from a real antebellum South disappeared in a hazy, romantic glow. In her "absorption" of the mammy figure, Irwin can be seen as *separate from* and *superior to* the coon character she portrays. This identity is also clear both in the songs performed as the Idealized Coon and in those performed as an outside narrator.

The Idealized Coon clearly reflects a paternalistic form of racism, fostering a desire in some to "lift their little brown brothers." In this view, new Negro citizens were likened to children who must learn from their white betters. Older histories, sympathetic and supportive of the Negro's role in American theater, lauded Bert Williams's simple-minded coon character with remarks such as "Somehow or other laughing at Bert Williams came to be tied up in people's minds with liberalism, charity, and the thirteenth amendment."[36]

If audiences could feel morally superior watching Irwin perform her Idealized Coon, they might also, however, slip into a romanticism and "whitewashing" of the past that denied the *need* for the Thirteenth Amendment and the Emancipation Proclamation as well. Guilt over slavery could change, then, to nostalgia: "To have heard [some] talk, you would have thought that the sole reason [they] held on to slavery was love and duty to the black man. . . . [H]e was a child who somebody had to look over. . . . a contented, loving child." Historian James Oakes has pointed out how the conditions that had been common in slavery reinforced the idea of black-as-child by the fact that, in 1850, the average slaveholder was forty-three years old and the average slave was under eighteen years of age. (Hardly "contented, loving children," these slaves were victims of child labor and overwork that reduced their life expectancy to fewer than forty years.)[37]

On the one hand, these numbers in which May assumed the voice of the outside narrator united Irwin and her audience, deprecating an "inferior" society. "The Frog Song" also included a potent warning to that society—stay separate or risk death—a death that would be approved of even by others *in* that society. After all, it is the black preacher who explains to his congregation the "reason why dis young frog is dead" and cautions them that they "bettah stay at home wid their fambily." The contrast between the tragedy of the frog's death and the bounciness of the song (as in the contrast between the Bully's murderous success and Irwin's happy strut "round, round, round" the levee) supposedly added to the humor of the ludicrous situation. Tellingly, however, when white newspapers reported serious accidents in the black community, they did so in a comic tone. In his seminal work *The Betrayal of the Negro,* Rayford W. Logan presented his comprehensive study of newspaper stories and reported dozens of instances of this occurrence. In one example, the collapse of a cellar floor and the serious injuries of the guests at a dance party were reported with quips such as "Miss Clara Bell Brown received a tight squeezing, but not at the hands of any of the male guests." In another instance, the *Kansas City Star* reported, under the title "An Earnest [*sic*] Hogan Item": "A Chicago policeman shot the wrong Negro during a row. . . . His only excuse was 'All niggers look alike to me.'"[38] Thus, the probable murder of an innocent man is linked to a comic song.

Irwin certainly reinforced this attitude of superiority with jokes in her cookbook and in interviews. Typical was her joke about her black servant, whose son (as Irwin related the story) stole a chicken and cooked it. The mother was supposedly more worried about how well her son prepared the bird than his crime of stealing. Irwin said she sympathized with her cook because her own son had been having trouble with an isosceles triangle—a remark that not only underlined the moral laxity of blacks, but also clearly elevated her own status over her help's. Presumably, her maid's son's cooking inadequacies were equivalent to Irwin's son's inability to get high marks in geometry.[39]

The jokes Irwin told in defense of women's suffrage were often comparable to the jokes in the coon songs featuring an alternative "coon" universe. The antiblack sentiment that caused a rift in the women's movement in the late

1860s when the Fifteenth Amendment passed was put to service for more than fifty years until 1920, when women finally gained the vote through the Nineteenth Amendment. On September 30, 1915, for example, Irwin spoke to the Employees' Club of the National Bank and told a racist joke to point out the absurdity of the existence of suffrage for black people but not for women. She said that she had been speaking to the black elevator boy on her way up to the meeting and asked him if he was going to vote in the next election. "'Deed I am," he replied. "Do you understand the Constitution, then?" she queried. His answer was, "'Deed I don't, what, do you think I'se some sort of doctor?"[40] In similar fashion, she began her work as head of the suffragists' "Bureau of Laughter" with a story making fun of the ignorance of a black preacher:

> "The anti-suffragists remind me," said Miss Irwin, "of the story of an illiterate colored minister who preached against the wearing of chignons from a text he said he found in the Bible: Top-Knot Come Down."
>
> "He did find it in the bible, too. He found it by exactly the method that the anti-suffragist uses when he or she finds a 'menace to morality' in the writings of such women as Charlotte Perkins Gilman, or an attack on woman suffrage in the statements of Judge Ben B. Lindsey.
>
> "Let him that is upon the housetop not come down."[41]

But even though Irwin's songs, in one way, reinforced her (and her white audience's) separation and superiority to the "coon," these portrayals of an alternative, carefree universe could also show what Eric Lott has defined, in his masterful study of minstrelsy in the antebellum era, *Love and Theft,* as "a sneaking envy, a wistful longing to be able to relax and be free, like the mythical levee lounger with his watermelon and banjo." Lott maintains that whites in minstrelsy engaged in "cultural robbery," which he likens to Karl Marx's term *expropriation,* an action that "troubled guilty whites all the more because they were so attracted to the culture they plundered."[42] His conclusions certainly bear on the coon song as well.

Lott's idea of love and envy is related to the "vitalist" impulse in late-nineteenth-century American racism. Vitalism contains an admiration of the so-called natural qualities of inferior races. As Jackson Lears puts it, "Just when white Americans were murdering the last remnants of Indian resistance at Wounded Knee, and lynching scores of African-Americans throughout the South, they were also discovering new vitality in those despised racial groups."[43]

These songs were part of how America clung to the past, even as it marched forward. No better symbol of this mixed impetus was one of the main attractions at the 1893 Chicago World's Fair, the "faithful enslaved mammy personified by Aunt Jemima." The only real "modern" representation of colored America was this fictitious character touting the new, easy-to-make pancake mix packaged by the Davis Milling Company. That the "original" recipe was "created" by a "trademark character suggested that slavery itself had been a necessary stage in the progress of capitalist civilization."[44] In a potent way, the figure of May Irwin served a similar function: she spoke as a modern city woman living in the abundance of the present but containing the comforting and carefree past of a fantasy antebellum South, where lazy afternoons were spent watching happy Negroes sing and dance.

Poised on the brink of a new century of modernity, African Americans complained that the advances of their race were not represented at the 1893 World's Fair. Even the renowned Frederick Douglass was relegated to the "Haitian Exhibit," one of the features of the "Midway Plaisance," which included replicas of villages of Native Americans, Africans, and Asians. Alongside these villages, visitors could eat ethnic foods at stalls and listen to African Americans playing new ragtime tunes. The Midway Plaisance drew much larger crowds than the "refined arts of the White City." The lure for whites was surely not only the chance to feel superior to other races. Crowds were also attracted as voyeurs of primitive, natural people, and whites envied "black performers as transmitters of an authentic folk tradition [ragtime music] their own culture lacked."[45]

Sometimes these conflicting attitudes resulted in a song that simultaneously called on the audience to laugh at *and* identify with the coon character. Nowhere is this clearer than in May Irwin's performance of "The Opera Rag." In the "coontown" presented here, a painter, Sam Johnson, dares to rise above his ragtime roots and fancy himself an educated devotee of opera. As music critic Larry Hamberlein has illustrated in his in-depth analysis of the piece, when Irwin sang this song in Booth Tarkington's play *Getting a Polish*, she evoked complex and conflicting responses.[46] As she sang Irving Berlin's music, Irwin imitated a black male whose "ragging of the classics" included obvious mismatches between operatic melodies and their composers. Irwin's audiences would have recognized the very familiar arias and laughed at Sam Johnson's misidentifications that render him unfit to join the white society he so covets. But Irwin's singing of ragtime music in a play that lampooned the snobbish pretensions of European culture would have also aroused identification with an American culture that joined blacks and whites together.

Irwin's remarks about using coon songs in her own versions of Shakespeare worked in a similar fashion. (Late-nineteenth-century entertainment offered many blackface burlesques of Shakespeare.) Making fun of her own inability to succeed at Shakespeare *and* lampooning the "high culture" of

Shakespearean tragedy,[47] she simultaneously referred to songs that made fun of black society. Irwin claimed that she wanted to play Desdemona, if only to get the chance to sing "All Coons Look Alike to Me" to a real coon. Then, she added, Othello could end the play by "changing the sex and sing[ing, instead of "I've Got Him Dead"] "I've Got Her Dead."[48]

In her identification with the coon character, Irwin was in a sense transformed *into* the "coon." Her physical characteristics actually helped her *become* the coon. Blackness has long been linked with "a child's eye view of sexuality, . . . fat lips, gaping mouths, . . . enormous bustles." Thus, who better than Irwin to portray a coon without makeup or disguise? The numerous reviews that mention Irwin's large derriere and the attendant caricatures of her form and mouth that so delighted the newspapers designated her as an apt model for the coon stereotype. Her occasional avowal that she was just naturally like a Negro and did not need to study them helped confirm this idea. Her childlike delivery of the coon songs reduced her to the childlike status of the coon. Perhaps most tellingly, critics noted that in her performance Irwin appeared unconcerned about the social problems revealed in coon songs. She was carefree and oblivious, just like the Negro: "Miss Irwin seems to see in every situation the humor of it so thoroughly that *the particular point escapes her*—she does not see that a thing is unconventional, improper, sad, funny, or illegal, because she sees beyond the immediate situation. Her large mouth and frame and voice all go to say, well, it's all right, anyway, in the beyond. These things don't mean what they seem. Let's enjoy."[49] What is the *particular point* that escapes her? How are things *not* what they seem to be? She is allowed to present a situation that is "improper" as long as the "reality of the situation" escapes her. Indeed, there is a harsh reality underlying these "coon" songs—one that Irwin not only excuses but also exacerbates with blatantly racist imagery. The very ubiquity of the numbers indelibly stamped their caricatures into the American consciousness. (By the mid-1920s, the coon song was being touted as au fait for any vaudeville performance, and even as early as 1897 critics noted, somewhat wearily, that "'coon shouter' is as explicit a term now as is 'song and dance artist.' Nearly every vaudeville programme introduces 'Miss So-and-So, the greatest living lady coon shouter.")[50]

As the oft-quoted Sterling A. Brown, one of the first black critics of the stereotypes of blacks in literature, noted, the constant repetition of a stereotype and the "sincere unremitting harping upon an argument will finally make it seem plausible." Brown sees this as most dangerous in the descriptions he cites of the "Negro as Brute," described, as Thomas Nelson Page did in 1900, as the freed slave who represented a "general depravity and retrogression of the Negroes at large . . . intemperate, insolent, and [lacking] the most rudimentary elements of morality." He culls physical descriptions from nineteenth-century literature that could be applied directly to the illustration from Irwin's "The Bully," the black man having a face "principally composed of a pair of protuberant lips, whose luxuriance seemed intended as an indemnity for a pair of crushed nostrils," and a "leg placed so near the center of the foot as to make it sometimes a matter of disguise whether he was not walking backward."[51]

Because "The Bully" was Irwin's most popular song, its relationship to the emergence of a new racism (sometimes termed *naturalist*) that grew in late-nineteenth-century American white society is paramount in understanding her success with coon shouting. Naturalist racism ushers in a new dangerous urban Negro, ready with a razor to cut anyone who dares encroach on his territory.[52] He has become the wild animal depicted in Charles Carroll's 1900 book, *The Negro Is a Beast.*

Naturalist racism may have partially been a response to the growth of large black settlements in more than thirty northern cities during the latter years of the nineteenth century. Many northern whites had never seen African Americans and were uncertain how they were to be integrated into white society. Backlash was in evidence everywhere. It did not help the black image or promote social tolerance that cities in the North experienced a fourfold increase in murder between 1880 and 1890.[53] Lynchings were on the increase throughout the 1890s, and unpunished killings of blacks were commonplace through the Red Summer of race riots in 1919 that broke out in Chicago and Washington, D.C., as well as in Texas and South Carolina.[54] Gradually, the ugliest forms of southern racism spread northward: "More and more the South formulated its creed: it glorified the old aristocracy that had flourished and departed, and definitely it began to ask the North if it had not been right after all."[55]

The new image of the murderous urban Negro, often represented by a character named Zip Coon (in contrast to the early pre–Civil War Zip Coon and to the more ragged and benevolent Jim Crow), grew out of three important and intertwined factors. The first was a growing emphasis on the idea of manliness, reacting to the anxiety that soft urban living had turned white men into flabby "neurasthenics." In the late 1880s, "Manliness became less a condition to be cultivated than a goal to be pursued. It acquired a therapeutic dimension, reshaping the desire for revitalization into a lifelong project, sending men in search of new sites for self-testing, new frontiers." This idea of manliness could be applied to men of all political stripes, to blacks as well as whites, and even to little boys. (*McGuffey Readers* around the turn of the century are full of stories of appropriate "manly behavior.") But it became a useful tool in the hands of racists, who believed that Negroes, without the civilizing influences of slavery, had regressed to an animal state. As animals blacks could not master their bestial instincts—and such mastery was truly necessary for real "manliness."[56]

The second factor was the ideal of Victorian womanhood, especially as embodied in the southern belle, whose virtue needed to be protected at all costs. Indeed, this rarefied, delicate creature became the symbol of the South. Following the ravages of the Civil War, which turned the South into a frontier to be conquered by "manly" men, this "creature" was ravaged as well. It was natural, then, that the "South should inevitably translate the whole battle into terms of her defense."[57]

These two ideas combined and helped promote a third—the rape myth of the South that spread to the North. Seemingly, suddenly freed black men could not contain their beastly sexual nature when tempted by the very sight of the unattainable white woman—though in truth the chance of a white woman being raped by a black man was something "less, for instance, than the chance that she would be struck by lightning."[58] The rape myth became an important tool for political power. Neo-Confederate groups of men and women blamed the murder of blacks by mobs of whites in 1898 on President McKinley's use of African American men in government positions. To Sumner Archibald Cunningham, editor of the *Confederate Veteran,* these positions of prominence caused the black civil servants to become so "insolent" that "white ladies could not walk the street in safety"; clearly, white men must stand by their "sacred oaths" even if "blood ran in the street."[59] The possibility of rape—no matter how remote—undeniably affected a practice that began to grow alarmingly in frequency:

> Sex (or the fantasy of it) was the crucial piece in the puzzle linking radical racial theory to the rising tide of lynching that engulfed many parts of the South from 1889 through the first decade of the twentieth century. Between 1882 and 1888, throughout the United States, 595 whites were lynched, compared to 440 blacks. In 1889 the ratio shifted to 76 whites and 94 blacks, and three years later the discrepancy had nearly doubled: 69 whites were lynched, and 162 blacks. For the next decade and a half, about 85 percent of all lynching victims were African-American men.[60]

The great black reformer Ida B. Wells-Barnett certainly understood and analyzed the "rape myth" in her antilynching campaigns of the 1890s, and her work resulted in the destruction of her home and flight to the North.[61]

In her remarkable analysis of the ritualized aspects of lynching, Amy Louise Wood shows convincingly that lynching in the South was not primarily a backward, rural activity but an expression of the tensions of modernization rapidly occurring throughout the country: "As southern towns and cities developed, largely because of industrial and commercial expansion, they produced new kinds of occupations, new social arrangements, and new forms of recreation that many emerging white working and middle-class men and women embraced. Even so, these people feared many of the consequences of those changes, particularly those that threatened the social authority and advancement they desired. Above all, they feared that urban crime, as well as the consumption of alcohol—phenomena that were regularly racialized—placed white women and white homes in peril."[62]

It was in this context that Irwin gained such fame with her Bully song. She struck a chord in her audiences in a way that helped assuage guilt over increased racial tension and lynchings, by painting a picture that seemed to justify the white backlash: "Audiences at *The Widow Jones* could plainly see Miss Irwin's detachment from the action: she sang as an actress, she sang without blacking up. She was no minstrel from a pastoral setting. She was a modern woman shouting about savagery near at hand, here in the big city. She was like a street news vendor announcing the latest bloodthirsty edition of the *Police Gazette.*" At the same time, then, that Irwin's rendition of "The Bully" calmed the fears of her audience by its very ludicrousness, it may have, as Samuel Denison suggests, through "her imposing figure literally challeng[ed] the listener to deny the accuracy of the stereotype."[63] Contemporary critics illustrated their receptiveness to the stereotype when they worried about what might lie behind Irwin's fun-loving imitations:

> The Southern negro [May Irwin] impersonates in "Crappy Dan" and "The Bully" is not the old plantation darky, happy in his bondage, primitive in his simplicity, but a product of the new civilization, the bad town darky of the age of transition. That he is susceptible to humorous treatment Miss Irwin proves, and the manner in which she thus puts him before us in all his badness and audacity, without the aid of make-up or scenic effect, is, in its small way, a triumph of art. But this same crappy Dan, with his dice loaded for "sebens" and his "'quaintance wid a gun," *represents a grave social problem.*[64]

Irwin's humorous style, by disconnecting her from the content of the material, may have become the most important aspect in making these songs acceptable. If there is an underlying fear of the Bully, the capturing of the image by a white female comic emasculates it and, thus, takes away its power (especially in her depiction of the Bully as childlike). This metaphorical emasculation can even subconsciously mirror the literal emasculation that occurred in approximately one-third of all lynchings of African Americans during this period.[65]

In a related way, May Irwin's performance plays into the violence that holds sexism and racism together.[66] That is, as a white female coon shouter, she was appealing because she could in effect become the focus of both the racism and the misogyny of white males. Critic Janet Brown has proposed that both women and blacks are victims of the projected self-hatred of the dominant group, but that women tend to internalize this message. That is, although blacks are victims of overt and life-threatening prejudice, they have their own separate societies in which they *are* the dominant group; therefore, they are more apt to *know* that the stereotype created by (and performed for) white people is not real. Because women are integrated within the group (be it the dominant group or not), they are taught that certain submissive characteristics are always desirable, and so they tend to absorb these characteristics.[67]

Critics like Brown might suggest that Irwin's success as a coon shouter depended in part on her gender. That is, when May Irwin performed as a coon, she may have been able to undercut her own powerful status as a star by projecting her "womanly" role onto the coon she was portraying. Thus, she rendered the racist image less threatening and more palatable and simultaneously assured her audiences that, despite her immense wealth and power, she was just a sweet, jolly, harmless, fat woman. Her act demonstrated to the mass audience that, just as it is "all right" and natural for a woman to display certain characteristics of the inferior sex, so it must be "all right" for the coon to display certain characteristics of an inferior race.

To summarize, a comprehensive survey of Irwin's coon songs reveals marked characteristics in her choice of and success with different stereotypes. Irwin's Idealized Coons fueled her popularity by exploiting her audience's taste for naive romanticism. At the same time, the appeal of her Pathetic Coon and Greedy Gal is reflective of her own and her audiences' condescension toward and separation from black culture. The narrator of the fantasized "coontowns" is certainly separated from the race she describes, but can also join with that race's qualities and love of "low culture" to stand against Old World "high culture." Although Irwin sang many more songs depicting the Idealized Coon and the Pathetic Coon, her greatest successes were coon songs that stressed the violent image of the Bully. Even her most triumphant Pathetic Coons, as represented in "Mr. Johnson, Turn Me Loose," inhabited songs filled with violence and premature death. The point of view from which Irwin sang was overwhelmingly that of the black male; she even moved in and out of the male voice in half of her depictions of the Greedy Gal. Only in a small collection of Female Victim songs did she exclusively use the female's point of view—and, interestingly, most of her own compositions were of that type.

The coon songs that Irwin sang contain multiple ambiguities that parallel the equivocal attitude toward the coon that was an essential ingredient of white racism in general and of May Irwin's own racism in particular. This contradiction between the white woman coon shouter and the coons that were her subject need not negate the power of either image—for Irwin could be identified as both sympathetic to and aligned with the black images she portrayed *and* separate from and superior to them. One moment she is the Bully, childishly marching around in triumph, the next she is a hapless female victim asking for justice, and then she becomes an outsider—a parental figure—warning the little frog to stay in his own place. She is both powerful and submissive, empathetic and condescending, threatening and reassuring.

Irwin clearly mirrored these opposing impulses in her own differing versions of how she learned to coon shout and cakewalk. In one account, she said that her ability to sing these songs in black dialect stemmed from intuition and that she had never seen a "colored" man or woman until she came to America and had only seen a few since. In another, she maintained that she heard singing at a hotel and spent a long time studying African Americans before mastering the art, once throwing a party to entertain them and learn from them. At one point, she claimed that the secret of the tune was not in the words but in the particular thumbing of the banjo; conversely, at another time, she insisted on the primary importance of words and themes, asserting that coon songs would never die because "the coons we sing about are our own product and their troubles are familiar to us." In one article, she described how she learned to cakewalk by sneaking into a black reception and observing, emphasizing that she couldn't really grasp the steps until a "colored" woman who was as heavy as she was executed them, whereupon she identified with the dancer and felt that she could imitate her accurately.[68]

That May Irwin had some awareness of the objectionable nature of coon songs is illustrated in a short story she wrote, "Ole Miss Cyarter and the Ghost." This story explores what happens when May invites her maid, Miss Octavia Magnolia, to her show. Much to Irwin's surprise, the maid is insulted by the coon songs that her employer sings. The maid suggests that Irwin's "Bully Song" is an insult because it doesn't describe in detail the noble African battle that a razor fight can be. She further complains that the number "I Ain't Gwine ter Work No Mo'" gives away precious tips to white people about living without working. When the maid comes up with her own song, which depicts a white person longing to be black, Irwin can hardly contain her laughter at the absurdity, and the maid quits, dubbing Irwin an "insulter of our race."[69] The obvious joke of the story is that the maid does not object to the racist portrayals for the reasons expected. Instead, she objects to the secrets about the black race that Irwin is giving away and the failure of Irwin to understand that razor fights are actually admirable. Her reaction indicates that blacks are so foolish and childlike that they cannot discern the offensiveness of the songs. If that is true, then the songs must contain real illustrations and not be defamatory after all.

Irwin's treatment of her own longtime cook and companion, Sarah, also highlights her ambivalence. She frequently praised Sarah with compliments that contained allusions to Sarah's race, such as her comment that Sarah was "a pearl, a black pearl, and for that reason, more precious." Many of Irwin's articles and interviews contain glowing referrals to her cook's intelligence and ability. Sarah is often included in photographs, such as the one picturing Irwin working on a number while Sarah watches, in which the caption states "May Irwin Trying a New Coon Song in her City Apartments with her Cook Sarah as the Critic."[70]

In an article on the maids employed by famous stage celebrities, Irwin emphasized her love of black servants. She told the story of her first maid, Ida, whom she could not keep when she left the city. Later she heard from Ida's sister that the young woman had died of pneumonia with a locket with May's photograph in it about her neck. The reporter noted that "May Irwin can't tell the story without tears of real grief coming to the eyes for the little colored girl who loved her so well."[71]

Of course, Irwin's treatment of her maids is part of a paternalistic type of racism—as an individual, Irwin heaped praise on the race, maintaining that she would hire only colored maids: "All her servants are colored people, and all are from the South. The sympathy she puts into the darky songs she sings are [*sic*] real and she loves the land where they originated and the people." But even in her own profession, Irwin tried to further the careers of black musicians on many occasions, and she took care to advertise that fact. When *Mrs. Black Is Back* opened, she used full orchestrations arranged by a black composer and claimed that, although black composers had had songs that had "time and time again been interpolated freely in the most successful comedies, never has the orchestration and incidental music been done by one. And so Miss Irwin feels that she has brought the colored man another step forward in the profession of amusing the public."[72]

Accordingly, Irwin could feel that her coons of song had nothing to do with the reality of actual "colored gentlemen." Certainly, as critics of popular music know, the addition of music to lyrics or scenic material creates a spectacle that "exaggerates content and adds a dimension of artificiality." Indeed, Irwin never used (in articles or writings) the words *coon* or *nigger* to refer to blacks, outside of her use of those words in songs or in reference to songs.

No newspaper journalist in a prominent paper would do so either. Under cover of spectacle, Irwin could present something the audience might consider indicative of reality or simply a ludicrous performance—as long as "the particular point escaped her." In the area of real life, woe to any Negro who mistook "spectacle" for reality—as famous early-twentieth-century fighter Jack Johnson did: "Entering the ring in a silk robe, blue trunks, and American flag belt, Johnson prolonged the fight to humiliate his aging opponent, taunting him with cries of 'How do you like it?' Finally, after two nine-count knock-downs, the champion finished off his rival with a fifteenth-round knockout. In response, white race riots broke out across the country, and fifteen states and the District of Columbia banned all boxing films to preserve public order. Newspaper editorialists now warned that African Americans were incapable of distinguishing between a sports contest and social reality."[73]

That coon songs like "The Bully" promoted stereotypes that could result in real harm to black people would have been a foreign idea to a performer like Irwin in the times she lived in. Although Irwin may have helped her audience *fail* to recognize a social reality, that is, that reality was not the "grave" problem one reviewer worried about—the existence of real, murderous urban Negroes. That "problem" was made all too evident in Irwin's performances, even as she fueled the spread of a much deeper and more serious problem—the existence of murderous, illegal threats to the lives and livelihoods of black men and women. In a dark and bitter satire, Washington, D.C.'s newspaper the *Colored American* drew the connection in this way, imagining a lynching as a performance: "A big burly Negro will be artistically roasted until life is extinct. During the exercise and before the torch is applied, there will be a cake walk and Miss _____, the daughter of the injured lady, will sing a number of spicy coon songs."[74]

To understand the success of Irwin as a coon shouter, we have to tackle the racism of the times she lived in and the conscious and unconscious effects racist ideology may have had on her and her audiences. Her triumph depends on a remarkable synthesis of contradictions. Irwin was able to win her audience by simultaneously *identifying with* and *separating herself from* the coon character. Like her Bully figure, she was powerful, took what she wanted, and succeeded in her endeavors. But like other coon stereotypes, she was also childish, foolish, and laughable; her admirers really had nothing to fear. In addition, she used the fact that she was a woman as a license to perform such material and still defuse its hateful overtones. Another of May Irwin's uses of her female identity is the subject of my next chapter.

"All Coons Look Alike to Me" (1896), by Earnest Hogan. Courtesy of Music Division, the New York Library, Digital Collections.

"I Couldn't Stand to See My Baby Lose" (1899), by Will D. Cobb and Gus Edwards. Courtesy of Karen Killian's private collection.

"May Irwin's LuLu Song" (1896), by Summit L. Hecht. Courtesy of the Lester S. Levy Collection of Sheet Music, Sheridan Libraries, John Hopkins University, Baltimore.

"The Bully" (1896), by Charles Trevathan. Courtesy of the Lester S. Levy Collection of Sheet Music, Sheridan Libraries, John Hopkins University, Baltimore.

Second cover for "The Bully." Courtesy of the Lester S. Levy Collection of Sheet Music, Sheridan Libraries, John Hopkins University, Baltimore.

The "Frog Song" (1896), by Charles Trevathan. Courtesy of the Lester S. Levy Collection of Sheet Music, Sheridan Libraries, John Hopkins University, Baltimore.

Postcard advertising *Reconstruction to Ragtime* (2008). Design by Austen Gage. Courtesy of the author.

5

Unbounded Domesticity

Her hands have wrought with such a wondrous skill
Not song, nor plastic form, nor rhapsody,
But greater joy without its myrrh or rue—
A thing on which Olympic cards could fill,
An art to praise with sweetest melody
May Irwin fair, I sing to your beefstew.

—Laurence Anhalt, untitled poem

As Irwin grew older and embarked on a long series of "retirements" (not unusual for star performers even to this day), her domestic life became more and more important to her.[1] But even in her younger days, her cooking and housekeeping were strongly associated with every aspect of her public persona. Newspaper headlines often coupled Irwin's performances with her domestic work, usually with an emphasis on the latter. Allusions to her domestic life intruded on and sometimes overwhelmed descriptions of her stage career. More than three-quarters of contemporary articles written about Irwin mention her housekeeping or cooking abilities, often assuring the public that she was fulfilling her domestic responsibilities.[2] She was lauded for declaring herself "a better housekeeper than actress," and in her interviews she explained how she "worked hard on stage and knows how to make chutney and bait a mouse trap." When she married Kurt Eisfeldt in 1907, the wedding announcement noted, "Young Mr. Eisfeldt to Marry a Famous Actress and Cook."[3]

Certainly, in making sure that her public closely identified her with domestic pursuits, Irwin was not exceptional. As Benjamin McArthur has noted, "The invocation of domesticity served to reassure the public that actors and actresses lived lives not so different from everybody else's. . . . [T]he domestic strain in American culture, which had defined women's social role since the early nineteenth century, still carried great weight into the twentieth." In 1913 *Good Housekeeping* featured several stories about actresses and their home lives, and throughout the period of 1880–1920 innumerable articles appeared in magazines such as *Collier's, Green Book,* and *Theatre,* stressing the domestic nature of individual actresses. Descriptions of home visits presented an idealized setting: "A deep, shady porch carefully screened against insect invasions . . . looked out across the fertile rolling acres of Miss Bates' [actress Blanche Bates] farm, to a skyline of serrated hills beyond which the placid Hudson gleamed, here and there between the blue crests. Here sat the actress in a summery gown of fluff and foolish little flowers. . . . Against her lap leaned a big-eyed tot, whom not even the severity of an interviewer's frown sufficed to awe out of her insistence for another 'tory.'"[4]

Media news about the home lives of celebrities—particularly female ones—continues to this day. We need only to remember the angry response to Hillary Clinton's remark in the 1990s about not having time to bake cookies to see how important an image of domesticity still is for women in the public eye. Indeed, in 2014 some pundits speculated that Mrs. Clinton planned the birth of her own grandchild in order to advance her political career!

Yet in her day, May Irwin stands out from the crowd of actresses as someone who managed to connect her professional and domestic life in *every way possible.* She certainly had the credentials to back up the publicity—as the author of not only a series of articles on homemaking but also a cookbook that still sells online today. Through the years, she also acquired and maintained a working dairy and farm in her retirement home in Clayton, New York.

Irwin's success in projecting her domestic image publicly helped endear her to an audience increasingly defined by its female members. In an important way—which I discuss further in both this chapter and the next—Irwin's domestic traits allowed her to extend her activities into a public space in the same way that female activists of the time used their domesticity to legitimize their work in public. As critic Richard Butsch has written, the "acceptance in theatre [of a respectable female audience] was justified on domestic grounds, just as the legitimation of extended domestic duty allowed middle-class women reformers more political incursions into public space."[5]

One way in which Irwin used her attachment to domestic duties was to portray a fondness for them as completely natural to her—something prompted not so much by preference as by instinct. For example, her reason for taking a large apartment rather than a hotel room when she stayed in Manhattan, as she told a theater journalist, was that "I've got to keep house or die." She maintained that she was "a housekeeper by instinct. . . . Household duties came naturally to me, I never had to learn any of them." Likewise, she was never taught to cook. "[My mother] had peculiar ideas upon some subjects. She said if we did not know how to work we would not have to do it. I don't know how I learned [to cook]. It must have come natural to me. Perhaps I inherited a taste for it."[6]

Irwin herself was careful to blend her domestic life with her professional one, thereby making her attentions to each mutually supportive. Her tendency in conversation to interject disconnected remarks about cooking preparations was humorously noted by interviewers. In the middle of an interview concerning her work with Augustin Daly, Irwin leaned forward and let the interviewer know that she felt bell peppers were a much-neglected vegetable, highly suitable in omelettes.[7] Another time she reported that she once dashed home on a Sunday, right after her opening season outside of New York, so that she could be certain to make chili sauce while her tomatoes were at the peak of ripeness. And when in 1915 she was phoned by Martin Beck, the prestigious owner of the Palace, and asked to replace the ailing singer Emma Calvé, she had him hold for a minute while she removed her special grapefruit shortcake from the oven. (Irwin promised to give the recipe to any woman in the Palace's audience who might want to try it out.)[8]

Indeed, Irwin defined herself as "a thorough home woman . . . never intended for the stage." Lamenting her need to work, she insisted that "99 out of 100 business or professional women would prefer the home life to a more public one. There are a few freaks, of course, but I am speaking of the large majority of women with normal hearts and level heads on their shoulders." Interviewers would sometimes evince great astonishment when the usually unflappable Irwin suddenly turned to them with eyes full of tears: "'Women weren't made for business,' she said. There was a slight but still perceptible quiver about the unsmiling lips. 'People call me a good businesswoman. Maybe I am, but how I hate it. If I had my way I would be a housekeeper. Such women don't know how well they are off.'"[9]

If Irwin labeled herself as one who would prefer home life to a more public one, why did she abandon her "true calling" for the stage? Her reason was as compelling as the one she gave young women for learning a trade or occupation—an unavoidable emergency. As noted in chapter 1, Irwin was just a young girl when her father died; she and her sister, Flo, took to the stage to support their mother. She spent most of her marriage to Frederick Keller (1878–1886) caring for him and their two sons. After Keller's death from tuberculosis, she provided sole support for both boys and her mother, and she often cared for her sister, who suffered intermittently from ill health. Her difficult beginnings impressed upon her the need to acquire financial security, and she embarked on a lifetime of business acquisitions and investments: "I learned years ago that it is important to have money in this world. If you haven't money, you might as well be dead. I had to go on the stage as a child, because when my father died it was found that everything had disappeared. It hasn't always been plain sailing for me. Why, I've gone hungry many a time."[10]

Irwin's need to make money expanded as she became the sole support of more and more people. In 1905 she told a reporter that she was presently responsible for the well-being of thirty-three individuals: "The thirty-three are relatives or servants whom it is my duty and my pleasure to help. My mother, for instance, whom I support, my brothers, who have families, and there is Sarah. It was Sarah who brought you upstairs. She has been with me for seventeen years. She has four children, three daughters and Bobbie. If anything happened to Sarah, of course I would look after them. Yes, I may be said to be the head of a family of thirty-three, white and black."[11]

If the need to acquire money to care for herself and others propelled Irwin out of her beloved domestic world, her homemaking abilities helped her to secure that wealth in the public world. Thus, although Irwin's natural instincts were initially thwarted when she had to go onto the stage, they resurfaced to aid her performing career and to provide other avenues for lucrative ventures.

Just as May Irwin was a triple threat onstage (as an actress-singer who could perform an inimitable cakewalk), so her proficiencies in homemaking clustered in three major areas: First, she presented herself as competent in managing a household and servants, with its attendant duties of saving, shopping, and planning. Second, she celebrated her status as a mother, responsible not only for raising two children to adulthood but also for providing the livelihood and care of her own mother and other members of the family (and her servant Sarah's family). Finally, she enjoyed widespread publicity for her expertise as a great cook.

May Irwin was proud of her capability in managing her household and servants. When the press asked her what her alternative choice of career would have been if her current glamorous occupation had been closed to her, she had a ready answer:

> May Irwin would rather lecture on household economics today than act. But she can't sing her lectures and she can't get much of her inimitable comedy into them. Or she would have been glad to become that personage, a visiting housekeeper, setting things right in great houses for the return of the owners from the country or from Europe, and directing the corps of servants as a general directs his army. But domestic economics in her own family required

> that Georgie Campbell, aged 12, should sing for a living, and that singing and acting she has lucratively done.[12]

Irwin prided herself on her excellent relationships with servants, which she credited as a substantial part of her facility in household management. She made suggestions for additions to servants' rooms—comfortable chairs, lamps, and reading material, noting that "people who help you like to read too." She even gave up a reception room in her house for her maid's convenience: "Its future will be my cook's bedroom. Yes, I mean it. I've had my cook for seventeen years and she deserves consideration. I saw her one evening after a hard day's work climbing to her room on the top floor and I said, 'Four flights are too many to climb. I am going to give you this reception room to sleep in.'"[13]

Irwin's most complete explanation of her belief in the Golden Rule is contained in her own prelude to a recipe for bread:

> The majority of people, men as well as women, think of the ones who help them with their work as beneath them socially, made, perhaps, of different and not so fine a quality of clay and they act towards them accordingly and that is where they are all wrong. Of course it wouldn't do for us all to think alike. "Difference of opinion is what makes men race horses" but where, I'd like some wise person to tell me, did the idea originate that one person is any better than another and what is the meaning of the word "servant"? In the bible the word is used several times but in a different sense from that of today. There we are all servants doing our duty, or supposed to be.[14]

She continued in this vein, suggesting that those who could afford servants try an experiment. By spending one week doing the work they expected of their servants, these household managers could learn to value their "Mary or John." In giving this suggestion, Irwin may have been sincere but was also certainly carefully fashioning a persona who was humble and "of the people."

This strategy was reflected further in her tendency to identify *herself* as a servant. Interviewers marveled at the positions they found her in when they arrived at her home to chat. She was "on her knees before the fire" checking on the efficiency of a gas log or was bent over in a "well-starched lavender apron" doing the morning cleaning herself, even though "a slim and willing mulatto maid" was standing by.[15] Irwin once expressed delight at being mistaken for kitchen help when she stopped by a local restaurant for lunch.[16]

At times Irwin even placed herself below her servants in competency and seemingly enjoyed reporting episodes in which she learned humility through the superior abilities of her hired help: "You would think by the way my servants look after me and care for me that I was about five years old." She maintained that even though she *thought* she fried chicken very well, "the last time I did it, Sarah, my cook, said 'I guess you better let me do that next time, Miss May,' so maybe I have forgotten how."[17] In a recipe for baking bread, she credited her cook with all of the know-how:

> One day, some years ago [Sarah] said to me "You're supposed to be a pretty good cook, aren't you, Miss Irwin?" I think I blushed but it is so long ago I have forgotten, but anyway, as my press agent was absent I had to reply 'Well I don't know. My husband and boys and friends think I can cook.' Then she asked me how I made my bread and right there she had me! I didn't know how to make bread and was ashamed to say so, so I hedged by saying 'I'm not so much on making bread but my biscuits and pies and cakes!!' That was her cue to hand me a broadside—not that that's where I got mine—you know what I mean. 'Well, she said, I don't think anyone should pride themselves on being a cook until they can bake bread!' and I agreed with her. She taught me to bake bread and this is the way she does it.[18]

Irwin's concerns for the well-being of her servants did not imply that she could not be "exactin'"—as she said herself, she expected top-quality work from her servants. She maintained that past servants always came to visit her, even if she had earlier sent them away for their incompetence.

Irwin's care of her servants was mirrored by her care in saving and shopping, two other parts of household management in which she took pride. Careful saving and shopping at home, Irwin thought, prepared women for successful money management in general. In this way, according to Irwin, a woman who took care of every aspect of her household could expect to reap benefits in the public world as well, should she venture into it. For example, in a series titled "How a Woman Can Make and Save Money," Irwin began with an article emphasizing "care." She insisted that all women start by assessing their own possessions, their own household, and their own domestic habits. Only through considerable care and economy at home could a woman expect to learn the skills necessary to enter the public world of real estate. Only through careful saving and avoidance of extravagance could a woman expect to put aside the initial sum of money needed to start her on the path to moneymaking.

Noted for her Scottish thrift, Irwin scolded young housewives for not examining their garbage cans, where they could learn from their extravagance in not using last night's entire roast. A roast's bones should be "scraped [and the excess meat] used in a hash."[19] Such abilities served her well when she worked under her own management, for a time taking over the exclusive control of the Bijou Theater.[20] But her actors were not always pleased, as when she refused to pay for a canceled Monday-night performance: "May, if you were hard up, or hadn't been making money, or were unlikely to do business, we'd meet your proposition in a minute. But under the circumstances, not in a thousand years." (The actors who refused to accept the short paychecks were Ignacio Marinetti and John G. Sparks.)[21]

In the second article of her series, Irwin introduced the topic of "dare." Here she praised the habits of the astute female shopper who "makes the rounds of the shops and inspects what each has to offer. She takes what might be called a bird's-eye view of the stock of the articles she wants in the various shops. Then, provided with samples, or merely with memories, she goes home and thinks it over. She weighs the merits of the different articles of her preference, their cost, their durability and their special fitness for her needs. Then she goes back and buys, one might say, in cold blood. For so all buying should be done."[22] Irwin herself combined the skills of thrift and shopping in her own purchases of real estate. As noted in a previous chapter, she had begun investing wisely as a young woman, long before her salary soared to the twenty-five hundred dollars weekly that she was earning by 1907.[23] Her holdings grew until, a few years before her death, she was reportedly able to sell a block of property on Lexington Avenue in New York City for more than one million dollars.[24]

Pairing shopping with real estate, Irwin urged women to take the radical step of buying their own homes. She noted that these women already had all the requisite skills necessary to acquire real estate, for "if you are a good shopper, you will be a wise home buyer. For the same methods should be employed. The good shopper goes out prospecting as a miner goes and looks about a region to find promising land."[25]

So in managing a household properly and in obtaining her own household to manage, a woman combines the empathy and interpersonal skills she can use to manage servants with the "cold-blooded" skills of saving and shopping. She "cares" for her household and her servants, but she "dares" to enter the public world and drive a hard bargain.

Irwin's ventures into real estate often included plans to utilize the property in a way that would make use of her facility in household chores. In 1922 she planned to establish an inn in Clayton, New York, at which she would supervise the cooking and serve milk from her own Jersey cows.[26] More than twenty years earlier, she had considered turning property in New York City into a "bachelor's home" that would provide good meals and rooms for luckless single men. In so doing, she planned to combine her skills of nurturing with those for moneymaking: "I'm going to turn philanthropist and make a lot of money."[27] (Neither of these plans materialized—Prohibition, which began with the ratification of the Eighteenth Amendment in 1919, played an important part in her decision not to open the inn.)[28]

Irwin viewed her nurturing abilities as linked more to her duties as a mother than to her obligations as a wife. Interestingly, she did not consider her status as a wife—in either of her two marriages—as one of particular importance. She often joked about marriage, claiming in 1906 (just one year before she remarried) that she wasn't thinking of marriage because widowhood had too many charms that "cannot always be predicted of married life."[29] She held the view—radical in her day—that divorce was a necessity if there was unhappiness or lack of love in a marriage,[30] and she featured in her published cookbook a monologue by writer-actor Clay Greene that parodied Hamlet's famous soliloquy with "Divorce or No Divorce":

> Divorce or no divorce, that is the question:
> Whether 'tis easier for the wife to suffer
> The stings and blushes of her lord's misdoings,
> Or to assert her woman's independence,
> And, mildly raising seven kinds of cain,
> Assure him that she's tumbled to his curves,
> And by divorcing end them. To love! To weep! No more!
> And by that weeping prove to man unworthy
> That she knows not how she can help herself.
> To love! To weep! Perchance to spoil
> The waxened fairness of her powdered face.
> Aye, there's the rub; for with a face bereft of beauty
> How can she other men attract and have revenge
> Upon her lord unworthy, and bring home to roost
> The many wicked chickens he has hatched
> By paying him tenfold in his own coin?
> Who'd his flirtations bear! To moan, to sigh,
> And cry herself into a wretched thing,
> When she might herself his sure quietus make
> In a divorce court, and perhaps provide
> Against the ever-present rainy day
> By liberal and frequent alimony.
> So, after all, can injured wives secure
> Protection 'gainst the things they know not of;

For whether knowing them, or knowing not,
Since she can seek her haven in the law,
Can cut no ice.[31]

Jokes about marriage and husbands and wives have provided ample fodder for comics from Aristophanes to Joan Rivers and were innumerable in vaudeville acts of the late nineteenth century. Irwin's cookbook was certainly full of these jokes, but even the wealth of charitable cookbooks that blossomed after the Civil War—communal books created by women's charitable organizations and churches to raise funds for good causes—included mild satire. A recipe called "How to Cook (or Preserve) a Husband," which admonished the cook not to "stick any sharp instrument into him to see if he is becoming tender," appeared in dozens of these books, albeit in slightly differing versions.[32] Of course, Irwin's stance on divorce carried no personal sting for, unlike Trixie Friganza, Sophie Tucker, Marie Dressler, and Eva Tanguay, she was never divorced and suffered no disastrous love affairs or infidelities (as far as her public knew—and thus far borne out by research).

Although she did not highlight her position as a wife, Irwin did feature her maternal traits in many of her projects, from the causes she took up on behalf of her employees to the court cases she attempted to influence and to the organizations she joined, such as the club meant to improve the welfare of young actresses.[33] She claimed that motherhood was essential to her professionally: being a good mother enhanced her ability as an actress. She even went so far as to declare that "every successful actress in the history of the stage has been a mother," and being a good actress enhanced her ability as a mother. She explained that a woman's "work as an actress would enlarge her knowledge of various phases of life and give her a better understanding of the things her child must face in later years. Then, being a good mother, she will naturally try to train her child to meet the problems that are to come, and which she sees much clearer because of her experience as an actress."[34]

In associating good mothering with good acting, Irwin not only implied that both vocations required similar qualities, but also maintained in a more general way that a woman pursuing a profession she enjoys is less likely to be bitter with her lot and so actually more likely than the stay-at-home mother to be present for her children: "There is nothing in the world sweeter or better than the happy mother of a happy family, but stagnation is not necessary to produce this happiness—it destroys it. There are many women who 'live at home,' who see their children less than does an actress, who has only two months out of twelve at home."[35]

Irwin also had clear views on how a mother should raise her children. Her method of child rearing emphasized mutual respect. She insisted that she never whipped her boys and always preserved an honest relationship with them, taking it upon herself to explain the facts of life when the time came. She allowed them to try cigarettes and liquor in front of her so they would not be lured by the forbidden to become "sneaks." Her boys came to see her onstage often and wrote to her daily when she was on the road. Her stated philosophy was that a "mother should make herself a companion, chum and adviser, not a mentor." The picture of family life that she presented to interviewers underlined this philosophy: "'There is only one room in this house that has not been disturbed,' said Miss Irwin. 'That is the boys' den upstairs. We flee there from the wrath and dust of housecleaning. You should have seen us last night. One of the boys was playing a guitar, and I sat at the table with a cigarette and a gin fizz that my other boy had gone downstairs and made for me.'"[36]

May Irwin strove to produce a public perception of herself as a good mother whose maternal instincts and performance skills were mutually reinforcing—a mother who gained respect from her sons, not through inspiring their fear but by treating them as friends and equals. She considered her two grown sons to be her "greatest achievement" and readily credited herself with their success as "fine, manly specimens of Americanism."[37] The scattering of her personal letters available for perusal attests to her concerns, not only in smaller issues—such as making sure her sons had available seats to see quality shows at Daly's long after she left the company[38]—but also in dealing with major financial problems. When the Knickerbocker Trust Company closed and Irwin lost a great deal of money during the recession of 1907, she wrote to a friend, "But there is no use in worrying about money. I have worried so much about Walter [who suffered ill health] that it took the money concerns out of my mind." The fact that Irwin had managed to raise two white male Americans protected her from the charge that she was neglecting her duty to the race, as some actresses were accused of by this early writer: "If President Roosevelt wishes to know where in this country Race Suicide is to be seen at its best (or worst) let him look for it in our theatres. The number of American actresses who are mothers is in almost ludicrous ratio to the number of women on our stage."[39]

Irwin's nurturing skills were best exemplified, however, by the third area of her domestic prowess, her cooking. Allusions to Irwin's homemaking nearly always included some reference to her cooking. She took great personal pride in her culinary skills, saying, "If I ever leave the stage and have to work I'm going to hire out as a cook, and you can bet I'd be a good one," and others agreed with her assessment: "Should the stage prove fickle, should the houses from which she receives large rentals in New York, the house she owns in the Canadian town where she was born, Whitby in Ontario, disappear in some convulsion of nature, the comedienne could draw a large salary as head-cook in any big hotel in the land, for her fame in this field is as wide as the land."[40]

Articles on Irwin often included photographs of her taken from her cookbook, *May Irwin's Home Cooking,* published in 1904, or in some other cooking pose in her kitchen. Filmmakers came up to Irwin Island to catch the actress going about her "typical day" that comprised mostly "cooking and preserving."[41] Most of the papers salvaged from her home and now held in the Thousand Island Museum are simply stacks of recipes. Even her notes for a performance idea (jokes, songs, and monologues) open with "You may or may not know I am interested in cooking—I always try new recipes" and continue with a joke about how the new beauty masks of her day remind her of a New England boiled dinner.[42]

In an intriguing article titled "Eating and the Stage at the Fin de Siècle," Laurence Senelick moves from a consideration of dishes named after stage celebrities to "the next step in increasing intimacy between the performer and the audience" as showcasing the performer as cook. In this endeavor, Senelick names *May Irwin's Home Cooking* as the earliest example of actor as celebrity chef. He points as well to the contrast in the cover shot of Irwin holding a splendid silver chafing dish as she leans over a stove: "The juxtaposition of the homely woodstove and high society's favorite appliance is significant."[43]

May Irwin's Home Cooking featured recipes "like mother used to make" and was reviewed in both the *New York Times* and the local papers around her home in the Thousand Islands.[44] This work was commended as "a cookbook, a joke book and a picture book all in one," "piquantly spiced with wit, humor and epigrammatically expressed wisdom," "a jolly combination of sense and nonsense," and "strong on such incidental trimmings of happy and convivial times as deviled eggs and anchovy toast."[45]

This cookbook was a unique project. The recipes included not only "several of her own" but also those "pried away from reticent chefs and head waiters, and others that the author's friends have generously contributed."[46] Illustrations were provided both by a well-known caricaturist of the day, Frances Farley, and by May Irwin herself.

The cookbook's most salient feature, however, was the way in which it placed Irwin's domestic life, both literally and figuratively, beside her professional career: Irwin coupled every recipe with a joke, song, or story (from her own performances or from friends). For example, all of the words of "The Frog Song" are printed alongside a series of fish dishes. Irwin's aforementioned popular monologue "A Painful Memory!" that alluded to her developing girth appeared opposite a recipe for California Indian pudding. Every recipe, from "Hoffman House Onion Soup" to "Rhine Wine and Champagne Punch," included a song, poem, or joke on its opposite page. Irwin completed the connection between her cookbook and her stage life by passing out copies of the book to her audience for Christmas gifts in 1904.[47]

In analyzing recipes, scholars often examine and compare standard commercial cookbooks with community cookbooks, noting that "these varying texts, once considered decorative and/or private and/or trivial, have served the communication needs of women."[48] Of course, in Irwin's case a very public figure is not only sharing recipes with her audience and banking on her own popularity to sell her new book (much as celebrities do today), but also advertising her public persona in as favorable a light as possible. To achieve this, besides including some of her most beloved songs and performance pieces, Irwin connected to her audience in three important ways: in the diversity of her dishes, in her language choice and tone, and in the illustrations used throughout the book.

The diversity of Irwin's dishes lies not as much in the selection of ingredients or cooking techniques used as in the setting and characters involved.[49] Although the book is titled *May Irwin's Home Cooking,* the recipes originate from a wide variety of sources that mark Irwin as a well-traveled person of importance. Generously scattered throughout May's own recipes and a few from her family and servant Sarah are those from, to name a few examples, Mrs. Ellen Bynner of Boston, a Chinese chef from San Francisco, Robert Stites from Chicago, chefs in Oklahoma City and Kansas City, chef St. Charles from New Orleans, and the famous staff of Rector's in New York City.[50]

Just as her recipes came from all sorts of places, Irwin tailored her recipes for cooks everywhere. She suggests substitutions for those who "live in an apartment with a chafing dish for a stand-by and a cook stove 'twenty miles away,'" and, again, "This can be easily done in a chafing dish and with clams instead of oysters."[51]

The same combination of worldliness and simplicity dominates Irwin's language in both her recipes and her added material. Critics have remarked on the difference between celebrity authors of cookbooks who tend to write often in the first person ("with no interest in his audience except how they get to know him") and one who "spotlights not herself but the recipes and her sources (self, friends, and fellow chefs)."[52] Although most critics focus on the boom in celebrity cookbooks of the twenty-first century, the comparison of the self-focused cookbook to the audience-focused cookbook can also be used to look at *May Irwin's Home Cooking.*

Irwin's cookbook abounds with anecdotes about herself, opening with her signed photograph ("Always leave them smiling when you say goodby—May Irwin") and an illustration signed by Buster Brown's creator in which Buster resolves that "I'm going to be May Irwin's own adopted child" and closing with a quote from Bill Nye:

> Go little booklet, go! bearing an honored name,
> Till everywhere that you have went.
> They're glad that you have came.[53]

Her recipes stay in the second-person imperative, as most recipes must ("add this, soak that, fry this"), and her tone can sound bossy and rather particular, as in "Don't use those food chopping machines, they'll mash it to a pulp" and "Half a pound of Italian spaghetti (the kind that comes in small short packages is decidedly better than the others").[54]

But Irwin undercuts her pronouncements and courts her audience in three important ways. First, her recipes are all simple and clear—even to the present-day cook—and she peppers them with reassurances. For example, in her recipe for Southern Chicken Pie, she opens with "This looks like a lot of bother, but it's worth it." And, in concluding that any cook can successfully make mincemeat just like May's mother's, she urges her reader, "Cover it up, so they won't eat it until the appointed hour!"[55]

Second, Irwin highlights recipes given to her by others, even when she does not know the originator: "I can't remember where I got this, but I do recall that it was couched in such flowery terms it sounded appetizing . . . so I tried it, and it is all that it promises." She is not afraid to admit that one of her recipes came from a "clipping from the *Evening Sun*," and, under one of the several recipes attributed to her friend Julia Roberts, she pens: "We've known each other now for forty years. / And it don't seem a day too much."[56]

Finally, Irwin includes a large number of jokes about poor cooks. They are the usual fare: the customer who wants to make sure that the doughnuts he is ordering are not like the ones his mother used to make—since those were awful; the wife who gets her husband to stop betting on races by letting him know that if he loses any more money, she'll do all the cooking herself; and advice to the weary husband whose wife gives him hash every night: "Be brave and stand it every day of the week if necessary. Wait until Sunday, and if she puts raisins in it and serves it for plum pudding, kick, and kick hard! I don't blame you!"[57] The effect of these jokes is to disarm her readers and help them join May in not taking any cooking fiascos seriously. The entire package—the jokes, the thanks to others, and the reassurances—softens her celebrity. She does not pass herself off as a know-it-all chef.

Almost all the illustrations in the cookbook are done by Frances Farley. They are winsome little pen-and-ink sketches of ingredients, kitchen utensils, stoves and pantries, and little figures. The figures place the cookbook squarely in the age of blatant ethnic stereotyping. African Americans with chickens hidden in their coats "shuffle" through the pages. Chinese "coolies" lie on their backs and spin balls with their feet. Native Americans whoop it up while wielding tomahawks. An Irish painter with an apish face bears the title "The mick that threw the brick" under a recipe for stuffed potatoes.[58] Irwin's audience in vaudeville would feel familiar and comfortable with all of these images.

Only a few illustrations in the book are drawn by May Irwin herself, and most remind the reader of her famous caricatures of unintentionally drunk temperance leaders. That is, her sketches spoof inebriation. The recipe for Rhine Wine and Champagne, for instance, features a drawing of two "drunken" bottles with spindly arms and legs and unkempt hair slugging it out in boxing gloves. Her directions for making Home Brewed Pickled Onions include two onions, arm in arm, seemingly engaged in a drunken serenade while waving top hat and cane.[59] And her illustration for the recipe from her 1904 cookbook depicts the bracing power of a claret concoction:

Sketch accompanying "Good for a Cold (Night)," in *May Irwin's Home Cooking* (1904).

GOOD FOR A COLD (NIGHT)

One pint of claret
A few pieces of cinnamon
A dozen cloves
One lemon, sliced
About four lumps of sugar

Boil everything; while it is boiling, light the claret and let it burn until all the alcohol is burned out. Drink it while it is hot.

Rene Stretti (opera singer)[60]

In 1914 Irwin announced from her Thousand Islands home that she would be putting out a second cookbook, one that would include recipes directed toward the low-income consumer: "The first one was written before the higher cost of living was a problem. Only a small millionaire could follow my receipts, I used thousands of eggs in that book. So now I'm compiling one on substitutes, or just as good things. And, believe me, any little bride can find meals for two in my new book. In the other one, the wealthy can cook, and they have as much need for the book as I have for a brochure on how to keep slender."[61]

This second cookbook was never published, but there does exist an intriguing copy of the first cookbook in which plans for another book have been outlined in May Irwin's inimitable handwriting. These plans for a new cookbook contain only jokes and stories instead of performance pieces, and songs and recipes attributed to creators other than Irwin are limited to the five ascribed to Irwin's mother. It is highly probable that the plans *are* for the new cookbook—the format is similar, with new jokes, and cheaper recipes are often written below the recipes in the original cookbook. For example, a recipe for "mashed potatoes" is substituted for "potato soufflé," and directions for making "corn meal gems," which require only one egg, replace those for "California Waffles," which use four eggs. The front matter begins with a sentimental poem, "All Earthly Good," and continues with lists of helpful cooking hints and tables of weights and measures. This work is much more detailed and practical than the published cookbook. It ends on page 236, thirty-one pages short of the ending for the original cookbook. In her first cookbook, Irwin included a poem by James Clarence Harvey, titled "Eat, Drink, and Be Merry," in the section she called "Drinkables." In her plans for the never-completed second cookbook, Irwin included a copy of this poem, and beneath it she wrote, "Eat, Drink, and Be Bilious." What she intended to include further shall remain unknown, for here her pen falls silent.[62]

Irwin continued to yoke her performing life with cooking in a series of articles she wrote for the *New York Evening Journal* in 1922. She sent them to Manhattan from her home in the Thousand Islands. These articles included advice for young brides making a dinner for four in a tiny kitchen, ice-cold desserts to make for hot days, and tips on preserving jellies.[63] She often related her recipes to memories of her performing career. In "There's a Time and a Place for All Soups," she recalled a delicious soup course enjoyed by her troupe during a one-night stand in New Hampshire. Her advice on delicacies to serve during the "coffee and tea hour" described the differing habits in Europe and England concerning tea and coffee time and how she observed these differences during her tour abroad. And in an article titled "May Irwin Dramatizes Potatoes," she included a little scene between husband and wife in which the husband, after being served boiled potatoes for too many evenings in a row, exclaims, "Boiled potatoes and chops bore my wife and they bore me!" But when the wife learns to fix Irwin's scalloped potatoes, happiness reigns and the wife and husband fall blissfully into each other's arms.[64]

For Irwin, cooking also served as a connection between her performing career and her weight. Irwin's heaviness was inseparable from both her presence as a cook and her persona as a comedienne. Irwin's jokes about weight were often linked to her cooking ability. Little asides, like her remark about her cook's cue to "hand her a broadside," are sprinkled throughout her discussions on cooking. The preface to *May Irwin's Home Cooking* includes this dedication: "This book is dedicated by the author to those who have laughed at her serious efforts to be graceful and sylph-like for their benefit; to those who failed to laugh; and to those who said 'go ahead and eat it' when she should have been adhering to her saccharin tablets and dry toast, with the hope that they may be tempted into eating 'not wisely but too well.'"[65]

Cooking, then, served many functions in Irwin's public life. It was associated with her nurturing skills and her own jolly, overweight demeanor. Not only did her recipes for food relate to her recipes for jokes and songs, but, with the publication of her cookbook, her talent for cooking also translated into additional success in the public sphere. Furthermore, the cookbook combined other aspects of her domestic image. Her practical recipes required organized and detailed instructions; her articles on cooking—and particularly the plans for her second cookbook—emphasized thriftiness. Cooking was associated with her family and friends and her expansive, maternal nature. She cooked for her sons and guests and—as mentioned previously—included recipes from her family, as well as those of famous chefs, in her cookbook.

Nowhere did Irwin's ability as household manager, mother, cook, real estate tycoon, and professional woman show through more clearly than in her devotion to her domestic haven in the Thousand Islands. A down payment had initiated her purchase, and her last payment of one thousand dollars, made with the help of a fellow actor, Henry Miller, completed it.[66] Once she acquired her island, she continued to add to her holdings; although she occasionally considered moving closer to Manhattan, she always returned to the Thousand Islands.[67]

So central to her domestic life did the island become that several of Irwin's recipe articles contained references to the joys of her Thousand Islands home. In "Make Breakfast a Festival," for example, Irwin paused to describe the natural beauty surrounding her: "Oh, the sunsets! In that clear sweep of Western sky above the wide shore I have seen coloring that in New York would make you call out the fire department, thinking Hackensack was ablaze."[68]

The lack of performance pieces in Irwin's plan for her second cookbook parallels Irwin's slow retirement from the stage into her world in Clayton and the Thousand Islands. Here she raised cattle and became one of the first female members of the American Jersey Cattle Club, she opened her own dairy and harangued city folk about their ignorance concerning milk prices, she won prizes for her cocks at the Watertown Chicken Show, and she even harvested her own hay.[69]

Indeed, Irwin presented her getaway in the Thousand Islands as a paradise incomparable to any other place on earth: "I have been to Scotland, where my ancestors were born, and in every country, all over the world, and all of you who have not seen the other countries can believe what I tell you—that there is nothing anywhere else like our Northern New York, the St. Lawrence River and the Thousand Islands."[70]

As Irwin grew older, she spent more and more time in the Thousand Islands, where she continued to demonstrate her homemaking skills in a highly public manner—publishing recipes and advice columns, producing prizewinning cattle and poultry, and appearing at local fairs and events.

Thus, throughout a long and varied career, May Irwin's domestic occupations permeated both her public image and her professional life. In fact, the trajectory of Irwin's career provides a nearly seamless blend of the domestic and professional. Because of unavoidable circumstances, she was made to leave her home to earn a living. But in so doing, she brought her domestic interests and skills with her, where they became an inextricable part of her public life. They served as aids to her professional career and showed the public her true nature as a homebody. In her own way, Irwin was following temperance leader Frances Willard's dictate: "Make the whole world Home-like."[71] Moreover, she was able to return to her domestic turf—not only untainted by her life in the theater but also better able to embark on a second profession as a publisher of recipes and advice columns and as a successful dairy farmer.

Undoubtedly, a major influence on Irwin's distinctive combination of public and private life was the period of social upheaval during which she lived. Over the course of her long career, Victorian notions of the woman's private sphere were giving way to the radical ideas of the "New Woman" of the 1890s. Therefore, Irwin, like the feminist leaders of her day, lived in two competing worlds. On the one hand, she "remained entrenched within the familiar, gender-distinctive assumptions of Victorian society. . . . In a world unkind to the notion of [a] . . . powerful, independent woman, women . . . would have been foolhardy to rush into the stream of modernism without any anchors." Yet on the other hand, Irwin could use her domestic values as an anchor for her public life because "the cult of domesticity created a new respect for the private sphere, [and women could begin] to carry domestic values outside the home."[72]

So the "sense" of Irwin's domestic skills (as evidenced in the recipes of her cookbook) supported the "nonsense" of her career in comedy, as these two aspects were labeled in a review of her cookbook. And in justifying her entrance into her profession on the firm ground of necessity, she was utilizing her talents in a way that would have been lauded by America's champion of "domestic economy" and renowned educator Catherine Beecher. (As early as 1851, Beecher had maintained that women must have the skills to "secure an independent livelihood.")[73]

To succeed in both the professional and the domestic spheres, Irwin was able to employ two seemingly contradictory traits satisfactorily. First, she was practical and efficient, with a no-nonsense, methodical approach to work. Second, she was intuitive and nurturing, a loving mother who was compassionate in her treatment of others.

Her advanced abilities in the first area meant that she was not *just* a housewife; she was one who could "lecture on household economics" or direct a "corps of servants as a general directs his army."[74] In equating household work to the professional world, she was in harmony with the contemporary rise of the culture of professionalism in America. It had been as recently as 1908 that women had gathered for the first meeting of the American Home Economics Association.[75] As an organized and efficient manager of the home, Irwin was in the perfect position to become an organized and efficient manager of her own theater company. In 1916 when Ada Patterson interviewed Irwin about her interests in "household economics," the culture (or "cult") of professionalism had taken firm root in America. Along with an enormous increase in men (and a few women) entering the already established fields of law and medicine, America saw a threefold increase between 1870 and 1910 in employees "in finance, accounting, and management."[76] This "professionalism" extended to the art of household management. Hence, as noted previously, Irwin could have made a living giving a "lecture on household economics" or directing a "corps of servants." And Irwin did, indeed, pride herself on her relationship with servants.

In an era during which the availability of good servants was diminishing,[77] it was only practical to foster loving, nurturing relationships with the household help. But the notion that relationships with servants should be personal *and* democratic was not widely accepted. Irwin hinted at the possibility that her views might raise objections when she interjected "Of course it wouldn't do for us all to think alike" into her arguments for better treatment of servants.[78]

In fact, the relationships between servants and housewives had undergone a marked change during the course of the nineteenth century. Early in the century, domestic help was apt to enjoy personal relationships with employers. Both urban and rural families hired help on a temporary basis to assist with spring cleaning and other added seasonal chores and in times of illness or death: "The hired girl, sitting and eating at the family's table, shared their food and their family circle. Usually, she had been recruited through a network of kin, neighbors, or friends."[79]

By 1890, however, gaps in religious backgrounds and ethnicities between servants and employers had widened. Women hired "domestic servants" through want ads or employment agencies. And "Unlike the hired girl, the domestic ate alone, in the kitchen, usually the leftovers of the meals she had cooked and served that day. Her mistress often dictated her diet. If, for example, she worked for employers who were food reformers, she might be forbidden to drink coffee, tea, wine, or beer."[80] And long before the 1890s, back staircases were being built for homes to keep "more physical distance between servants and family."[81]

If a blend of practicality and democratic feelings helped Irwin manage "the servant problem," practicality ruled to make Irwin an expert on two attributes often coupled in the period—those of thriftiness and acquisitiveness. Irwin wasted nothing but continually acquired more and more money and real estate. Thus, her advice to housewives to scrape excess meat from a roast's bones echoes the advice of John D. Rockefeller to reduce "from forty to thirty-nine the number of beads of solder used to seal his five-gallon kerosene cans." In the same way, her initial investments in one-dollar mining shares, which slowly built to a great wealth of real estate, could be compared with Andrew Carnegie's rise from a Scottish immigrant "of twelve with scarcely a penny in his pocket" to the undisputed leader of America's steel industry, already clearing profits of more than one million dollars annually by the 1880s.[82]

The culture of the period certainly paired saving with shopping. By the late nineteenth century, with the complete separation of the worlds of production and consumption, women were becoming the principal intermediary figures between these two worlds. That is, they were developing into shoppers. The growth of consumer capitalism reached a fevered pitch by the late nineteenth century. Large business corporations proliferated. The years from 1890 to World War I witnessed the birth of major department stores such as John Wanamaker's of Philadelphia, Marshall Field's of Chicago, and Macy's and Bloomingdale's of New York City. With the introduction of consumer credit, customers with smaller sums of ready cash could purchase goods from Sears, Roebuck or from Woolworth's.

In 1904 the Advertising Federation of America was formed,[83] adding to the push toward consumerism. Advertising focused on the dreams and desires of the American public and actively sought to foster those needs and desires that would lead to increased consumption. Perhaps one of the best representatives of the new world of advertising was L. Frank Baum, whose background in both theater and business helped him develop the idea of using store window displays to "arouse in the observer the cupidity and longing to possess the goods" so artfully arranged for his or her pleasure.[84] In 1900 May Irwin contributed to this aesthetic when she used her show *The Belle of Bridgeport* for the "brazen advertising" of a "brand of whisky and a make of typewriter." She also included plugs for particular products in both her published cookbook and her plans for a second one. In *May Irwin's Home Cooking,* she suggested the use of Uneeda Biscuits in a recipe with a wry note, "For this advertisement I get two dollars." In her plans for her new book, she advised cooks to only use Gold Medal Flour.[85]

Thus, Irwin was part of the nascent advertising push to connect the new brand names to celebrities. Coca-Cola began to feature actress Hilda Clark and opera star Lillian Nordac to promote their new drink. New brand names were added rapidly—from Goodyear rubber in 1839 to Coors beer in 1873 and from crayon wax Crayolas in 1903 to Wrigley Doublemint gum in 1914.

By the 1920s, "9 out of 10 screen stars" were claiming they used Lux Toilet Soap to care for their skin.[86]

Critic Andrew Erdman has connected the development of brands to the idea that new shoppers experienced anxiety in selecting products that were mass-produced. Therefore, new brands "stressed the authenticity, originality, or uniqueness of the products in question. To connect their *care* with their *dare,* May Irwin was ready to help new shoppers "weigh the merits of the different articles . . . their cost . . . their durability."[87] May had her work cut out for her because shopping was a complicated issue:

> Women had to learn how to read through enticements and to assess the "authenticity" of claims by "interested advertisers and shopkeepers" who endowed goods with every kind of association. Women—especially mothers—had to discover how to distinguish their individual desires from the needs and desires of their families. For men it was different and easier; for men, "making money" was confined to their workplace, not their homes. Most women enjoyed no such distance; the demands of "spending money" and providing love were inextricably intermingled in one place. Yet women needed to maintain distance to see clearly, in the interest of their families' well-being, the "true" worth to them of the goods on sale.[88]

"Maintaining distance" was certainly not part of the new methods of child rearing, and May Irwin's beliefs in child rearing were in keeping with the times. The importance of the "mother's heart" had gained undeniable strength by the late nineteenth century.[89] How this maternal affection displayed itself was connected to a new theory of child rearing that stressed the very tenets that Irwin purported to follow in raising her own sons. For instance, in Jacob Abbott's *Gentle Measures in the Management and Training of Children* (1871) or Newton Riddell's *Our Little Ones* (1895), whipping or any form of corporal punishment was rejected; instead, mothers were to guide their children gently and treat them with the same respect with which they treated their adult friends.[90]

Finally, if May was an indulgent mother, she was certainly also an outstanding role model of self-indulgence. As such, she was able to remain a good and moral married woman who performed in clean shows, while simultaneously enjoying the bodily pleasures of food and drink. In this way, she appealed to both her male and her female public, avoiding any association with women involved in the powerful temperance movement. She was an independent, strong woman who did not indulge in what critic Suzanne Marilley has called the "feminism of fear": "Feminists of fear make . . . the assertion that most behaviors oppressive to women derive from the inherent evils in men. This sort of moral cruelty crept into Willard's [Frances Willard, president of the Woman's Christian Temperance Union] feminism." In contrast, Irwin certainly extolled the fun of a good nip now and then. In her cookbook, she not only includes her amusing sketches of inebriated figures, but also includes a recipe for gin fizz associated with one of her well-known stage characters, Widow Jones.[91]

Although Irwin came of age in the 1880s, this love of pleasure and fun helps to place her more in the age of the New Women who followed in the 1890s. The latter have been described as putting "more emphasis on self-fulfillment, a bit less on social service" than the former.[92] Irwin's impetus for remaining on the stage and often neglecting some of her beloved duties at home may have been much more radical than her stated reason of mere necessity:

> Personally, I do not particularly dislike washing dishes, and I like to cook, but since many people agree with me that I can act a little bit, and since I have agreed with myself that I can act and sing just as well as I can wash dishes, it would be foolish for me to stick to the kitchen or the sewing machine or the wash tub. I am happier, my husband is happier, our friends are happier; and the public should grant us ungrudgingly, the right to be happy as we choose, so long as we do not disturb others.[93]

In summary, Irwin combined the practical, business-oriented side of her domestic skills with the nurturing, maternal side to create the image of a woman who was both successful and acceptable, both capable and feminine. She then was able, at times, to further her less popular opinions (for example, championing the rights of servants) by carefully extending her accepted beliefs in one realm to those of another. This strategy paralleled that of leading feminist activists of the time who projected their roles in the private sphere to activities in the public sphere. In this respect, her choice to champion the rights of servants made her seem even more lovable and "of the people." She was someone who, despite her immense wealth and fame, did not fancy herself superior to others; she remained aligned with the "common folk."

Did Irwin use her strategies not only to enhance her own reputation with her public but also as a gateway to effect change in larger issues? That is, did she celebrate her Scottish thriftiness, domestic efficiency, and mother's intuition in order to gain entry into the world of social activism? I will explore this idea in my next chapter.

6

Causes and Compromise

Many epoch-making ideas that man claims to have originated all by himself, were nursed in the quiet solitude of women's tender care, and passed on to the man without his ever realizing that something was being handed over to him.

—May Irwin, "My Views on That Ever-Interesting Topic—Woman"

May Irwin was an ardent supporter of women, even if she may have shied away from direct identification with the early women's movement, claiming, "I am not a suffragette, but I believe in absolute freedom, fresh air, vegetables, and laughter."[1] But even the most cursory review of Irwin's life indicates that she was an active supporter of suffrage. And like many in the women's movement of the early twentieth century, she was also a staunch advocate of pacifism. Although suffrage and pacifism were Irwin's most significant causes, she was also involved in other political activities, from economic reform and labor issues to animal rights and capital punishment.

Just as the growth of consumer capitalism bolstered Irwin's contention that women must learn to be economically independent, so it led to conditions that would add urgency to the causes she and a new generation of women championed. The rapid expansion of American industry continued unchecked in the years before 1900, resulting in the creation of trusts headed by powerful businessmen. Chief among these millionaires were J. P. Morgan, whose backing enabled a small group of men to take over the greatly expanding railroad industry; Andrew Carnegie, the steel magnate who joined with Morgan in 1900 to form U.S. Steel; and John D. Rockefeller, head of Standard Oil.

During this period, industrialization had its greatest impact in urban centers. The rampant power of the trusts led to bloodshed following labor attempts to strike for fairer conditions and wages. Urban deterioration (and the appalling amount of child labor) worsened living conditions for a large portion of city residents. In the resulting social and economic upheaval, the ideals of progressivism began to stir, and many Americans began to demand action against monopolies.

Early efforts against the trusts that controlled large portions of the economy had been watered down by court rulings that limited their effectiveness. For example, the Sherman Anti-Trust Act of 1890 was rendered toothless by the Supreme Court ruling in 1895 that protected the sugar trust by declaring that the E. C. Knight Company, which owned 98 percent of America's sugar-refining capacity, was a manufacturing monopoly—not one of commerce. For another—and even more notorious—example, the Supreme Court, in *Wabash, St. Louis and Pacific Railway Co. v. Illinois,* allowed the antitrust laws to be used *against* railway strikers.

Change, however, was in the wind. In 1904 when Theodore Roosevelt ran for his first full term as president, he emphasized his desire to work for reform and to give everyone a "square deal." Following his victory, he enacted many reforms, including the Pure Food and Drug Act of 1906 that, along with a series of subsequent amendments, began to halt the interstate transportation of food products contaminated by harmful additives and produced in unsanitary conditions. But as Grover Cleveland had before him, Roosevelt relied on the vast resources of J. P. Morgan to steady the American financial system during the recession of 1907 and was forced to assure Morgan that he would not interfere in purchases by U.S. Steel meant to assist New York banks.[2]

When Roosevelt returned to politics in 1910, eventually forming the Bull Moose Party when he lost the Republican nomination to William Howard Taft (a progressive himself, as were all three of the major candidates in the 1912 election), he redoubled his efforts on behalf of progressivism. He now asserted that America needed a "New Nationalism" and that those who thought only of their own profit "must now give way to the advocate of human welfare."[3]

Progressivism, however, was destined to go forward instead through the new leader of the Democratic Party, and one of May Irwin's political heroes, Woodrow Wilson. Initially, Wilson expressed the desire not merely to regulate monopoly, as Roosevelt had hoped to, but to destroy it completely. After only a short time in office, Wilson changed his idea of "New Freedom" and edged closer to the idea of regulation of the trusts. In 1913 Wilson passed perhaps his most important single piece of legislation, the Federal Reserve Act, which granted significant control of national banking to the federal government but allowed bankers to keep control of local funds. And in 1914, he signed the Federal Trade Commission Act into law, creating a bipartisan committee to police corporations found to encourage unfair trade practices.[4]

Middle-class concern for "human welfare" over the profit motive had been growing throughout the nineteenth century, perhaps culminating in Jacob Riis's widely attended lectures accompanied with photographic slides of conditions in New York's Lower East Side tenements. Riis began his lectures in the late 1800s and published his photographs and commentary in 1890 and again in 1901. His oft-cited work still makes fascinating reading. Despite prejudices and attitudes that sometimes startle the contemporary reader, his words reveal a paternalistic outlook on poverty that was an essential part of the progressive spirit: "The readiness with which the tenants respond to intelligent efforts in their behalf, when made under fair conditions, is as surprising as it is gratifying, and fully proves the claim that *tenants are only satisfied in filthy and unwholesome surroundings because nothing better is offered.*"[5]

Middle-class women in particular were ready to offer something better to the poor, and their involvement in the reform movement often took place through the new informal political power they wielded with the proliferation of clubs during the second half of the nineteenth century. One of the earliest women's clubs was Sorosis, founded in 1868 and developed for initiating social ties between women in an atmosphere of serious intellectual discourse: "Important to the clubs was the judgment that such intellectual and social activity would enhance women's ability to effect social betterment. Sorosis proposed to help its members 'to think for themselves not so much because it is their right, but their duty.' And *duty* had a very special meaning—to encourage women to assume their proper responsibilities, to enlarge women's sphere of interest both for self and for communal improvement."[6]

During the next quarter century, the growth of women's clubs accelerated. Most of these organizations were bent on "communal improvement" and strongly relied on the notion of female moral superiority. Thus, Josephine Shaw Lowell of the Charity Organization Society emphasized the importance of women in philanthropic organizations, because of their strength in avoiding the great danger of being corrupted by the people that they intended to help.[7] Grace Dodge, led by unswerving moral and religious beliefs, helped launch a movement among working girls in New York that led to the formation of the Association of Working Girls Societies. These societies sponsored a series of "practical talks" for working girls on such subjects as "Purity," "Womanhood," and "Money—How to Get It and Keep It."[8]

As a working girl herself, May Irwin learned early how to "get and keep" money. In this, as I have noted before, she differed from many star performers of her day. In a way, her "Scottish thrift" may indeed be traced to her ancestors in Clan Campbell. In a scrupulously researched study, Charlotte Erickson uses the letters and diaries of Scottish and English immigrants to the United States to highlight their differences from other immigrants in the nineteenth century. (Although the study was done on immigrants to America, I am assuming similarities. The Campbells lived near the border between Canada and America, and many relatives found homes in America.) Their language and race were undeniably foremost in assisting their rapid assimilation. But two additional factors were important as well. First, they were not fleeing cruel regimes in order to seek freedom; rather, they were looking for places with lower taxes. Second, instead of sending money home, as was usual with the immigrants from continental Europe, they brought money with them and often wrote letters requesting more money from families left behind.[9]

Whether Irwin inherited a bit of Scottish practicality about her resources or not, she was certainly generous. As she gained wealth and status, her charitable activities clearly underlined her generosity and compassion for the poor and underprivileged. Irwin claimed that, although she fervently believed in women's clubs, as a busy professional she herself didn't have "time for Clubs. I wish I had."[10]

Another of Irwin's concerns was the welfare of animals, particularly those used in the entertainment field. The American Society for the Prevention of Cruelty to Animals was formed in 1866, and Irwin was known for spying on suspicious animal acts on the vaudeville circuit and reporting cruelties to the organization.[11] She made public statements against cruel practices: "I loathe the custom of docking horses' tails," "I wouldn't wear a bit of baby lamb for the world," and "I don't believe in sacrificing our beautiful songbirds for our hats."[12]

Irwin showed her populist colors when she defended the rights of the masses to affordable entertainment and blamed the system in general for their sometimes rude behavior in public: "That most Americans lack refinement and good manners is not their fault entirely: I am just enough of a socialist to believe that such a state is due to an unfair and unsatisfactory economic system."[13] Irwin dubbed high ticket prices for the theater and the abuses perpetrated by ticket scalpers the "two great evils besetting the theatre today." In order to combat ticket scalping, she sent a letter to Elihu Root, then president of the state constitutional convention in Albany, New York, in 1915, "suggesting the passage of an amendment to the State Constitution which would make it unlawful for the manager of any place of amusement or his employee to accept tickets of admission for which premiums had been paid."[14] Almost fifteen years earlier, she had fought to hold ticket prices to one and a half dollars, instead of the proposed new price of two dollars, conveying antitrust leanings in her argument: "Miss May Irwin . . . has been lying awake o'nights recently thinking what a shame it is to charge $2.00 for an orchestra chair in these days when the necessities of life make living so expensive, with the price of oats way up, the Sugar Trust raising the ante till you can't afford to have more than one lump in yours, and Standard Oil magnates hoisting the price of kerosene till you have to give up burning oil and try to grope your way to bed by electric light."[15]

Despite Irwin's solidarity with the poor and struggling, she had a protective attitude when it came to two of her chief financial interests—farming and theater. For example, although she defended the farmers for raising the price of milk, noting that the increases barely covered price rises in feed supplies,[16] she sometimes showed little sympathy for the itinerant farmworker: "Help is the most serious problem confronting the farmer today. . . . It is next to impossible to get anyone to do any farm work, and for that reason, a good share of the crops and the produce has not been as profitable as in other years. A farm hand asks $8 a day to do ordinary farm work, and when one is fortunate to find one, he works all day with his eyes on the clock."[17]

In a similar spirit, she was an opponent of the Actors' Equity Association (AEA), saying that she believed in "labor unions for labor, but not in art." In this she identified with many of her fellow vaudevillians, who "believed they were primarily independent creative artists rather than exploited workers in need of collective action. In 1919, the average factory worker's annual wage was $1,300 while a vaudevillian who was paid $75 a week earned $3,150 on a 42 week tour."[18]

There were early attempts to unionize vaudevillians through the White Rats, an all-male organization with a separate unit for women. Lillian Russell is often associated with the female "Rat Lambs" (later renamed the White Stars). Although Irwin is *not* usually associated with this union's activities, a curious article in the *Chicago Tribune* does indicate that she was initially a member: "It was decided at the meeting to admit women to the organization, with the title 'Ratlambs.' Lillian Russell, Jenny Yeamans, and May and Flo Irwin were elected by a unanimous vote. Two hundred applications for membership from women are already on file."[19]

In any case, the White Rats—with the women as lambs, stars, or what-you-will—merged with the American Federation of Labor, and, in 1912, trust buster President Teddy Roosevelt even threatened antitrust measures against vaudeville's powerful manager E. F. Albee on behalf of an actor, thus equating unionization with antitrust activities.[20] In *Weavers of Dreams, Unite!* however, Sean P. Holmes puts forward the thesis that the AEA's formation in 1913 had much more to do with the desires of a select group of actors to raise artistic standards in theater than to improve conditions for working actors. He maintains that "the theater trusts had actually done a great deal to improve their [working actors'] lot by stabilizing a notoriously volatile employment market."[21] The resulting membership rules excluded men and women in choruses and most vaudevillians.

Irwin stated that she would quit producing rather than join the organization, claiming that her reasons for opposing Equity had a lot to do with her sympathy for out-of-work actors:

> Miss Irwin is still off the stage and she re-iterated today her intention to remain off the stage as long as the Actors' Equity and closed shop dominate the situation. "The theatrical conditions in New York are very bad," she said. "In the first place there are four or five plays which are attracting good crowds. The others are merely hanging on. Then there are hundreds of actors and actresses out of employment because of conditions brought about by the Actors' Equity. In all of the shops where I go in New York I see someone whom I have known on the stage working as a clerk."[22]

Irwin's stance against Equity and for the individual farmer reveals an important quality of her politics. She was an individualist who believed in personal responsibility and gave this advice: "Do things yourself instead of delegating them to others."[23] Of course, as a star who produced her own shows, Irwin was in a position to fight Equity personally—she could refuse to hire Equity actors and even shut down productions of her own shows. And as a popular personality who also happened to be a farmer, she was in an ideal position to explain to the public the necessity for raising prices on farm goods.

Although the importance of Irwin's own financial interests should not be underestimated, neither should her concerns about the dangers of a closed shop for the individual actor. For Irwin, Equity shut actors out of the business rather than allowing each individual to succeed or fail on his or her own in a difficult art. To Irwin, an actor could not win by delegating professional responsibility to a union. Instead, Irwin joined George M. Cohan, Otis Skinner, and others to create the Actors' Fidelity League. (Other stars—such as Ethel Barrymore, Lillian Russell, and Marie Dressler, pledging their greater allegiance to the working actor—supported Equity.)[24] The Actors' Fidelity

League evidently played a part in trying to get Equity to allow nonunion actors in shows. In 1924 actress Frances Starr wrote an acerbic piece in the *New York Times,* making fun of the union's "highly amusing proposal to allow the employment of one nonunion actor to every fifteen union actors. One wag has tried to figure out just what would happen if the cast only called for seven actors."[25]

Even today, the AEA's policy keeps many of its actors from gainful employment in nonunion work and shuts out nonunion actors from Equity auditions. Hence, in 1988, the National Labor Relations Board declared the AEA's audition process illegal, which resulted in the temporary issuance of so-called AEA Priority Cards to nonunion actors who could prove a sustained history of professional employment. The cards allowed these actors to audition alongside Equity actors. The ruling was reversed in 1996.[26]

Accusations that the Actors' Fidelity League was primarily composed of relatives of business managers overlooked the membership of stars like May Irwin and Minnie Maddern Fiske. Fiske had certainly been an active critic of the Theatrical Syndicate.[27] Further, actors who became successful and took their own shows on the road often found themselves in disagreement with Equity, even if they had previously been ardent supporters of the association. Perhaps the best example of this state of affairs is the experience of Marie Dressler, a leading figure in the actors' strike of 1919 who nonetheless became embroiled in a fight with her cast and representatives of the AEA when she took *Tillie's Nightmare* on tour. These problems led to Dressler, the "Joan of Arc" of the strike, "resign[ing] from her post as president of the chorus auxiliary and inform[ing] her cast that she was through with the AEA altogether."[28]

Irwin's politics sometimes even colored her own acts of kindness. In 1916 a series of articles covered the remarkable escape of two German prisoners held by the British government in Canada to the Thousand Islands area, where they received considerable care and protection from Irwin and her husband.[29] Several years earlier, she interceded on behalf of a steamboat captain who had accidentally run down two couples on the St. Lawrence River—making certain she was able to influence the judge on his behalf.[30] Her personal defenses of others accused of murder supported her position against capital punishment, especially if the alleged murderer was young. She defended a young girl accused of homicide and also angrily confronted the governor of Indiana during a train ride after she had called him to ask him to pardon two young men awaiting electrocution: "You may think it was officious to call you up on the phone the other day, but I do not care. I never did like you and now I hate you."[31]

Irwin's generosity was such that, in her adopted home of Clayton, New York, family members who had profited from her kindnesses still remembered her gifts in the mid-1990s. She often helped to pay the court costs of those whose causes she took up; in the case of Robert Bertrand's family in Clayton, she loaned five thousand dollars for the purchase of a hotel and never asked for the note to be paid back, and she generously paid medical costs to help nurse residents of Clayton through a flu epidemic.[32]

Of course, May's stance as an "individualist" may lie behind some of her tendency to distance herself from the suffragist movement, even though it was to become one of her chief causes. At other times, she called herself a "new woman" rather than a "suffragette"[33] and replied to the question "Are you a suffragist?" with the equivocal, "Well—not exactly. I don't like the word. I hate to tell you [how it sounds to me]—but aren't we having nice weather for this time of year?"[34]

Just as critics implied that Irwin was the "exception to the rule" in her comic abilities, sometimes she positioned herself as an exception to the rule in deserving the vote that other women might *not* deserve. The cultural message is clear in this critic's review of Kate Sanborn's popular lecture on women and comedy given in the late nineteenth century: "Miss Kate Sanborn has a lecture which has been much approved by clubs of her own sex, the object of which is to prove that women are witty. Whether she has proved her thesis, I don't know. . . . I am still in doubt as to whether women are witty; but I am in no doubt as to whether May Irwin is funny."[35]

When Irwin defended her own rights while separating herself from other women, especially those who exhibited stereotypical female vanities, she was using the same logic as the above (male) admirer. Thus, Irwin described herself as a practical woman with financial responsibilities, a woman who owned property and paid taxes and, therefore, deserved the vote. Only a woman with qualities like hers should be allowed to vote, certainly not one of those "little, frilly perfumed things. . . . All she does, anyhow, is vote the way somebody tells her to, the little idiot." She disdained women who occupied their time with petty concerns and "cry if a seam is turned wrong on the lining of a dressing jacket." Sometimes she blamed such women for the failure to win women's suffrage: "It's the women who can't see the need for suffrage, and who won't permit themselves to be made to see it, who keep millions of their sisters suffering for the want of the ballot. Men would give women suffrage; it's the other women who won't. The more mischievous 'antis' are the lap-dog-in-the-manger class. They do not wish the ballot themselves. If they had it they would not know what to do with it; they are bereft of sufficient gray matter to learn what to do with it."[36]

Yet even as Irwin distanced herself from certain women, she connected herself to women who displayed positive female virtues—such as compassion and caring. In fact, Irwin took care not to identify with women who did *not* possess these traits and who did not show sympathy for others. In this spirit, she refused an interview with a female journalist who had written harsh articles against a young woman on trial for murder: "It is the first time in my life I have declined to help a woman when I could do so. But that woman doesn't deserve the name. Her sex was an accident."[37]

By aligning herself with the supposedly caring and compassionate nature of women, Irwin was, as indicated in the previous chapter, pushing for the independence of women under "cover" of what were deemed positive feminine traits. In so doing, she took her place in the growing clamor for women's suffrage. Irwin profited from changes in American politics that had occurred before her birth. From the 1820s, "Governments largely gave up the tasks of regulating the economic and social behavior of the citizenry." At the same time, the rise of mass political parties, which solidified the political participation of white males, pushed male and female politics further and further apart. Women were no longer seen as worthy participants in traditional politics as practiced in the public sphere; instead, women's "emotional and guileless nature provided strengths in pursuing the important tasks of binding community divisions and upholding moral norms. Through selfless activities in the home and community, women could provide stability."[38]

Thus, from the 1820s, as their traditional role in the public sphere diminished, women's domestic role began to extend into the public sphere. Women brought their qualities of nurturing and moral support to volunteer work, and a fusion between domesticity and politics began to grow. Women were increasingly active in the public arena, as long as that arena had something to do with the social welfare of women and children or with the womanly support of fallen males (as in nursing those wounded in war or lifting up those who had succumbed to sin and alcoholism).

By the 1880s and 1890s, women's political roles further expanded in two important aspects. First, the new idea of professionalism, with its increasing faith in the practical application of scientific method to social problems, added legitimacy to women's political actions. Second, the social movements that women had been spearheading on the local level enlarged so as to affect public policy. As summarized by historian Paula Baker, "The domestication of politics, then, was in large part women's own handiwork. In turn, it contributed to the end of separate political cultures. First, it helped women gain the vote. Suffrage was no longer either a radical demand or a challenge to separate spheres, because the concerns of politics and of the home were inextricable."[39]

By the 1890s, the suffrage movement was the most visible political movement involving women. In 1890 the two factions of the earlier suffrage movement—the National Woman Suffrage Association and the American Woman Suffrage Association, both organized in 1869—united. The AWSA was originally led by Henry Ward Beecher and focused on attaining voting rights for women on the state level; in contrast, the NWSA, headed by Elizabeth Cady Stanton, had more broad-reaching reformist concerns—from divorce laws to women's wages.[40] Together, the AWSA and the NWSA became the National American Woman Suffrage Association. Elizabeth Cady Stanton was NAWSA's first president and was succeeded in 1892 by Susan Anthony. Many years and many battles would pass before women's suffrage was actually won in America. In 1907 American suffragettes conducted their first outdoor rally in New York City; in 1913 President Woodrow Wilson was met in Washington, D.C., by several thousand suffragettes marching down Pennsylvania Avenue; in 1916 at the Republican convention in Chicago, about five thousand women marched to demand that suffrage be put on the Republican Party platform; and in 1917, New York became the first state on the East Coast to grant women full suffrage. (Wyoming was the first state to award women suffrage; other western states followed, and in 1910 Illinois became the first state east of the Mississippi River to grant voting rights).

In 1916 the Republican platform included this somewhat watered-down statement: "[The party] favors the extension of suffrage to women, but recognizes the right of each state to settle this question for itself." From 1914 on, pro-suffragism was a mainstream cause. By 1917 the ranks of NAWSA had grown to nearly two million people.[41] In greater numbers than ever before, women began to stand up for their rights, ignoring attempts by friends and family to dissuade them: "I didn't walk in New York's first suffrage parade because my mother wouldn't let me. Next year, in 1913, I wanted to march, but my husband asked me not to. This fall I decided that it was 'up to me' to suffer for democracy."[42]

Even though more and more of the population backed women's suffrage, Woodrow Wilson moved slowly on the issue. Perhaps his need to keep the country squarely behind him in a time of imminent war caused Wilson to view the suffrage issue as one that should be deferred for a time. In the fall of 1916, he wrote to the Woman's Democratic Club of Portland, Oregon, "regretting the partisan use of the suffrage issue 'at a time so critical as this when the question is about to be determined whether we shall keep the nation upon its present terms of peace and good will with the world or turn to radical changes of policy which may alter the whole aspect of the nation's life.'"[43]

Even recent biographers defend Wilson's inability to push through a national suffrage amendment: "Pressing for a woman's suffrage amendment, Wilson moved against a wall of political apathy, as well as against what seemed often an excessive ardor on the part of the women themselves." (If the author of a book written in 1991 can view years of peaceful demonstration for a fundamental right as indicative of "excessive ardor," one can imagine the frustrations faced by the early suffrage movement!) Nonetheless, by 1917 women in the suffragist movement had started to feel betrayed by Wilson and his inaction. Eventually, of course, the movement did succeed, and women's suffrage was finally gained on August 20, 1920, when the Nineteenth Amendment was ratified by Tennessee, the thirty-sixth state to do so.[44]

Of the many traditional reasons women used for supporting their fight for voting rights, one of the most prevalent arguments was based on the idea of the natural purity and moral superiority of women. Some suffragists asked for the vote so that women could "use their power to purify and amend society. If a woman be herself pure and noble-hearted, she will come into every circle as a person does a heated room who carries with him the freshness of the woods."[45]

As noted earlier, in purifying society, women brought their domestic abilities into the public sphere. That is, they took the moral virtues of a good home and family into politics and society, thus civilizing a world gone awry in an age of rampant industrialism. Women's objective was, then, "not that the world should come into the home, but that the home, embodied and impersonated in its womanhood, should go forth in the world."[46] Conversely, by bringing the home out into the world, women would be saving the world *inside* the home:

> In a crowded city quarter . . . if the street is not cleaned by the city authorities no amount of private sweeping will keep the tenement free from grime; if the garbage is not properly collected and destroyed a tenement-house mother may see her children sicken and die of diseases from which she alone is powerless to shield them. . . . In short, if woman would keep on with her old business of caring for her house and rearing her children she will have to have some conscience in regard to public affairs lying quite outside her immediate household. . . . May we not say that American women need this implement [the ballot] in order to preserve the home?[47]

Like many of her contemporaries, Irwin portrayed women as the vanguard of civilization. (I covered much of her strategic use of the private sphere–public sphere debate in the previous chapter.) The important work of wives and mothers was the foundation of the advancements of society: "Mr. Adam awoke to that fact [that women were essential in the progress of civilization] after his wife or his daughter had become a priestess in one of the temples. Woman has always taken the lead in religious reforms. Since that time woman has been engaged in a constant struggle to enlarge the borders of her world and become a more important factor in the development of the civilization which she had started, without relinquishing any of her duties or privileges as a mother." Indeed, as noted in chapter 5, writers often directly related Irwin's domestic and maternal duties to her concerns for suffrage: "Certain of her enthusiasms for cookery and for suffrage have kept the woman-and-mother side of this comedienne as much in the public eye as the vocalist and actress side."[48]

Suffragism went along with the "actress side" for many women in the theatrical profession. Perhaps the most important actress-suffragists of the period were Mary Shaw and Lillian Russell. Shaw was in one of the first pro-suffrage plays introduced in the United States—Elizabeth Robins's *Votes for Women*—in 1909. Lillian Russell, whose mother had been a suffragist in the 1880s, was a leading proponent for the cause and an avowed feminist as well, from at least 1907.[49]

Author Susan Glenn has noted, in *Female Spectacle,* that comic performers, such as Trixie Friganza and Marie Dressler, supported suffragism but "worried that their irreverence, so willingly embraced in the theater, would not be acceptable on the streets." Indeed, Friganza was ridiculed for public appearances at a 1908 city hall rally, and Marie Dressler expressed "anti-suffragist" and "anti-militant" sentiments in 1913 but performed in a pro-suffrage play in 1916 to raise funds for suffrage activism.[50]

In contrast, Irwin was able to successfully appear in public and onstage in support of suffragism. When Irwin came to Chicago to march with Illinois's Equal Suffrage Association members, she used her status as a mother to support her rights: "'Mother knows and she should vote,' that's what my two big boys say." And in her article on women published in 1912, Irwin even implied that a good mother was one who was active in public affairs: "The fact that a woman is a mother should not bar her from taking part in the world's activities. In fact, if she is the right sort of mother, she will not let it."[51]

In this article, however, Irwin went much further in expounding her feminist sensibility than simply urging that women, by virtue of their domestic and maternal qualities, must have the vote and take more action in public affairs. Here she argued not only that "woman's sphere is the same as man's—and that is the whole world"—but also that women are often nothing more than "household slaves" and "piece[s] of household machinery" to men. Additionally, she made a very modern argument against the double standard applied to fathers and mothers: "It always seems strange when I hear a man or woman say a mother has no business being on the stage. Why not say the same thing about a man? Has a father any less responsibility? Has a father any right to shirk this responsibility and put it all upon his wife? A great many of them do, I know, but that doesn't make it right. Can a man be a good father and an actor at the same time? Then why cannot a woman be a good mother and an actress at the same time?"[52]

Irwin's desire for a world without sex-linked limitations might also be inferred from an interesting juxtaposition of an excerpt from this article and a photograph. Here, she notes that men initially only killed and hunted for food, while women cultivated the more civilized skills of raising "grain and vegetables." The accompanying photograph, however, shows Irwin with a gun, hunting for food! She also hinted at a more radical outlook when she supported the right of European women to resort to violence when they were mistreated and then noted, in a comment seemingly designated to soften her support of violence, that a Parisian woman cabby proved to her that even if "there may be sex in throwing a stone . . . there is none in driving a cab."[53]

One way in which Irwin cleverly supported her more radical views on women was by her constant praise of women's sense of humor and the connection of this humor to self-awareness rather than feelings of superiority. A woman might be vain or foolish or petty, but she stood a much greater chance than a man of recognizing these qualities in herself because she had a sense of humor:

> Don't talk to me about a man's sense of humor! I never knew a man who realized how funny men are. I know any number of women who see the funny things in women. The men think that women are awfully amusing. That is one of their stock theories, but they haven't the faintest idea that they are even more amusing. No matter how absurd a man may be other men take him seriously because he's a man. Now women think that they themselves are funny and know that the men are. That's where woman's sense of humor is broader and keener than man's. That's my opinion, but there's no use telling it to the men. They haven't enough sense of humor to recognize the truth of it.[54]

In this, Irwin's connection to other women and her belief in their innate self-awareness helped her more effectively voice the contention that women were as deserving of the vote as men (perhaps even more so!).

To Irwin, male vanity was extremely funny. She included innumerable jokes about men in her cookbook and in articles. This decidedly aggressive verse has been attributed to Irwin and was placed in her own scrapbook:

I love to watch the rooster crow,
He's like so many men I know,
Who brag and blush and run and shout,
And beat their manly chests without
The first damn thing to brag about.[55]

More important, combining male vanity with male political ambitions helped add starch to Irwin's stance on women's political rights. In 1916 she attended the Republican National Convention. She could not help but note that even the most powerful, clean-shaven politician would retreat and pout if a woman praised beards and mustaches in his presence.[56] By comparing men to children who needed a woman's care, she humorously attributed their reluctance to allow women to vote to their own desire to have a party without women there to discipline them: "It's all done to such a boyish accompaniment of hot air, and more hot air, anecdotes, and more tobacco smoke. It's nice for the dear men: there's nobody about interfering to tell them it's time to go to bed if they want to get up early or to be careful not to fuss the furniture or smell up the curtains. Oh, yes, yes, indeed, it's all a great grand layout. No wonder some people don't want the ladies to vote."[57]

Irwin not only makes male vanity the butt of her humor, but places women above men in their appreciation of comedy, for "it is only very sensible or very honest people who laugh as freely at their own absurdities as at those of their neighbors. In general, the contrary rule holds, and we only laugh at those misfortunes in which we are spectators, not sharers."[58]

According to Irwin, the laughter of women was the laughter she most coveted. Once, after telling a male interviewer that she felt that a woman's sense of humor was more spontaneous than a man's, she snapped, "I'd rather play to women than men anytime. . . . You can put that in your hat and wear it out with you." In many articles, she stressed this point again and again: "Of course I would [rather play to women than men], infinitely rather. . . . [T]he women respond so quickly and heartily to every shade of humor I throw into my act and are so sympathetic that I can just turn myself loose. . . . Give me a house full of women and I'll do my best work."[59]

Not only did Irwin champion women's sense of humor, but she also professed to believe that women had more sadness than men in their everyday lives and, thus, more need for comedy. This is what gave her a particular joy in making women laugh:

> [Women's] lives are more tragic than men's. . . . I believe women have a keener sense of the humorous than men, but it isn't always in working order, because they have a keener sense of the tragic, too. They are more emotional all around, feel everything more intensely than men do. They can't throw off worry and sorrow and deep emotion of every kind and be funny to order as easily as men can. It isn't because they don't see the funny things, but because, so often, their hearts are too full to make room for humor. Men go racking along and do not feel anything very deeply.[60]

Here Irwin is also cleverly playing on opposites by connecting women's sense of humor to their innate emotional nature and sense of tragedy. This depth of feeling, which Irwin believed she shared as a common bond with other women, rendered a sense of humor a crucial asset for women. This humor was "born in [woman] and keeps her alive." It needed only proper stimulation: "When I can make a woman laugh and forget her troubles—and the dear lord knows she has enough, with suffrage and corsets and hobble skirts—I feel that I am doing something worthwhile. The men I don't care about. Anybody could make them laugh. I always play to the women."[61]

The troubles of other women were hers as well. She often referred to her own life: "Tragedy would seem too real to me to do well." She opened one interview with "I am a serious woman. It is true . . . there is not a woman in the United States who has had a harder time in life than I." Ada Patterson, who interviewed Irwin on a number of occasions, noted that "often, after one of the scenes that set folk rocking with laughter [Irwin] goes to her dressing-room and cries from sheer nerve exhaustion—an unguessable reverse side of the comedienne's shield." Irwin once told an interviewer that it was probably a good thing that the audience was unaware of how, at times, she was very close to tears.[62] Irwin claimed that she viewed her ability to get laughs—even when she herself was ill or in the depths of despair—as a mixed blessing. Although it helped her through difficult times, it sometimes deprived her of the support she yearned for. She expressed this perhaps most completely in an article in the *New York Times*, "May Irwin's Tale of Woe," which included the subtitle "She Gets Laughter Instead of the Sympathy She Needs."

With these public statements, Irwin was "allowing" her audience to see behind the comic mask and playing on the long-standing story of the "sad clown." At least as early as 1827, when Henri LaTouche wrote his popular fiction imagining a harlequin actor whose comedy obscured a melancholy disposition, comedians, writers, and actors have clung to the idea of tears behind laughter.[63] From Ruggiero Leoncavallo's *I Pagliacci* to children's stories to kitsch painting, the image of the sad clown persists.

Beyond helping her audience to identify more closely with her, combining humor with an innate sense of tragedy in her own life helped Irwin underline the importance of comedy itself as an art. If comedy is a serious art form, then those who are skilled in it are serious, important people whose political and social opinions carry weight.

In using the idea of the sad clown and the tragic nature of life to enhance the importance of comedy, Irwin was behaving as many comics have through the years. As Woody Allen once remarked, comics often feel that they have been relegated to the children's table and that their art is *not* taken seriously. (That's why comedians insist, somewhat defensively, that it's so much harder to play comedy than tragedy.) Part of this idea is expressed in the bromide that Irwin offered whenever she felt anyone slighted the importance of comedy: "An onion can make people cry, but there has never been a vegetable invented to make them laugh." Comedy was essential for both men and women because it helped them through the tragedies of life—it was less *like* life than tragedy. This quality also rendered comedy more important than tragedy, as its purpose was to assist audience members in "seek[ing] a moment's respite from the tragic pressure of life."[64] Irwin claimed that, although she initially yearned to be a tragic actress, life taught her that comedy was actually the nobler calling:

> The natural trend of life is tragic, not comic; all the things which tend to dispel care and drive away sorrow are to our natures like the precious rays of the sun in the spring to the flowers. They charm out to the surface all our more lovable and more beautiful qualities, and make us more worthy in the eyes of mankind. It did not take me long to find out that life was not a continuous performance of the realization of one's fondest dreams, but rather one of their continuous shattering and that one gained sunlight and happiness in this world by giving it to others.[65]

But even as she revealed her solemn side, Irwin retained her self-deprecatory humor by undercutting her own seriousness with humorous remarks, and her interviewers played along: "'Women's lives are more tragic than men's.' For one-tenth part of a second Miss Irwin looked grave, then her irresistible laugh came to the surface again. 'The women have to put up with the men, you see. There's tragedy for you. Seriously, though, I meant what I said.'"[66]

Irwin maintained that "suffrage is the one question in the world that can't get a laugh out of me."[67] Yet when the eminent suffragist Ida Blair, treasurer of the Equal Franchise Society of New York, noted Irwin's suggestion to Woodrow Wilson that she be appointed "Secretary of Laughter" and wrote a letter asking that Irwin begin a Bureau of Laughter for the suffrage movement, Irwin was quick to volunteer.[68] Blair courted Irwin by assuring her that the committee "will welcome the assistance of the woman who has demonstrated to the country that even under the most distressing national strain our sex possesses that safeguard of the mind, a sense of humor."[69] Irwin replied with fervor:

> Dear Mrs. Blair—Thank you indeed for your kind letter and your invitation to me to head a Bureau of Laughter. I accept your offer with enthusiasm, since you believe in my ability to be useful in this work, and if it were not for this hot weather I should wear a coat for the satisfaction of pulling it off and rolling up my sleeves. The energy I will be able to bring into this fight will be propelled by a deep sympathy for the grand idea and a sincere conviction of its justice. Results count: and I am already at work and can promise you two votes on Nov. 2. They will be the votes of my sons. . . .
>
> . . . With a deep immovable yearning for the success of "The Cause," permit me to report for duty.
>
> May Irwin[70]

Irwin not only used laughter to "put a sane sense of humor in suffragists' campaign" and help her fellow protesters keep a sense of perspective, but also became fully active in the movement, not limiting her support of women's rights to making statements in newspapers. She used her persuasive skills to "convert a Supreme Court Justice to equal suffrage,"[71] marched in parades in New York and Chicago, and spoke at the aforementioned 1916 Republican National Convention.

Most important, Irwin used her theatrical profession to support women's rights. Perhaps May did not have time for the women's club movement, but she could use her play *33 Washington Square* as a vehicle for the suffrage movement. After returning from Washington, D.C., in the fall of 1915, she began a run at New York's Park Theatre: "'33 Washington Square' has opened as [*sic*] Suffrage Headquarters, and all this week speakers for the cause will be heard between the acts, while a percentage of the receipts will go to the funds of the Empire State Campaign Committee." This performance was part of a major campaign in New York, which included a protest advertised one month earlier in the *Suffragist:* "The Empire State Committee is planning, for late September or early October, as a practical demonstration of the weakness of the anti-suffrage argument that woman's place is in the home, a woman's one-day strike. Women will be asked to stay home for one day, to show the present-day extent and variety, as well as the social value, of the work they now do outside the home."[72]

Although it is true that by 1915, the suffrage movement had gathered enormous momentum, there were many people who worked tirelessly against it. One of their tactics was to connect the suffrage movement with socialism. (Of course, it *was* tied to that movement in America—as were many important advances such as the prohibition of child labor and the development of strong unions. But just as today, people can't always see that they are benefiting from many ideas gleaned from socialism. Most of us have seen photographs of demonstrators in front of the White House during President Obama's tenure. They are waving signs against government programs. My personal favorite was one protester demanding the government not take away his Medicare!) Newspaper articles as late as 1918 decried the "notorious" connection between the woman's movement and socialism. The Anti-Suffrage Party also tied socialism with another "evil"—pacifism: "Some of the most illustrious torch bearers of feminism in the United States are, or have been, tainted with these twin maladies."[73]

May, of course, had no compunction in being a "little bit of a socialist," as quoted earlier in this chapter. As I have noted before, the women's movement that Irwin *did* distance herself from—and one that may have cost her some support—was the temperance movement. Any taint of stridency was apt to alienate Irwin. Critics have maintained that Frances Willard, leader of the Women's Christian Temperance Union, was really more interested in women's rights than in temperance and used temperance as a "means rather than an end."[74] However, after Willard's death in 1897, the WCTU became an organization much more focused on the fight to establish Prohibition.

For Irwin, as for other feminists of the time, the issue most closely linked to suffrage was pacifism. To Irwin, America's entrance into World War I could be stopped only by women voters: "Over in Europe cannon and schrapnel are razing civilization to the ground. They'll do it here, too, if women don't get the vote."[75]

When Irwin agreed to assist Blair in heading the "Bureau of Laughter" for the Women's Equal Franchise Society, she offered a proposal that also indicated the strong connection she made between impending war and women's rights: "May I make a suggestion for the parade in October? Let there be organized a marching brigade of women as a feature. Each woman should wear the dress of an army nurse, the cap and the insignia of the Red Cross on the sleeve, and the organization should be called 'The Women Who Watch and Wait.' By this object lesson let us show our men that the women who suffer for them and with them ought to have the franchise right to vote with them. I'd like to be in that brigade."[76]

Irwin's pacifism was reinforced by her nationalism, which often revealed a marked xenophobia. She was shocked by the treatment of women in Europe and found anti-suffragist sympathies there to be much harsher than those in the United States. She also expressed anger at the British, specifically in their treatment of American actors and theater, arguing not only that American theater should not hire British actors, but also that British theatergoers in general "look upon [Americans] as curiosities to be looked and laughed at, but never taken seriously. . . . [W]hen our players go over there they do not succeed unless they present some freak tendency or some social amenity different from that to which England is accustomed. They never have treated the American stage with anything but contempt."[77] And in 1922, after the passage of Prohibition, Irwin suggested to Secretary of State Frank Polk that a ten-mile dry zone be set up between Mexico and the United States to prevent Americans from being lured south to drink such concoctions as "mescal," which, she said, could turn a white man insane. This drink was "more nefarious than the Philippine 'bino,' which caused the permanent mental breakdown, and in many cases the death of our soldiers during the occupation." Nationalism is undeniably coupled with racism in this ludicrous remark, especially since she notes that the Canadian border does not present a problem because the "climate is cold and the citizenship friendly."[78] (Anti-immigration sentiments coupled with racism and nationalism had been building at least since the 1880s in America, and Congress attempted to pass literacy requirements for immigrants in 1896, 1903, and 1915. All were vetoed by the president.)[79]

President Wilson initially provided great hope for pacifists—many of whom were women like May Irwin, who did not want to see their sons go to war. Originally, Wilson sided with the pacifists against the interventionists and, in 1914, delivered his Appeal for Neutrality, asserting that "every man who loves America will act and speak in the true spirit of neutrality, which is the spirit of impartiality and fairness and friendliness to all concerned." Indeed, at the Democratic Convention of 1916, a speaker created the slogan that was to prove instrumental in Wilson's reelection: "He kept us out of war."[80]

Irwin's work for pacifism is perhaps most clearly revealed by the central position that her command performance for President Woodrow Wilson held in her memories. In 1931 when Irwin looked back over her years as a star of American vaudeville, she pointed to this performance in the fall of 1915 as the unquestioned climax of her career. In the same article, Irwin was introduced as "the only American player who has ever given what might be compared with . . . a command performance, in the United States." This performance of Scott LeRoy's farce *33 Washington Square* and the president's subsequent invitation for Irwin to come to the White House to be appointed "Secretary of Laughter" remained central in numerous articles, reviews, and obituary notices. In later years, Irwin recalled the performance as an interruption of a tour:

> We were playing Detroit, or some such place at the time, . . . and to my surprise, a few days later I got a telegram from a high official, asking when it would be convenient to bring the company to Washington—the President had need of a hearty laugh. I wired back, saying that we would be glad to break our tour and come at once. . . . Next day I was invited to meet the President at the White House. I went all alone, but evidently my coming was well announced, for although the President had an important delegation waiting, he received me at once, and I remained with him for an hour, both of us cracking jokes and having a big laugh.[81]

This story of a sudden cancellation of her tour and her rush from Detroit to Washington is repeated in her obituary in the *New York Times.* But an examination of the press coverage surrounding the event reveals that Irwin was performing the farce in New York at the Park Theatre and interrupted her run for one night to perform in Washington, D.C. She and her troupe arrived in Washington, D.C., late in the afternoon of September 24, 1915, attended a reception in her honor at the National Press Club, and performed the show that evening for an audience at the National Theatre. The audience did include President Wilson and most of his cabinet, but there is no indication that Irwin had time to visit Wilson the next day at the White House. She and her entourage left early the next morning to return to New York.[82]

Woodrow Wilson does not mention any visit from May Irwin in his detailed personal calendar. His only note occurs on September 24, a reminder to himself to arrive at the National Theatre by 8:15. Furthermore, a memorandum dated September 21, 1915, indicates that Wilson was unaware of Irwin's plans at that time: "May Irwin plans to come to Washington this week to present at the National Theatre her new farce comedy '33 Washington Square.' . . . [Her representative] said that Miss Irwin was especially anxious to have the President see her play. She plans to come Friday or Saturday, and if the President can attend, she will put on the play on the night which most suits his convenience."[83] At the bottom of this memorandum, Wilson wrote that he couldn't make it on Friday but might be able to come on Saturday.

Contrary to Irwin's recollection, then, it was she and her press agent who made the initial moves toward securing the command performance. In a letter sent by her press agent to the president in order to elicit an invitation, Irwin suggested that "the president, worried by world war, needed . . . a good laugh."[84] Many reviews of Irwin's performance and subsequent articles on her life viewed the move as a publicity stunt and quoted the sections of this letter that proposed that the president create a Department of Laughter and make Irwin its secretary, touting the curative powers of laughter in dark times. However, the *Washington Bee,* subtitled "Washington's Best and Leading Negro Newspaper," interpreted the letter more directly as a political move. This paper named Irwin a "suffragist who campaigned ardently for the president" and quoted the following portion of her letter:

> In these times, when our beloved country is facing the most crucial problems of its history, you [President Wilson] have shown yourself as great a patriot and statesman as ever had the executive office. But, as usual, there are some agitators and self-seekers who, for the sake of notoriety, are attempting to handicap the work of the president, even to the extent of hurling this nation into the bloodiest war of all history. I am only a humble almost citizen, but I think it is the duty of every woman, child or man to encourage you with a direct approval of your course, hence, this letter.[85]

In an interview, Irwin underlined her purpose in performing for Wilson: "I have two sons and a husband, and I don't want any war." Tellingly, the interview, given to a female reporter while Irwin unpacked costumes at the National Theatre, was placed in the fashion section of the newspaper, close to articles dealing with such issues as velour hats, which eliminate the necessity of hat pins, and problems that attend the changing waistlines of the latest fashions. It is worth noting that even the staunchest feminist-pacifists, who did not want to fall into the trap of being seen as "patriotic mother-citizen[s]" or "passive and defenseless creatures[s]," still could not and did not completely "reject a self-image as a pacifist moral mother."[86]

Nevertheless, events, notably the sinking of the *Lusitania* by the Germans in 1915, inflated tensions and inexorably led to the U.S. entrance into the Great War. When Wilson prepared the nation for the inevitable, he appealed to his constituents' reform spirit:

> The United States, Wilson insisted, had no material aims in the conflict. The nation was, rather, committed to using the war as a vehicle for creating a new world order, one based on the same progressive ideals that had motivated a generation of reform efforts in America. In a speech before a joint session in

> Congress in January 1917, he presented a plan for a postwar order in which the United States would help maintain peace through a permanent league of nations—a peace that would ensure self-determination for all nations, a "peace without victory."[87]

After Wilson asked Congress to declare war on Germany on April 2, 1917, women reacted swiftly and angrily. Irwin's personal ire was expressed in a telegram she sent to President Wilson. Although the contents of the telegram are lost, Wilson's reply is not. Dated April 3, 1917, it reads:

> My Dear Miss Irwin,
>
> Your telegram of March thirtieth came to my notice only after I had addressed Congress. It disturbs me very much that you should have found the sentiment as you represent it. I need not assure you that I would not have come to the conclusion I stated last evening to the Congress if there had seemed to me any way of escape in the circumstances as I unhappily know them.[88]

Irwin was above all a political pragmatist. Trying to influence where she could, but accepting defeat gracefully, she repositioned herself to ever-changing circumstances. Therefore, Irwin did not allow her anger over the country's entry into World War I to prevent her from working with the Red Cross over the next few years or from telegraphing the president again in 1917 to offer her home in Clayton as a refuge for soldiers who were recovering from illnesses brought on by war conditions.[89] She was always able to live in the present—"To us who live in the present, the past is little or nothing"—and to make the best of difficult circumstances. She viewed this as an essential ingredient of being an American and in keeping with "the spirit of the times . . . [and] our national character with which I myself am imbued to the core."[90]

In summary, May Irwin was politically active in a variety of causes, of which by far the two most important were suffragism and pacifism. As a champion of women's rights, she aligned herself with the traditional virtues of women while simultaneously distancing herself from the petty vanities of "little, frilly perfumed things." She used mainstream arguments connecting women's maternal and domestic qualities with the need for the vote as a springboard toward more radical feminist expressions—such as her objection to the double standard applied to mothers and fathers. Irwin was personally active on behalf of women's rights, marching in suffrage parades and inviting suffrage speakers to present their views between the acts of her plays. She used comedy to inject humor into the women's movement, to ridicule anti-suffragists, and to underline the absurdity of granting voting rights to black men but not to white women.

As a pacifist, Irwin supported Woodrow Wilson and linked her plan to create a Department of Laughter to the cause of peace. Her strong reaction against U.S. entry into World War I indicates that she felt her influence on Wilson should have been greater than it was. Irwin's pacifism, connected to a fervent nationalism, did not prevent her from doing charitable work during World War I. Ever the pragmatist, she made the best of her circumstances.

Irwin's political activities also included individual acts of kindness toward others, civic assistance in the Thousand Islands community, and work against cruelty to animals. Irwin was also an adamant supporter of the individual farmer. Irwin believed that citizens must take personal responsibility in aiding those less fortunate than themselves. Her own individual acts of generosity showed that she believed in helping people—both strangers and friends—in achieving their goals. Therefore, she was quick to offer a loan for a worthy cause, always recalling that her initial real estate purchase might never have occurred without the assistance of a fellow actor. (As mentioned before, Irwin's fellow actor Henry Miller loaned her one thousand dollars when she was out of money and time in making the final payment on her island real estate.)[91] Finally, she worked against the formation of the actors' union Actors' Equity Association—denying that artists could operate well and profitably under the same types of labor unions so necessary in other areas of work.

Irwin's diverse political actions, then, stemmed from an impulse that was at once collectivist *and* individualist. Her sympathies were sometimes paradoxical, and, in this respect, she was similar to a politician she supported throughout her life—four-term governor of New York and Democratic candidate for president in 1928 Alfred E. Smith. Just as Smith was both a Tammanyite and a progressive, Irwin was both an urbanite and a farm woman rooted in the rural populace. Like Smith also, Irwin was in favor of progress in women's rights, but against Prohibition and the excesses of temperance leaders.

Irwin's balance of opposites revealed a political nature that was dependent on compromise. For example, when the United States entered World War I, she did not join the small minority of women who continued to actively oppose the war, such as the group led by protester Crystal Eastman, who opposed all women's relief efforts.[92] Neither of Irwin's sons became conscientious objectors.[93] Nor did Irwin suddenly switch and become a prowar crusader.

Instead, she dealt with the situation pragmatically—with a compromise that supported Red Cross efforts to alleviate the sufferings of war while still disapproving of America's entrance into that war.

Irwin's readiness to compromise also underlined her efforts on behalf of women's rights. She knew how to paint a picture of suffragism that was a familiar, popular, and friendly one. What Irwin injected into the suffrage movement were humor and perspective. Her distance from the Women's Christian Temperance Union separated her from those who were continually lampooned in the press as sour-faced extremists. (She herself lampooned an ardent suffragist and temperance woman when she performed in *Mrs. Peckham's Carouse.* She once jokingly noted that the president of the WCTU lived in her building and that neighbors had remarked on the close resemblance between the temperance president's bonnet and the one worn by Irwin's character Mrs. Peckham.)[94] Irwin showed that a woman could be pro-vote and still have a sense of humor and an attractive demeanor. She could even enjoy an occasional beer or gin and tonic.

Above all, Irwin was patient in her attempts to effect political action. She persisted in efforts to influence Wilson with the establishment of a Department of Laughter right up to the time of his declaration of war, ignoring such ridicule as the *St. Louis Globe Democrat*'s satire of her letter with a cartoon depicting England and Germany declaring a truce based on May Irwin's collection of jokes. Certainly, Wilson was responding to Irwin's real frustration and anger when he wrote to her after America's entrance into World War I. It was not, however, in Irwin's nature to give up. Several years earlier, she had declared that "when things go wrong, I don't cry anymore, I fight."[95]

Irwin's interest in politics was maintained into the last few years of her life. The last entry in one of her personal scrapbooks is a clipping of an article by journalist Walter Lippmann lamenting the failure of Alfred E. Smith and Franklin Roosevelt to compromise and work together effectively. According to Lippmann, each politician had traits that "supplemented the other's weaknesses," and a "union of such diverse but complementary temperaments" could not help but be fruitful.[96] The excerpt is an entirely fitting one for Irwin to preserve. She was a woman who knew the value of compromise in politics.

7

The Road to Rainbow's End

I wish you could have seen May in her place at Club Island. It had a stairway fit for a Queen. And it suited her. I hope you can write that book you're thinking of. We don't want her forgotten.

—Robert Bertrand to the author, November 1994

By 1915 Irwin was increasingly concerned with weighty matters—specifically, the war in Europe and the growing conflict over women's suffrage at home. May was beginning her gradual retirement from the stage. She was now a new grandmother to John C. Irwin, the son of her firstborn, Walter, and his wife, Ethel, who lived in Detroit, where Walter was a wholesale fruit dealer. Her younger son, Harry, had been married for just a year, and Irwin began to spend much more time with her growing family. But she still valued her audience and declared that their laughter provided her with a "tonic," and she thought of her times onstage as "reciprocal good will, an exchange of mutual optimism." These exchanges kept her alive and happy; she felt that "should [her audience] cease to like me, I am so dependent on their good will that I should become unhappy and unhappiness is the poison that kills." Irwin maintained that creating happiness in others was the most important objective any individual could have and that those who do not foster this "mental attitude" are "an obstruction."[1] (In this way, once again, Irwin underplayed her own importance as a comic by crediting her fans with giving her as much as she gave them.)

Although Irwin's performing career slowed during this period, it did not end. In 1918 she made a promotional film for Jersey cows entitled *Hearts and Jerseys,* which received a special showing in Watertown, New York, so that she could approve it before its release. Watertown, a small city less than thirty miles south of Clayton, is the county seat of Jefferson County. In May's time, it was an important place to shop and the site of the first Woolworth's Five and Dime. As indicated earlier, May was involved in Watertown's civic matters, such as the question of an affordable Watertown-to-Clayton bus line.[2]

In 1919 May appeared in *The Water's Fine,* a musical version of her earlier show *Sister Mary,* and when she was forced to close the tour because she was ill, she bristled at the suggestion that she might be ready for retirement.[3] Irwin then played in *On the Hiring Line,* which included music written by Irving Berlin, and she served as emcee of a vaudeville show, *The 49ers.* In 1925 she headlined at the Palace in New York City in *Old Timer's Week.* She even reprised her famous intoxication scene in *Mrs. Peckham's Carouse* for a benefit performance with English mimic Cissie Loftus in 1927.[4] This benefit took place in the Clayton Opera House,[5] which remained essentially unchanged until a $2.3 million renovation in 2007.[6]

Irwin spent many of her later years still acquiring and selling real estate. In fact, her son Harry started his professional life as an accountant and then shifted to real estate—perhaps partially to assist his mother in her property holdings.[7] After her marriage to Eisfeldt, May continued to purchase property in New York City, acquiring a house at 638 Lexington Avenue in 1910[8] and two houses at 152 and 154 West Forty-Fifth Street (purchased for $35,000), with plans to build "May Irwin's Playhouse" and install Eisfeldt as one of the major directors.[9] This plan was one of many that Irwin did not carry through (she also thought of building a theater in Philadelphia, a home for bachelors, and an actors' home).[10] Irwin's property on Lexington Avenue proved to be her most lucrative purchase. When she and her husband sold it in 1929, just before the Great Depression, they received more than $500,000.[11] (Her savvy timing is perhaps worthy of further research!) At that time, she had already sold—nine years earlier—properties at 152, 154, and another she owned on 156 West Forty-Fifth Street (along with an "abutting house at 155 West Forty-fourth Street") to a bankers' syndicate for $350,000.[12]

Irwin's role as a New York City landlord was a difficult one; she was the object of numerous complaints and lawsuits. In 1905 she lost in a foreclosure suit against her property on 144 West Twenty-Eighty Street.[13] In 1909 she was sued for repairs to her property on West Forty-Fifth Street.[14] She even filed suit herself, in 1916, against a tenant for exhibiting more than two women's waists in her clothing store window at a time. Irwin claimed that "she placed the restriction in the lease because she had previously leased another store in the same building to a dealer in waists and feared that if she did not restrict Miss De Hockman's display, 'It would bring about too great competition of rivalry and might cause the failure of one or both of the tenants.'"[15]

The most serious problem on Irwin's property occurred in 1917 when a fire destroyed a theatrical boardinghouse that she had purchased on West Forty-Fourth Street. Because of this fire, eight claims were filed against Irwin, including Charles O. Holman's suit for $100,000 because of the death of his wife. Tenants asserted that Irwin was negligent because fire escapes had not been installed in the building, even though a previous fire had taken the lives of five people.[16]

In the last twenty years of her life, however, Irwin focused most of her attention on her holdings in the Thousand Islands. Although she certainly did not need to earn her living, she used her land for farming, fishing, and hunting. At first Irwin lived in a bungalow during her summers on the island. Then she built the large home that was in the process of construction on her wedding day in 1907:

> The summer home, strikingly attractive from the St. Lawrence River, is a model of convenience. Most of the furnishings were picked up by the famous comedienne from odd corners of the globe—three fireplaces were removed bodily from European palaces. . . . The house has forty rooms and six baths. One of the most attractive and frequented rooms, both by the mistress and visitors, is the kitchen. . . ."You probably know," said Miss Irwin to a reporter, "that in the building of this place I was my own architect. Well, I planned the kitchen first and built the rest around it. I figured it this way: I do most of my 'receiving' with sleeves rolled up and enveloped in an apron" (it requires *some* apron too!) "and in these circumstances what better setting could be asked for than the kitchen?"
>
> Irwin Island has a well-stocked dairy, a pedigreed bull or two, three horses and half a dozen colts, a few hundred Orpington hens, a round dozen boats of different types, and without doubt the best gravel beach on the St. Lawrence River.[17]

At different times during her ownership of half of Club Island (her half is often called "Irwin Island" or "Irwin Isle"), Irwin made different plans for her large home. For a while, she wished to set it up as an inn, and postcards from as late as 1912 still designated the home as the "May Irwin Inn." Prohibition, however, interfered with her plans. In 1915 Irwin announced her decision to turn her summer mansion into a home for actors—but only those who were "retired comedians and comediennes."[18] This was one of her many ideas that did not come to fruition.

Beginning in 1913, Irwin intermittently announced that she was planning on selling her home, either to move away from the area altogether or to buy a larger farm on the mainland near Clayton.[19] With this move in mind, beginning in 1917 Irwin and Eisfeldt purchased farmland south of Clayton, adding lots throughout the year.[20] This land, where Irwin and Eisfeldt raised Jersey cows and operated a full dairy, was called Rainbow's End. It was at Rainbow's End where Irwin made plans for her second cookbook and wrote a series of recipes and household hints published in the *New York Evening Journal,* a supplement to the *New York Times.*[21] Eisfeldt died at Rainbow's End in 1940; as late as 1996, there still existed a remnant of the old farm in the form of a dilapidated barn.

Irwin's home on Club Island may have been on the market as early as 1913, but it was not sold until 1927, when it was auctioned off to "Mr. Zimmerman of Natural Bridge" for a mere $16,000 (it was estimated that Irwin had spent a minimum of $140,000 on the property).[22] However, there is no record of the registration of the transfer of title to Zimmerman. Instead, in 1943 there was a title transfer from Harry Irwin and Gustave Eisfeldt (Kurt's brother) to Beatrice Morgan Goodrich. Goodrich was related to David Goodrich, one-time chairman of the rubber firm and husband to Mrs. Pruyn, owner of the other half of Club Island. Author Stanley Norcom corroborates the transfer in his well-researched book *Grindstone: An Island World Remembered,* in which he asserts that Goodrich united the two halves of Club Island after Irwin's death.[23] The island later passed down to Elizabeth Dodge Haxall. Although Elizabeth died in 1998, the island still belongs to her descendants.[24]

As early as 1909, Irwin concentrated many of her political interests on the island area near Clayton. In that year, she volunteered to assist the board supervisor of Clayton in entertaining a large group of county officials and lawmakers. After treating her guests to good food and a boat trip, she made certain that she "chatted for a time with the county legislators, intimating that she hoped they would do all they could to hurry the building of a good road from Watertown to Clayton."[25] In 1920 she vehemently complained about Watertown's city manager and his plans to tax the Clayton-to-Watertown bus line:

> I never heard of such a thing! . . . The buses bring business to Watertown and the city ought to pay the operators of these bus lines, rather than tax them for the business they bring to Watertown. Who is this city manager and who employed him? . . . From Waltham, Mass., he comes? Really, I'm surprised that we couldn't find a man capable of managing our city in this community with all of its brilliant men. And from Massachusetts, too! Why, they used to burn witches in Massachusetts. They named Waltham after a watch, and I don't know whether that is a recommendation or not. I never had a Waltham.[26]

In the late 1920s she also organized a special committee for the illumination of the Thousand Islands.[27] As evidenced by her remarks on the Clayton-to-Watertown bus line, Irwin maintained her tendency, even in serious matters, to undercut her point (and simultaneously underline it!) with comic shifts from her major argument. In this case, she uses a ludicrous ad hominem attack on the city manager's origin and name—while slyly letting her audience know that Mr. Waltham was not from the area and thus could not possibly understand local civic needs.

We can also see May using her performance techniques in many of her later activities and writings. For example, even as she reached old age, Irwin often used a childlike assertiveness to win laughter during her public speeches. One such address has been alluded to previously. It was given to the joint Rotary and Kiwanis Clubs of Watertown, New York, on June 12, 1928. This address is particularly valuable, as it has notations of places where general laughter greeted Irwin's remarks. Recounting the events that led her to settle in the Thousand Islands area of New York, Irwin told of her first visit to the island she would later purchase, where she and her sister spent the night outdoors. The audience responded heartily when Irwin said she was confronted by a landowner, who said she saw Irwin and her sister put up a tent on her property the night before, to which Irwin retorted, in her famous pouting demeanor, "Well, why didn't you give us a hand?" She also exhibited her penchant for self-criticism when she poked fun at the famous frugality that enabled her to purchase an island at a young age, eliciting laughter when she explained that when she was traveling, though her theater company "for the look of things . . . had to live in the best hotels," she always got "the cheapest room in the hotel, you understand."[28]

In an enjoyable article in the *Watertown Daily Times* in March 1922, Irwin combined her jokes about her weight with both her frugality and her solidarity with other heavy women. "Seats Too Small for May Irwin" began with Irwin's outcry concerning the sixteen-inch seats that were provided for guests at Westminster Abbey for the recent wedding of Princess Mary to Viscount Lascelles. She found herself siding with some of the royal guests who were too large to fit in the chairs and claimed that nothing "less than a 20-inch chair will accommodate me." Calling for the swift punishment of the Lord Chamberlain for his decision by "sentenc[ing him] for life to sit on a chair 12 inches wide," Irwin continued with an alternative suggestion—supplied, she maintained, by her husband, Kurt Eisfeldt—of the creation of theaters in which both lower-priced sixteen-inch seats and more expensive twenty-two-inch seats would be provided. Big women who wanted to save money could squeeze into the smaller seats if they so desired: "Ushers might be provided with large shoehorns, and for a small tip, would help slip large ladies into small seats."[29]

In the same manner, she continued to make fun of the pompous, sometimes satirizing an individual who criticized another on a subject of which he had no knowledge. She used this tactic in her response to the editor of the *Utica (N.Y.) Observer*, who had the audacity to claim that Irwin was not a "real dirt farmer." She replied by comparing the journalist to Mark Twain, when he served as substitute editor of a farm journal: "When a subscriber asked what was the best way to harvest beets, Mark replied 'Send a little boy up the tree and shake them down.'"[30]

In 1919 Irwin celebrated the birth of her second grandson, William Irwin, to Walter and Ethel, although these years were also filled with loss for her. May's uncle Frank Campbell had died in 1915. In 1922, five years after Irwin's mother died with the family by her side, Walter died after an illness of only ten days. Irwin had her son's body brought back from Detroit to New York City for burial.[31] Irwin's sister, Flo, died in 1930 at the age of seventy-one. Then in 1933, Harry's wife, Mae McCosker, died in New York City. May arranged for all of these family members to be buried in her vault in the Kenisco Cemetery in Valhalla, New York. Later, they would be joined by May, Kurt, and Harry.[32]

Among her many other activities during this period, Irwin also traveled widely. She and Kurt took a journey around the world in 1927, and May took the time to get her picture taken atop a camel and send the photograph to the magazine *Theatre* for her fans.[33] In 1931 she traveled to South America with her husband, later declaring Venezuela to be one of her favorite countries in the world.[34] The following year, the couple toured Northwest Canada for nearly two months.

In the 1930s, Irwin began to cancel most of her scheduled activities. Determined to drive a horse at the Clayton County Fair in 1932, she nevertheless had to bow out at the last minute, perhaps swayed by the protests of friends. Irwin even tried, in 1934, to return to the stage in a special three-day engagement with the Summer Civic Center of Clayton, which was moving its location to Watertown.[35] But she decided, during rehearsals, that the theater engagement would be too tiring for her and canceled her performance.[36] She did, however, come to Central Park in New York City in 1935 to sing at a celebration of Mark Twain's one hundredth birthday, noting that she and Twain had been "dear friends for years." She was said to be "in superb voice" on this occasion as she sang her renowned "Frog Song."[37] In that same year, Irwin received the news that her famous film *The Kiss* was the showpiece of the newly established Museum of Modern Art Film Library in New York City. Irwin retained a copy of a bulletin from the Museum of Modern Art with a picture of the famous embrace. Her handwritten comment below the picture is a simple "Oh!!!"[38]

Irwin's last years were marked by growing absorption in her family and farm, including the trotting horses that Eisfeldt had begun acquiring. In 1934 she called herself "the most fortunate woman in the world" because she had "the best husband, the finest son, and the most perfect daughter-in-law in the world."[39] She stayed abreast of politics and contemporary entertainment, still following one of her favorite politicians, Al Smith, and favoring the acting of Walter Huston, Katharine Cornell, and Helen Hayes (she also loved Katharine Hepburn in the movies, but not on the stage).[40] Even in her last few years, Irwin remained alert to political affairs and the possible threat of another war. She kept, in the final few pages of her personal clippings, a poem focusing on the rise of Hitler. This poem, featured alongside a selection of cartoons from the newspaper, included stanzas such as this:

> The war to end wars?
> The war to make the world
> Safe for Democracy?
> World peace and the
> Brotherhood of Man?
> Versailles? . . . Geneva?
> The death of militarism?
> What of them now?[41]

In the spring of 1937, Irwin suffered a stroke. She regained some of her health and returned to her home at Rainbow's End. Then, at the age of seventy-six, on October 22, 1938, Irwin died of bronchial pneumonia at the Park Crescent Hotel in New York City. Many of her old stage friends paid her tribute and put her to rest in the bright-red dress she had requested for her burial. Her estate totaled more than one hundred thousand dollars. She bequeathed ten thousand dollars to her widowed daughter-in-law, Ethel Irwin, and left the rest of the estate to be divided between her husband and surviving son, Harry.[42]

In March 1940, Kurt Eisfeldt died, leaving not one penny to Harry, even though he bequeathed sums to Irwin's niece and grandniece.[43] (This seems to support Harold Kendall's contention that both of Irwin's sons disliked Kurt and interacted with him as little as possible.) A few months after Kurt's death, Harry remarried, this time wedding May's former secretary Nellie Carton. Harry passed away in 1947 without any children. Both of Walter's sons, William and John, served in the U.S. Army during World War II. William, however, suffered a brain aneurysm and died in his sleep in 1943, while he was in service.[44]

John Irwin had two sons, Scott and Todd, who are now in their sixties. Scott has a photo album of May's with pictures from the farm in Clayton and a collection of silverware engraved with the words *Irwin Inn.* Scott maintained that Irwin was very fond of her grandchildren and had hoped to send John to Europe and then pay for his college, but, either because of the Depression or for unknown reasons, she was never able to fulfill this promise. William's obituary states that he lived "with his Grandmother at her home in Rainbow's End for nine summers before her death." Scott's favorite story, heard from his father—who died in 1991—is how May organized dinnertime at her home when the entire family gathered: "She would ring the dinner bell and everybody had about fifteen minutes to get to the table or else they didn't eat."[45]

After Irwin's death, her name slowly faded from the pages of the *New York Times,* and when Harry died only four lines appeared in the newspaper, noting that the deceased's mother had been a stage comedienne at one time.[46] But Irwin's name never diminished in the Thousand Islands area. Stories and anecdotes about the comedienne appeared throughout the 1950s in local papers.[47] Many reprints of these old articles appeared in the 1980s and continue to be featured up to the present. In 1991 a local ragtime festival honored Irwin. In 1996 she was impersonated in costume for parades in Clayton. And, of course, I took part in a documentary of the life and times of May Irwin, Eva Tanguay, and Marie Dressler in 2008, and Archeophone Records released a CD with songs by May Irwin and Clarice Vance in 2011. In July 2013, a documentary titled *The Mysterious Origin of Thousand Island Dressing,* by Eric J. Roberts and Andrea Reeves, aired on WCNY, an upstate New York affiliate of PBS. May Irwin is prominently featured in the film, as she was reputed to have given the dressing its name (a rumor of doubtful veracity). Karen Killian, who was the manager of Spicer's Gallery in Clayton for many years, has created a beautiful line of stoneware based on Irwin's photographs and artifacts. May Irwin has been the subject of both new and old articles in the magazine *Thousand Islands* as recently as 2013.[48] The *Thousand Islands Sun,* Clayton's main newspaper, featured May in articles in July and August 2015.[49]

We know most of Irwin's life as a presentation of her public persona, sprinkled with a few memories and stories passed down through the years. In the 1990s I was fortunate to be able to talk with a few people in the Thousand Islands area who had met May. (These people have since passed on.) What emerges is a picture of a very tough and resilient individual, full of kindness and generosity—but also insistent on certain rituals and procedures. Robert Bertrand remembered that when May visited the Harold House in Clayton, she had a favorite chair, and "beware if you were in it when she wanted it." He also noted that when Lowell Thomas came on the radio with the 7:00 news, you had to "be quiet or take a tongue lashing regardless of who you were." Bertrand praised May's generosity and "lack of ego," even though "her husband Kurt waited on her hand and foot!"[50]

When I look at her home movies, I see a woman surrounded by family and friends and full of life and energy. That energy is what spurred her to try to do too many things—as I've shown in this study, her plans to build inns and homes for actors and many other schemes never came to pass. (She even once planned to build a skyscraper in Chicago!)[51] In her home movie, besides the scene I described in chapter 2, we see clues to her personality. There is a long ceremony and raising of the American flag; there are a multitude of dogs and children chasing each other and jumping into ready laps. Young people are shown dancing the Charleston, and the camera pans slowly and lovingly over a collection of every kind of liquor anyone could desire. At one point, pictures are held up to the camera—May in her early days and one of her deceased son, Walter—the latter held up for a long time at different angles as if to make sure that his presence is there and not forgotten. Near the end, we see a close-up of May smoking a cigar and chatting, with an enormous wry smile and a twinkle in her eye. She wears no makeup, is wrinkled with age, and has lost much of her hair—wisps of which blow in the breeze. But she fills the frame with confidence and good humor.[52]

Irwin is and was remembered for her talent, her toughness, her politics, her cooking, her humor, and her spirit. Typical of reprinted anecdotes about Irwin is one from 1950, in which a newspaper executive remembered being rescued when he was but a small paperboy by May Irwin from a cheating "customer" who hopped on a streetcar without paying. Irwin witnessed the mishap and came up beside the boy in her carriage, with tears in her eyes:

> "The blankety-blankety-good-for-nothing skunk. I saw the whole thing. Listen, kid, you stand on that corner and wait for us. We'll be right back. Mike"—she whirled on the coachman—"get going and paste the blankety-blank-blank out of that blankety, blankety, blankety guy." . . . Ten minutes later they had come back. The actress beckoned the boy to get into the Victoria and sit beside her. "Now, Mike," she said, "go on and tell him what you did." "I hung one on him," said Mike fiercely. "I blackened both his eyes and hit him one in the solar plexus. And I brought you something back." Into Bill Brede's grimy palm Mike laid a 5-cent piece.

> "Now, kid," said May Irwin, "There is something else I want to tell you. Don't ever let guys like that make you hate the human race. There are a lot of dirty devils in this world—but most people are just like you and me."
>
> On top of the nickel she placed a rose and a $1 bill.

The executive went on to recount how he later realized that the duo couldn't possibly have accomplished what they said they had, but that the "deception was part of a deep kindness." He felt forever grateful to "May Irwin with her roses, her tears and her swear words that kept me from growing up to hate the world and myself."[53]

Irwin's Strategies for Success

From Irwin's public life, we can discern five interconnected strategies that enabled her to establish and sustain her popularity. (Irwin herself was probably consciously aware of some of these strategies but not of others.) First, she grounded both her comedy and her political views in mainstream American tradition, and from this mainstream she extended into more dangerous and less familiar and acceptable spaces. Second, she enhanced her popularity through a careful balancing of traits that were both self-denigrating and self-affirming. Third, she employed shifting identities—identities that helped associate her with both the powerless and the powerful, the black victim as well as the white master, the helpless child as well as the capable mother. Fourth, Irwin allowed the public to see behind the jolly performer to another woman, a loving mother who really felt most comfortable in the home, not on the stage, a woman whose life reflected tragedy more than comedy. Finally, Irwin—as performer and person—embodied for her audience the developing American myth of success. That is, she was a poor child who had attained tremendous stardom and material success. Her direct contact and her regular alignment with her audience made them feel that such success might be possible for them as well.

In her day, Irwin was widely regarded as a tremendously funny woman—by both men and women—whether she was singing a coon song, starring in a comic role, writing down her opinions, or being interviewed by the press. Irwin's success as a comic was dependent in part on her use of comic techniques already familiar to her audience. Her humor was typical for her day in its use of puns and wordplay, its satire of the wealthy and pretentious, and its reliance on ethnic stereotypes. As an overweight female comic, she was also typical in her self-denigrating humor about her weight—shedding layers of clothing like her contemporary Trixie Friganza and poking fun, as Sophie

Tucker did, at her own inability to control her appetite. Her firm grounding in comic tradition allowed her to sometimes step out of the comic territory traditional for women—as when she turned her humor against white males.

Although she was active in a number of causes, from labor rights to animal rights, suffragism and pacifism were Irwin's major political concerns. As a suffragist, as in other areas, Irwin planted herself firmly on traditional ground and then branched out to more controversial territory. Thus, her arguments might begin with a mainstream cry for women's votes, based on the idea of women's moral superiority, and end with a diatribe against the double standard applied to mothers and fathers. Similarly, she might start by ridiculing the notion that black males could vote while women could not, but continue her argument by belittling white males who were against female suffrage. As a pacifist, Irwin emphasized the importance of women attaining suffrage as a way of keeping America out of war by connecting women's supposed moral superiority to the maintenance of peace.

It was in the use of her domestic life, however, that Irwin most effectively used a mix of tradition and innovation to bolster her popularity. Not only did she use domesticity as feminists in general did—to ground her support of suffragism and pacifism in the moral superiority and domestic needs and interests of women and mothers—but she also used it to support her professional work as a comic.

May Irwin's domesticity worked for her on a personal level in a way remarkably parallel to the general extension of the domestic sphere by women's groups during the period. She began as a woman who belonged in the private sphere but was forced by necessity to earn her living in the public sphere. She expanded her domestic sphere, by placing it side by side with her professional work as a performer: her routines appeared beside recipes in her cookbook; her audiences were challenged to compete with her cooking abilities. She combined traditional womanly values associated with mothering and nurturing with the new practical applications of science to domestic activities like home management, shopping, and saving. Finally, her domesticity became a profession in its own right. The concerns of her domestic life and her professional life were blended into one.

In her domestic profession, Irwin wrote articles on homemaking, published a cookbook, and operated her own dairy. She used her experience as household manager, mother, and cook to support her arguments for the necessity of combining "care" and "dare" in a woman's life. As just such a woman, Irwin appeared intuitive and nurturing, on the one hand, and practical and efficient, on the other. She needed to save with care but make bold purchases. She needed to look after her home life in the domestic arena but also go out and vote in order to maintain that home life.

Additionally, Irwin appealed to both men and women in her healthy embrace of hedonism and rejection of the temperance movement. In her suffragism, Irwin was careful to separate herself from certain women (the "little, frilly perfumed things" and the humorless temperance crusaders) and align herself with "good women" (mothers with a sense of compassion and duty). Small wonder that the suffragist movement wished to enlist Irwin's popularity with both men and women to inject humor into the cause and extend its appeal.

Irwin's second strategy for maintaining popularity concerns her specific balancing of traits that were at once self-denigrating and self-affirming. The power of a typical female comedic personality has been defined as a combination of comedic ability (simply the ability to elicit laughter), sexual appeal, and attractiveness. In brief, most female comics balance sexuality with intelligence—they perform characters who are *either* beautiful or smart, but never both. (As previously noted, this may be changing long after May's time—pretty *and* smart is often the requirement now.) Irwin, however, managed to achieve a balance of these characteristics—she could be heavy *and* beautiful; she was both assertive *and* coy; she performed well because of intuition *and* hard work.

Irwin also both supported and undermined her competence as an intelligent and economically successful woman. She displayed intelligence in both her sharp wit and her writing, but undercut it by her scatterbrained behavior and occasional proclamations, accompanied with tears, that women were unfit to bear the responsibilities of business. She underplayed her tremendous economic power by reminding her audience of her humble roots and ridiculing the affectations of the upper class. But Irwin always managed to use self-deprecating humor to align herself with her audience—particularly the women—assuring them, despite her immense stardom, that they were equal, and perhaps even superior, to her.

Irwin further enhanced her popularity by her stunning (perhaps unconscious) use of shifting identities. She concurrently portrayed opposing personae: she was both the child and the mother; she was both the idiot savant and the learned one; she was at once the character she portrayed and the performer May Irwin.

Irwin often juxtaposed the characters of the child and the mother. She portrayed characters who were at once naive and bold, confused and capable. Critics noted that her renditions of children's songs seemed to portray equally the protective mother and the small child.

Irwin was, as the idiot savant, the precocious child whose talent was pure, spontaneous inspiration and, as the learned one, the well-trained comic who had learned her craft through years of application. She was both the cook whose mother never taught her to cook and the baker who had to learn bread making by painful study at her own cook's side. And she was both the coon shouter who naturally sang and danced like a Negro and the singer who had learned dialect and rhythm through careful observation and study.

As a performer, Irwin was particularly adept at shifting back and forth from herself to her character and to the different identities taken on by her character. Of course, all performers are involved to some degree in different levels of identity. In Irwin's case, however, in an important sense she always played herself, standing outside of the character and inviting her audience to laugh with her and not merely at her. In this way, Irwin was simultaneously the object of laughter and the laughing subject. She may have sometimes posed as the "unlaughing at which men laugh," but she was also the laughing observer.[54] Her position as laughing observer added to her power as a female comic, for the more self-aware a comic is of the power of laughter that she controls, the greater is the power that she wields.[55]

Behind the comic self that Irwin displayed, however, was another, supposedly private, self that she encouraged her audience to believe in. This self was a vulnerable and home-loving woman who canceled performances to spend time with her family. She was a serious woman, one who perhaps more closely understood the black female victims whose songs she composed rather than the more popular "Bullies" whose songs were written for her. By her repeated insistence of her fundamental seriousness and her expressed viewpoint that life itself was inherently tragic, Irwin undercut her own robust comedy and aligned herself with a woman's supposedly more sensitive, less aggressive approach to humor, a humor women shared from "perceiving the blend of the tragic and comic which is life in its fullness and vitality."[56] Additionally, her stated altruistic purpose for being a comic—to bring happiness into the lives of others—softened the egotism and aggressiveness that could be inferred from her star performances in plays in which other actors were allowed very little comic focus.

Finally, Irwin was a living example of American success. She was a modern "New Woman," reflective of the new urban American. And she urged her audience to take her journey to success with her. If she turned nickels into dollars for a newspaper boy and that boy rose to great heights, perhaps she could make dreams come true for her audience. And she was both virtuous and fun loving, a mother with good values who still loved the sensual pleasures of life—

money, food, drink, and fun. Her success offered audiences "both an escape from the moment and a tangible promise for the future."[57] Unfortunately, this nineteenth-century view of American excellence was tied to a nationalism that revealed both the xenophobia and the racism of American society in that age: Irwin criticized the British for their snobbish treatment of the American theater and characterized Mexican and Filipino citizens as savages indulging in exotic drugged beverages that would render civilized white men insane.

It is surely also unfortunate that in performance, it was as a singer of coon songs that Irwin achieved her most skillful balance of power. This balance is difficult to discern, its interpretation an attempt to "read the subtext of the commentaries, and to understand audiences and performers only half-conscious of what is happening."[58] However, this study shows that Irwin's performance as a coon shouter operated on at least three distinct levels, levels that corresponded to the complex relationship between the white female performer and both the dominant male culture and the oppressed black culture.

On one level, Irwin as coon shouter certainly expressed the feelings of the dominant white culture and, as such, both enhanced her own status through the disparagement of another group and helped empower the dominant group by assuaging any feelings of guilt over the growing mistreatment of blacks during the period. Her "Bully Song" seems to ask white Americans: "Why suffer any pangs of guilt for the mistreatment of a race that mistreats its own—cheating readily on friends and bursting into razor fights at the least provocation?" In this respect, the point of view of the coon songs is backed by the virulent media coverage of the turn of the century, articles emphasizing the supposed lack of conscience on the part of blacks, sometimes creating an uncanny parallel between whites' treatment of blacks and blacks' treatment of animals: "The darky is happy because he does not recognize, does not realize, his duty to others. He lives simply to gratify his own cravings. He does not feed his mule or ox because he thinks the creature is hungry, but only because he has to have it to plough with."[59] So on this level, Irwin became a powerful force of the dominant culture and its need to "believe in the signified 'coon' as represented in the songs as a necessary sociopsychological mechanism for justifying segregation and subordination."[60] As this dominant force, Irwin was completely separate from the "coon" she sang about—as separate as were the white males in her audience.

At another level, Irwin was representative of Eric Lott's white culture that "continually acknowledged and absorbed black culture even while defending America against it." At this second level, Irwin, as the white maternal female, stole the black image through a desire to possess it, displaying a complicated mixture, as Lott has observed, of envy and love.[61] As the maternal figure, Irwin contained the black figure; her white female presence asserted its power. The conflation of "woman" and "black," with the attendant disappearance of the black woman, is a subject much studied in contemporary criticism.[62] The covers of coon-song sheet music tended to represent the South as a white female, even when the songs inside referred to a black female.[63] Irwin, performing without blackface and with an understated dialect, remained the female. Buxom and matronly, she was associated with the earth and fertility as a mother; she was the perfect vehicle to contain the black image. Irwin was sympathetic to the black image she portrayed because of her closeness to blacks' supposedly primitive, earthbound nature, yet remained separate because of her whiteness. She was still a condescending, superior parental figure.

On the third level, Irwin was absorbed by the black image she wished to contain. That is, Irwin *became* the coon. Associated with the infantilism of the female sex, Irwin could more easily become the childlike Negro she represented. Her occasional avowal that she was just naturally like a Negro and did not need to study the race helped confirm this idea. The caricatures of her lips and chubby figure implied that she did not need blackface to appear black. Her childlike delivery of the coon songs reduced her to the childlike image of the coon. Perhaps most tellingly, critics concerned about the social problems revealed in Irwin's coon songs noted that her comedy seemed based on her inability to understand the objectionable nature of certain behavior. (Her critics meant the antisocial behavior of the blacks being depicted, but we would also add the inherent racism of the depictions.) She was carefree and oblivious, just like the Negro: "While the white man worries over his state the coon lives the happiest life imaginable. . . . The happy-hearted, care-free children of the sun are the most contented beings on earth."[64]

In summary, Irwin's performance of the coon song may have been her most complex and nuanced balance of traits and identities, one that endeared her to her audience at the same time that it expressed that audience's most powerful prejudices and longings. Not only was she aligned with the dominant white male culture as a separate, controlling force, which defined the black image in order to justify its own actions against blacks, but she was also the powerful but loving maternal image, which absorbed and contained the black image—making it safe for others to enjoy. On yet another level, she became the image that she portrayed. The balance of these three images allowed audiences to admire her power and accept it at the same time; they could laugh *at* her as the foolish coon, a poor, simple, and oblivious child;

they could laugh *with* her *as* the foolish coon, at the simple child contained within us all; and they could laugh *with* her *at* the foolish coon, separate and satisfied in their mutual superiority.

The question that remains at the end of this study is how successful was Irwin in her strategies of influence? Certainly, she was successful in maintaining an enormous popularity during her lifetime. She was materially successful, able to acquire whatever possessions she desired for herself and her family. Artistically, she was less successful. She never acquired a vehicle that seemed to measure up to her promise. There does seem to be, at a point in her career, a trade-off between popularity and artistic growth—her audiences wanted to see her perform herself again and again.

Her political and social objectives likewise met with mixed success. She played her part in the suffragist cause and lived to see the fruits of her labors. Her pacifist hopes were dashed with World War I, and she died with the awareness of another impending war. She seemed, however, to have had a happy second marriage and a good relationship with her sons, though a troubled relationship with her sister.

Irwin's wish to be remembered as someone who made people laugh, rather than the originator of coon songs, did not quite come true. In fact, in the short run, she was remembered primarily as a coon shouter. In the longer run, she was probably ignored because of her association with a racist form of singing that is only recently beginning to be studied. And, sadly, her "Bully Song" surely negatively affected the treatment of blacks in more ways than she could have possibly realized.

Perhaps Irwin's biggest success in her endeavors was due to her adaptability to her circumstances. If she did not do well as a serious performer, then she decided that comedy was the noblest profession. If she could not stop U.S. entry into World War I, then she would offer her house to the Red Cross to help ease the pain of soldiers. If she could not stop the Actors' Equity Association from becoming a powerful union, then she would find more satisfaction in running a dairy than in running a theater company. In a letter she wrote in the 1920s, she recounted a conversation with a friend in words that aptly sum up Irwin's victory over the obstacles she faced in life: "'It's a glorious day,' I said. Friend: 'yes, but it's terrible underfoot.' To which I replied: 'Yes, but we're not going that way.'"[65]

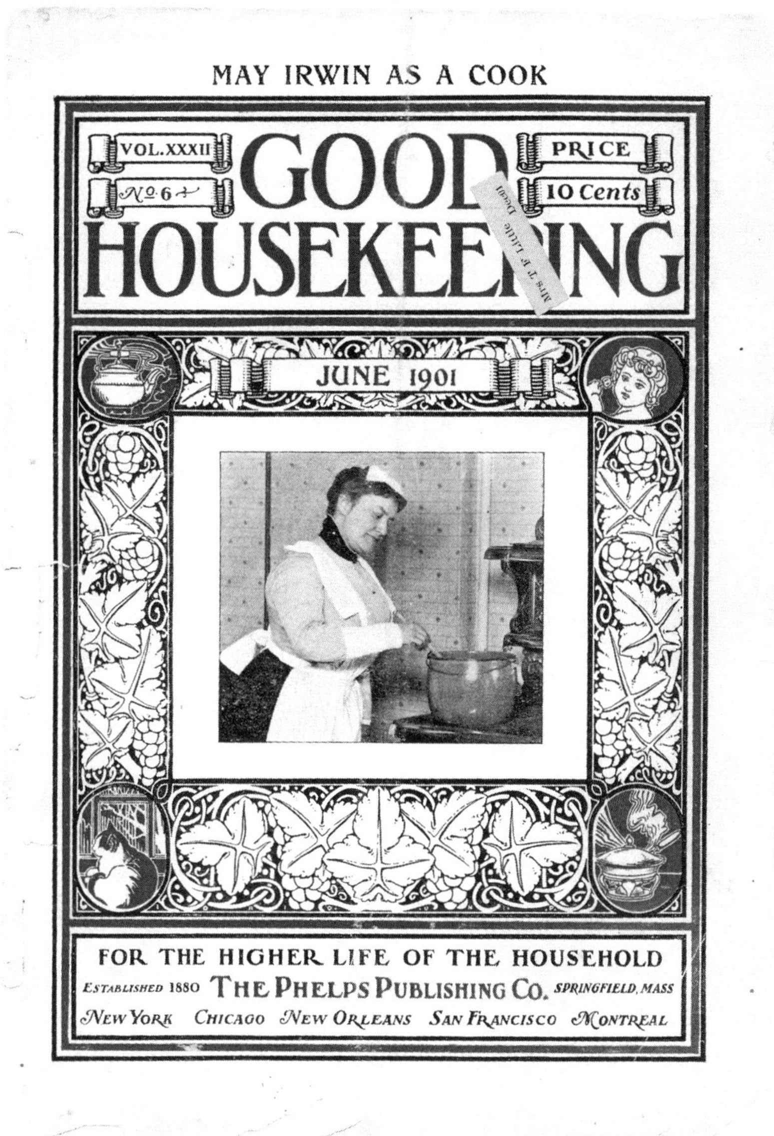

Good Housekeeping cover (1901), featuring May Irwin as cook. Courtesy of Karen Killian's private collection.

PROGRAMME.

BIJOU THEATRE

H. B. SIRE, - - - - - - - - - - - - MANAGER

1884—TWENTIETH SEASON—1904

WEEK COMMENCING MONDAY EVENING, DEC. 12, 1904

Matinee Saturday.

SIXTH WEEK.

MAY IRWIN

And Her Company

IN HER NEW OFFERING,

MRS. BLACK IS BACK

By MR. GEORGE V. HOBART.

Those Present on This Occasion:

MRS. BLACK....................MAY IRWIN
PROFESSOR BLACK, Mrs. Black's second husband....................A. S. LIPMAN
EMILY MASON, Mrs. Black's sister....................JANE BURBY
PRISCILLA BLACK, Mrs. Black's sister-in-law....................FRANCES GORDON
JACK DANGERFIELD, Mrs. Black's only son....................EDGAR ATCHISON-ELY
LARRY McMANUS, Mrs. Black's son's valet....................JOHN G. SPARKS
DON PEDRO DEGAZEBE, Mrs. Black's son's Nemesis....................NICK LONG
TOM LARKEY, Mrs. Black's physical culturist....................CHARLES LANE
MAJOR THORNE, Mrs. Black's broker....................ROLAND CARTER
BRAMLEY BUSH, Mrs. Black's neighbor....................JOHN JOHNSON
HANK, Mrs. Black's gardener....................CHARLES CHURCH
LIZZIE, Mrs. Black's cook....................MAY DONOHUE
PETER PATTER, Mrs. Black's letter carrier....................HENRY PATTEE
MARY, Mrs. Black's housemaid....................LILIAN KAVANAGH

Young Lady Students in Mrs. Black's Husband's College.

SARAH DALE....................VIRA RIAL
ELLEN LEIGHTON....................NEAL FRANCIS
ELIZABETH MORGAN....................SADIE WESTON
CAROLINE PATTERSON....................HELEN DUNLAP
AMELIA BRANT....................KATE GOTTHOLD
AGNES HAMILTON....................DOROTHY BANES

Programme continued on second page following.

Program cover for *Mrs. Black Is Back*, 1904. Courtesy of the author.

Postcard featuring May Irwin's home on Club Island. Courtesy of Karen Killian's private collection.

May Irwin in *33 Washington Square*, 1915. Courtesy of Karen Killian's private collection.

Publicity shot of May Irwin. Courtesy of Karen Killian's private collection.

Harry boating in the St. Lawrence River. Courtesy of the Harry Ransom Center, University of Texas, Austin.

May Irwin hunting ducks. Courtesy of Karen Killian's private collection.

May Irwin and Kurt Eisfeldt, ca. 1927. Courtesy of Whitby Archives, photograph 34-000-021, Whitby, Ontario, Canada.

May Irwin with baby from Siam (now Thailand), taken during her world tour in 1927. Courtesy of Karen Killian's private collection.

May's barn in Clayton, at Rainbow's End, 1996. Courtesy of the author.

Photograph of May Irwin collection of stoneware designed by Karen Killian, 1996. Courtesy of the author.

Button worn by visitors to the Spring Ragtime Festival in 1991. Courtesy of the author.

May Irwin is Back!

Scenes and Songs
from
Mrs. Black is Back!
by Eugene Hobart
(interspersed with May's timeless wit and wisdom)

Mrs. Black is Back was performed
on this very stage on August 15, 1904

Program for *May Irwin Is Back!* (1999). Courtesy of the author.

EPILOGUE

Me and May

I did not find any of the songs offensive. The singer explained the omission of the *N* word and I think the use of that word would have been offensive, but it probably wasn't seen that way in the 1890s. The "Bully Song" was just cute, silly, and funny.

—White audience member, *May Irwin Is Back!* Clayton Opera House, Clayton, New York, 1999, oral comment

It was very difficult for me to listen to May Irwin's "Bully Song." Whether or not the n-word was used, the idea that blacks randomly kill each other with razors and we're supposed to find that amusing is repulsive. However, in this case Dr. Ammen was trying to teach us something about the past and for that I am grateful.

—African American audience member, *Reconstruction to Ragtime,* Saint Mary-of-the-Woods College, Indiana, 2008, written comment

What is it like to perform May Irwin's material today—particularly her racist songs—and how do audiences react to it? I cannot pretend to be an entertainer of May's caliber. Nor, though I have performed May's material on numerous occasions, have I conducted a controlled quantitative analysis of audience response to her racist songs. When audiences viewed my performances, they were seeing a professional educator and actress present a scripted text carefully designed both to educate and to entertain. Nevertheless, the variety of responses I have received during performance and through discussions and audience surveys can offer valuable insights into Irwin's success onstage and on contemporary understanding of this historically important body of popular entertainment that is rarely offered today.

Objectives

My objectives in continuing to perform May Irwin's material as I researched her life and work are straightforward: to enhance my understanding of her as a performer, to share her life and works with new audiences, to see if contemporary audiences find the material funny, and to see how audiences react to and interpret the racist elements in her work. Of course, interpreting my findings is a complex undertaking requiring in-depth application of performance and reception theory. Such analysis goes far beyond the scope of this book.[1] But I would like to share a few ideas that can stimulate further research for performers of this type of historical material.

For many years now, my approach to theater performance has combined, albeit in an elemental manner, the areas that Marco de Marinas defines as essential in understanding the performance event: "the experience-comprehension of the theatre artist—in particular, the actor . . . the experience-comprehension of the common spectator . . . and the experience-comprehension of the theatrologist."[2] (*Theatrology* has become a broad, inclusive term, relating to performance studies, semiology, sociology, and, I believe, the kitchen sink as well.)

In performing Irwin's material, I am dealing with popular material with little literary value in the conventional sense, and I am arranging pieces that mix biographical material with performance play excerpts. Bearing this in mind, I can offer clues to the effects of Irwin's material on the contemporary audience.

Performances

I have chosen two performances to consider because of the differences in audiences and their reactions. I introduced these performances in my first chapter, but I will briefly review them here.

In 1999 I received a grant from the New York State Council on the Arts Decentralization Program to perform at the Clayton Opera House where May herself had performed. I adapted a program titled *May Irwin Is Back!* that included scenes and songs from her show *Mrs. Black Is Black*. The program was well advertised in local newspapers and featured side by side with articles on May Irwin's life and her importance to the community. This performance took place on the evenings of July 9 and 10, 1999, and required a modest admission price. The production was arranged with the head of the Thousand Islands Museum, at that time housed within the old Clayton Opera House.

The Opera House held four hundred when it was built in 1904, but by 1999 the seats had been removed and much of the space filled with exhibits. The proscenium stage was high, small, and raked and fairly close to the audience, who sat on folding chairs. I performed with two fellow actors.

We performed nine scenes from *Mrs. Black Is Back,* essentially the story of a woman who lies to her husband about her age; she is thirty-six but has told him that she is twenty-nine. Her lie is almost discovered when her son, Jack, arrives and turns out to be quite a bit older than the "little Jack" she has described to her new husband. There are many scenes of disguise and mistaken identity, and we interspersed them with commentary explaining the scenes and sometimes connecting them to our own lives and the present. Pieces of note for this performance included the automobile monologue (see chapter 2) and a scene in which Mrs. Black tries to get her son's simple servant (who is white) to memorize a cover-up story so she does not have to reveal her true age to her husband. The servant keeps repeating the story back to Mrs. Black in a highly contorted and mangled form. I also recited "A Painful Memory!," the piece about a woman's growing girth included in chapter 2, which Irwin often recited in her shows. Additionally, we included material explaining the racist nature of Irwin's coon shouting, letting the audience know when and where I would be replacing the *N* word that was in the original numbers. I sang "The Frog Song" and "The Bully."

The other performance I am discussing here occurred several years later. In the spring of 2008, I undertook what was certainly my most ambitious project with May Irwin's material. Associate professor of music John McIntyre and I received a grant from Arts Indiana and the Indiana Arts Commission to present a two-hour panel and a one-hour performance at Saint Mary-of-the-Woods College. The program was titled *Images of African Americans in the Arts: Reconstruction to Ragtime.* For this production, I enlisted the talents of a professional actress from Los Angeles, Anita Dashiell-Sparks. Anita, an African American, was in her early thirties and had been a student of mine at the University of Maryland. She had broad experience on television and stage (including Broadway credits) and a master's of fine arts from New York University. I thought it would be interesting and educational to have her portray May Irwin imitator Belle Davis. Professional accompanist Ronald Maurey played piano for this production.

I teamed up with the local chapter of the National Association for the Advancement of Colored People to help spread the word to the African American community; we also had extensive newspaper and radio coverage, and posters and postcards were widely distributed around town. We presented this event on the stage of Cecilian Auditorium at the SMWC campus. Built in 1913, it is a beautiful theater with a balcony, and it seats about four hundred people. The stage has a proscenium with a permanent thrust in front of the arch to push action closer to the audience. The floor of the house is raked. I filled the large foyer with displays, including information on coon shouting as a racist phenomenon; a labeled, framed piece called "The Troubling Art of the Coon-Song"; song sheet covers; photographs of May Irwin and Belle Davis; and a comparison of a print of the lyrical "Banjo Lesson" by Henry Ossawa Tanner with prints of the racist Currier and Ives series depicting banjo players and other African American stereotypes. (I discussed this iconography in chapters 3 and 4.) Audience members were also able to view a video from the Jim Crow Museum of Racist History.[3]

After an afternoon panel, we held a performance in the evening. In this performance, I was joined by some of my young students at SMWC as well as a colleague I had performed with previously in Clayton. We began with great gusto, moving from the scripted introduction that we had used previously to scenes from *Mrs. Black Is Back,* from my recitation of "A Painful Memory!" to a dramatization of the story that May told about her maid Octavia (included in chapter 5). Because Anita could not be present during the performance, she appeared on film. At one point, she appeared as herself—stopping the action and admonishing me for not dealing with the racism of Irwin's coon shouting. After I sang my "whitewashed" version of "The Frog Song," Anita appeared again on film as Belle Davis. We interspersed this with live performance of "The Bully," segueing into Irwin's own voice on her recording of this number. In this case, we did not censor the *N* word.

Adaptations/Frames

Willfried Passow has divided the interaction in theatrical performance into five sections: the interaction within the fictional world presented onstage, the interaction between the audience and that fictional world, the interaction between actors onstage, the interaction between the audience and the actors, and the interaction between members of the audience.[4] Because my adaptations of May's material are connected to my extensive background in Readers Theatre, there is little sense of Passow's fictional world. That is, actors carry scripts for the narration, and the audience is quite aware of the performers as *actors* who switch back and forth into a number of roles: "narrator" characters who introduce material about Irwin; critics and writers from the time period who comment on Irwin; "lecturers" who discuss historical matters; a variety of characters from Irwin's plays; actors themselves who share stories and jokes with the audience and speak to each other, using their actual names; May Irwin as herself; May Irwin impersonating a character; and other actors (primarily Belle Davis), whether performing in roles or speaking as themselves.

The desired effect is a collage of material "washing" over the audience to give the feel of performances and personae. The audience is seldom drawn into an entirely fictional world. Additionally, the separation between the audience and the actors is completely porous. The actor is encouraged to interact with the audience, just as Irwin encouraged her audience to interact with her. (The work Irwin did with Augustin Daly was of a different sort—he enforced the fourth wall, as I noted in chapter 1. However, I did not use any of this material in my adaptations.)

Although most of my scripts and excerpts were performed live, there were also instances of recorded accompaniment: recorded piano accompaniment for songs in Clayton, New York; the use of film (for Anita Dashiell-Sparks as she portrayed Belle Davis); and the actual recorded voice of May singing. These additions added to the complexity of the piece, creating frames within frames.

Success with Audiences

Two solo performances of nonsong material stood out as the most successful with the audiences. Anita's performance as Belle Davis on film was highly effective. The audience first saw her as herself and then, shortly afterward, completely transformed into a careful, controlled late-nineteenth-century black performer. Her mannerisms and voice were completely different as Belle than as herself, and the distance of the film media paradoxically added to her believability for contemporary audiences. Audible expressions of support came from the audience. African American audience members reacted more audibly to her "presence" than to the presence of the live actors onstage. They were drawn into her fictive world.

Also successful was my performance of "A Painful Memory!" I had complete command of this piece, having performed it many times in other venues. Additionally, I could feel myself more clearly inhabit the "persona" of this woman whose "hooks and eyes" would never meet again! I knew how to shape the material, and I knew that the root of its humor was the contrast between the tragic demeanor of the performer and the mundane cause of her anguish. Further, this is material well suited to my particular tendencies as a performer: I am naturally overly expressive, loud, and prone to caricature.

Audiences in Clayton and at SMWC each responded equally well to the monologue about the automobile. Not only are the nonsense words great fun, but older audience members compared this monologue to information they tried to understand about computers. The newness of the automobile and its strangeness in 1904 corresponded directly to problems many of us experience in the technological age. Because the Clayton performances included material overtly suggesting a connection between the past and the present, those audiences were more apt to laugh in self-recognition.

Throughout the performances, I developed a strong appreciation of how May used pauses effectively in her work. In the automobile monologue, pausing before declaring that the car had "barked" increased the audience's laughter. The recitation of "A Painful Memory!" wove pauses with up-tempo sections, as well as using a wide variety of vocal inflections and pitches. But the scene in which the use of well-planned pauses bore the most fruit was between Larry and Mrs. Black in *Mrs. Black Is Back*. When Larry mispronounced "Massachusetts" a number of times, and I paused right before the last time—looking ever so thoughtful, then giving up before saying, "That's right"—the laughter was robust. Then I allowed myself an exceptionally long pause, actually opening my mouth a few times with nothing coming out, before I responded to his long, garbled repetition of the information I wanted him to remember with "That'll do." The laughter was significantly rewarding. I was learning precisely how important delivery was in enhancing Irwin's rather thin performance material.

Finally, the attention I gave to physical work paid off in eliciting response. This was especially true when I used young college students in my performance. Because I was surrounded by actors who were so much more physically adept than myself, I could use their abilities to stylize the material to its maximum potential. There was also a marked contrast between their athleticism and my highly energetic but somewhat lopsided dancing that seemed to add to the hilarity.

It is important to add here that the rehearsal for these two pieces differed markedly. For the Clayton audience, I spent a lot of time structuring the piece and much less time rehearsing with my two colleagues. (Much of this had to do with distance and time.) So the performance became an entertaining "lecture" interspersed with excellent solo pieces but also scene work that lacked polish.

By the time I was working on *Reconstruction to Ragtime* in 2008, I understood the material much better and presented a well-rehearsed, layered presentation that I had been able to direct. Even though Anita was not present, we had a long time to work with her filmed appearances. Her advanced skills and the addition of a professional pianist added to the production.

Interpretive Communities

When Stanley Fish uses the term *interpretive communities,* he is referring to communities of readers who share strategies of how a text is written.[5] Their ideas of the possibilities of a text affect how they read it—or, in the case of a theater event, how they read the action onstage. These communities are unstable and can change according to culture, time period, and place. I am simplifying his ideas, but the differences in the groups for whom I performed and the context of those performances had a noticeable effect on responses.

The Clayton audience was heavily populated with individuals who shared a prior knowledge of May Irwin and viewed her as a community treasure—as their own "May." We performed in a theater in which she herself had performed, and we used excerpts of her own descriptions of the beautiful Thousand Islands area. These residents took great pride in their environment and in laying claim to one of the most beloved performers of the late nineteenth and early twentieth centuries. I don't think this audience was apt to judge critically our performance skills, as their primary reason for attending was to celebrate May Irwin. Their predisposition made it difficult for them to even consider the material of some of these songs as racist.

In contrast, the audience for *Reconstruction to Ragtime* was easily the most complex of all the audiences for whom I have performed this material. Most of the audience members seemed to have absorbed the background information we had presented concerning the racist history of the time period. During the evening performance, the African American audience mostly sat apart from the white and Asian audience members—and farther away from the stage. Therefore, it seemed as if there were two separate audiences. The entire audience felt a bit tense at the outset, but the comic material at the beginning of the piece eased them into laughter. The change occurred when Anita appeared on film as herself. The attention and response to her were heightened, particularly among the African American members of the audience. Audible commentary accompanied her accusations of my "whitewashing" and, later, her performance as Belle Davis. The thick silence of both sections of the audience during the scene with Octavia and the "Bully Song" did not dissipate until the final monologues that connected Belle and May to each other. The discussions afterward—both the formal one in the theater and the informal one that followed during the reception in the lobby—were absolutely vital in bringing the groups together and in finishing the event. As the lights came up and I encouraged everyone to come closer for a discussion, the two groups somehow blended into one, with African American spectators filling empty seats between white spectators.

Here I would like to touch on the demographics of our audiences. I did not make a formal tabulation of the Clayton audiences, but they were almost entirely Caucasian and mostly middle-aged or older couples. I saw one African American middle-aged couple and one Asian middle-aged couple during the two evenings we performed. Of course, that is simply my informal "eyeballing" of the audiences.

For the performance in 2008 at SMWC, I formally surveyed the audience. Out of a sample of fifty returned surveys, I derived the following information:

Audience makeup
- Students: 6
- Faculty: 14
- Community members: 30

Ages
- 18–25: 6
- 26–36: 10
- 37–50: 12
- 51–64: 14
- 64 and older: 8

Gender
- Female: 36
- Male: 14

Ethnicity
- Caucasian: 33
- African American: 11
- Asian: 3
- Biracial: 2
- Native American: 1

Because the last section of the performance evoked a lot of response, I would like to quote it here, along with some of the audience reactions:

> Near the end of the production, four performers—two young and two older—began to sing "The Bully" onstage with piano and tuba accompaniment, using the *N* word. As we sang and moved, the lights faded with the music, and we froze, our voices fading into a recording of May Irwin singing "The Bully." As she finished, and the lights went down, a spot appeared on a young actress downstage as May Irwin and the screen with Anita as Belle Davis came up.
>
> **MAY:** My name was Georgina Ada Campbell and I was born in Canada in 1862. My sister and I helped support the family by touring on the vaudeville circuit, and I had to drop out of school. The manager of that tour renamed me May Irwin. I almost became a legitimate professional actor with Augustin Daly's troupe, but I needed to make more money—my husband was dying of tuberculosis, and I had two small children to feed. I had to return to vaudeville

and make my own way. I was strong; I endured hardships—one of my sons died young, leaving his wife and two small sons in my care. My sister, Flo, stole some of my comic material, and we didn't speak for ten years. I learned that the natural trend of life is tragic, not comic; all the things which tend to dispel care and drive away sorrow are to our natures like the precious rays of the sun in the spring to the flowers. They charm out to the surface all of our more lovable and more beautiful qualities, and make us more worthy in the eyes of mankind.

BELLE: I was born in New Orleans—to a white father and a black mother. I was a recording pioneer and had an immensely popular song and dance group: "Belle Davis and her Pickaninnies." I never exploited my little orphan boys—I took great care of them. There was Irving "Sneeze" and little Sonny Jones. In those years, before I took my boys to Europe, booking agents in America told me I needed blackface. That's right, they wanted me to "darken down." You see, I was always so light-skinned, and they wanted to be sure I didn't try to "pass."

May Irwin may have been the original "coon shouter," but I was known as the undisputed queen of ragtime music. I had a voice that felt just as at home in jazz as in light opera. And—oh, yes—I could do a great impersonation of May Irwin. I was a charming mulatto pretending to be a white woman who was pretending to be a black man—as conceived by white men in blackface.

How would I have felt about May Irwin if we had met face-to-face? Would we have laughed at each other, shaken hands, hugged? Could we have met as equals, or would she simply have studied me as I studied her—as if we both were exotic parodies of real women?

Well, I didn't have the opportunity to meet Miss Irwin. She may have thrived in America, starring in her own vehicles, managed by her second husband. But I couldn't rise above my environment. So, I went to Europe, where I was billed as a "regular song and dance artist" and an "elegant representative of the Creole race." In Europe, I was known as La Belle Dame—the newspapers noted that the name was a perfect fit. I became a choreographer in Paris, and somewhere along the Seine my story ended. It was a full life and a beautiful one, but fraught with obstacles and peril.

MAY: (first line with Belle) It was a full life and a beautiful one, but fraught with obstacles and peril. It did not take me long to find out that life was not a continuous performance of the realization of one's fondest dreams, but rather one of their continuous shattering and one that gained sunlight and happiness in this world by giving it to others.

(From the recorded "Bully" number fading out into the comparison of May Irwin and Belle Davis, the audience was silent—not a stony silence, but a hushed, attentive silence. There was a pause and then much applause. Many audience members stood at the end and had tears in their eyes).

Directly after the performance, I gathered the roughly half of the audience that remained into the front few rows. The discussion began in the theater and then continued informally in the foyer, where we held a reception. The audience spoke of their impressions of the entire day. Many white audience members expressed the shame they felt after seeing the film from the Jim Crow Museum. African American members, especially older ones, told a few stories of being called "niggers" or "coons" and how painful it was. (I am now using the word *nigger* instead of *the "N" word* to emphasize bluntly how thoughtlessly it was used in May Irwin's day.) All audience members expressed how strange and chilling it felt to listen to the ragtime music and enjoy it so much—and then hear the word *nigger* delivered with such carelessness. There were many comments on the strength of the acting and portrayals of May Irwin and Belle Davis as themselves—especially their interchange at the end. They noted that they felt sad somehow for both women in that they could never know their common "sisterhood." Most audience members found the earlier scene between Octavia and May to be unfunny and offensive. (I discussed this piece in chapter 4.)

Most respondents said that the reason they attended was to learn more about the history of racism. A few African Americans said they came because they felt there needed to be a strong African American presence at any event discussing African American history. A few students needed class credit, and others came to support the artists involved. Interestingly, no one felt that the material should *not* be performed, but all noted that it needed to be placed in context and dealt with sensitively. Anger was expressed, by all ethnic groups, that this material was usually whitewashed, sometimes out of embarrassment, but ultimately working against racial tolerance. Whites tended to express shame and embarrassment. African Americans and audience members of other ethnicities tended to express sadness and pain, especially in the sense that the material brought up memories of personal past injustices experienced. Many respondents expressed mixed feelings because of their attraction to the music and also to the persona of May Irwin. Most commented favorably on the skills of the performers.

Racist Humor: Who Is Laughing?

Connected to audience response is the difficulty in perceptions of laughter—who laughs and why? This is especially true in the case of racist material. In the scene between Larry and Mrs. Black, Larry is funny precisely because he is so stupid and unable to understand or retain information. In the scene between Octavia and May, Octavia is supposed to be funny because she is trying to put black "culture" (that is, a white racist version of that culture) on an equal footing with white culture. Additionally, she is not smart enough to discern the real reason coon songs are offensive. This latter reason for humor would not be apparent to most audience members of Irwin's time because they did not see the offensiveness of the songs. (As I noted in chapter 4, many black critics of the coon song have found the idea that blacks did not understand the racism as offensive as the racism itself.) Nor are *either* of these supposed reasons for comedy appealing in any way to contemporary audiences. In fact, this material elicited the chilliest reception of any material, even "The Bully Song." Besides the overt racism in the scene, the stupidity of Octavia (including the over-the-top dialect), or any foolishness exhibited by a black character from this period, is offensive simply because it is one of the very few characteristics shown in black roles at the time and for many decades later. Larry is funny because all young white male characters are *not* like him. A later character, Stepin Fetchit, was a brilliant performer and very funny. But his foolishness was presented as a descriptor for all blacks. Only in the past few decades, with plays such as George Wolfe's *The Colored Museum* (first produced in 1986) and, more recently, brilliant comics like Key and Peele, have we seen enough variety in African American characters so that we can laugh *with* some and *at* some, including the foolish ones. (But white audiences are more apt to feel uncomfortable in laughing, lest they be mistaken for racists.)

This brings me to the question of why we laugh at material. Some African Americans in *all* audiences I have performed for laughed at "The Bully Song" and then stifled their laughter. (The white audiences in Clayton laughed wholeheartedly and unself-consciously at "The Bully Song" and "The Frog Song.") No whites laughed at "The Bully Song" in *Reconstruction to Ragtime.* When contemporary audience members laugh at "The Bully Song," usually they either are amused at the jaunty sound of the song and not paying attention to the words or laugh from embarrassment and from the ludicrous contrast between the music and the words. (Whites tend *not* to laugh if significant numbers of African Americans are in the audience and everyone understands the true content of the song.) In today's world, only overtly racist audiences would actually find the song funny because it accords with their image of a black man. (Reportedly, Dave Chappelle left his popular television show because he was afraid some audience members were laughing at his material for racist reasons—and not because of its satirical content.) Of course, there is a difference between material that *seems* to portray a racist attitude but is meant to function as satire and Irwin's material. Her material is not satirical (or ironic) on any conscious level. Instead, it is steeped in the racism of Jim Crow America and the time period in which she lived.[6]

The insidious nature of the coon song is that the music is so catchy that it is enjoyable to perform, notwithstanding its content. Whenever I perform "The Bully Song," I cannot get the chorus out of my head for a long time and find myself humming it everywhere. Additionally, I confess that I often find coon songs funny because they are so racist and ridiculous beyond measure. In that respect, these pieces seem almost to be satirical when they are being performed. For this reason, I almost laughed in Clayton when I caught the eyes of the other performers as I was singing "The Bully Song." The enormous absurdity of what I was doing hit me forcefully in that moment. In contrast, onstage, during *Reconstruction to Ragtime,* I felt a cold chill run up my spine when I had to use the word *nigger.* As May's voice took over, with her completely unabashed use of the word, she taught me more than she was ever capable of understanding. So much of Irwin's life is important to remember, but unwrapping the pleasant musical packaging of her coon songs gives us all a deeper understanding of our troubled past and its effects today.

Chronology

This is an abbreviated chronology taken from my more detailed history and performance daybook. Biographical information and performance history are derived from many sources used throughout this book, including Robinson Locke Scrapbooks, vols. 297–99, from the New York Library of Performing Arts; Special Collections from Hawn Memorial Library and the Thousand Islands Museum, both in Clayton, New York; articles and reviews from the *New York Times* and the *Watertown Daily Times*; the Jack Brown Scrapbook from Ontario, Canada; Whitby Archives in Whitby, Ontario, Canada; George Odell's *Annals of the New York Stage,* vols. 12–15; and material from the Library of Congress in Washington, D.C.

There are also online sources, but many have errors. A good source for dates and times of May's work on Broadway is IBDB, the Internet Broadway Database.

1862 On June 27, May Irwin is born as Georgina May Campbell in Whitby, Ontario, Canada. She is the youngest child of Robert Campbell and Jane Draper Campbell. She has four older siblings:

Adeline Flora (b. 1859)
Albert (b. 1856)
Frank (b. 1854)
Chester (b. 1853)

1874 Robert Campbell dies.

1875 The Campbell sons secure positions as clerks, but Mrs. Campbell decides to take her two daughters to America to try their luck onstage. Adeline and Georgina have their first vaudeville debut under Daniel Shelby in Buffalo and Rochester, New York, where he renames them Flo and May Irwin.

1876 The Irwin sisters tour the Midwest in vaudeville.

1877 After their first appearance in New York City (NYC) at the London, Tony Pastor sees the girls in Detroit, and they debut at Pastor's Old Met in NYC on September 13.

1878 May marries Frederick Keller on tour in Saint Louis. Flo marries John Morris. Both sisters return to perform in skits together and separately in NYC with Tony Pastor.

1879 The Irwin sisters continue in Tony Pastor's Company in NYC.

1880 May gives birth to her first son, Walter, on May 25.

1881 May gives birth to her second son, Harry, on August 28 and continues her work with Tony Pastor's Company, appearing in travesties such as *The Pie-Rats of Penn-Yan* with Lillian Russell.

1883 May leaves Tony Pastor's to work with Augustin Daly. Her first appearance is in *Dollars and Sense.*

1884–86 May continues to work with Daly's Company in servant roles for which she receives much praise, both in America and during two tours of Europe. Noted roles include Susan in *A Night Off* and Betsy in *Nancy and Co.* Her husband, Frederick Keller, dies of tuberculosis in 1886.

1887–90 May leaves Daly to return to vaudeville and work with Flo in *City Directory, Boys and Girls,* and similar pieces on tour and in NYC. Flo has divorced John Morris and marries Senator Thomas F. Grady in 1887.

1891 May travels to the Thousand Islands and makes her first land purchase there. She squelches rumors of her marriage to actor Hugo Tolland.

1892 May appears in *The Poets and the Puppets,* by Charles Brookfield (a burlesque of Oscar Wilde's *Lady Windemere's Fan*), in which she sings "After the Ball."

1893–94 May portrays Irene Dolan in J. J. McNally's *A Straight Tip* under the management of Rich and Harris and sings "Mamie, Come Kiss Your Honey Boy."

1895 May opens as Beatrice Byke in *The Widow Jones,* by McNally. She forms her own company and retains Rich and Harris for managers. She makes a hit with her song "The Bully."

1896 May appears in Vitascope, re-creating the kiss from *The Widow Jones,* with fellow actor John C. Rice. Late in the year, she opens as Dottie Dimple in *Courted into Court,* by McNally, singing "The Bully" and "A Hot Time in the Old Town."

1897–99 May continues in *The Widow Jones* and *Courted into Court* and also appears as the Countess de Cagiac in *The Swell Miss Fitzwell,* by Henry du Souchet; Kate Kip in *Kate Kip, Buyer;* and Alice in *Sister Mary,* the latter two by Glen McDonough. She adds several new "coon" songs to her repertoire, including "When You Ain't Got No Money, Then You Needn't Come Around" and "The Frog Song." Flo Irwin divorces Senator Grady after being involved in a scandal with a married actor.

1900–1902 May opens in *The Belle of Bridgeport,* by McDonough, and *Madge Smith, Attorney,* by Ramsay Morris, and begins another run of *The Widow Jones.* In 1902 she collapses from overwork and goes to Europe to recover; she does not return to the stage until 1904.

1904 May publishes *May Irwin's Home Cooking.*

1904–7 May begins a long run as Mrs. Black in *Mrs. Black Is Back,* by George Hobart. Irwin's new manager is Kurt Eisfeldt. In 1905 she performs as Mrs. Black for President Roosevelt. She also opens in *Mrs. Wilson, That's All,* by Hobart. (The title changes to *Mrs. Wilson-Andrews* during the run, and *Mrs. Peckham's Carouse,* by Otis Skinner, is added as a curtain raiser.) New songs include "Don't Argify" and "'Tain't No Sense in Lovin' Dat Way."

1907 May marries Kurt Eisfeldt on May 26 in Clayton.

1908–9 May records the following songs for Victor: "Moses Andrew Jackson, Goodbye," "The Bully," "When You Ain't Got No Money, Then You Needn't Come Around," "Don't Argify," "Ma-tri-mo-ny" and "May Irwin's Frog Song." In 1908 "Don't Argify" is combined with "You Splash Me and I'll

Splash You" (sung by Alice Lloyd), and in 1909 "The Bully" and "When You Ain't Got No Money, Then You Needn't Come Around" are combined (in double-sided recordings).

1907–13 May tours in vaudeville and appears in other productions despite frequent "retirements" to the Thousand Islands and intermittent illnesses. In 1910 "Ma-tri-mo-ny" and "Moses" are dropped by Victor. In 1911 Irwin's son Walter marries Ethel Thompson. In 1913 "The Frog Song" is combined with "I'm Wise" (sung by Clarice Vance) by Victor. Also in 1913, Irwin's son Harry marries Mae McCosker.

1914 Irwin's first grandchild, John Irwin, is born to Walter and Ethel in Detroit. May closes as Gloria Grey in *Widow by Proxy,* by Catherine Cushing, a play she has been appearing in off and on since 1912. Film of *Mrs. Black Is Back* is released by Paramount. (No copies survive today.)

1915 May opens as Matilda in *33 Washington Square,* by Scott LeRoy. She performs for President Wilson on September 24. Her beloved uncle Frank dies.

1916 May tours in *33 Washington Square.*

1917 May and Kurt buy land in Clayton and name the farm Rainbow's End. Irwin Island is put up for sale.

1918 Irwin appears in the industrial film *Hearts and Jerseys* for dairy-cow breeders.

1919 Irwin's second grandchild, William Irwin, is born to Walter and Ethel. All of May Irwin's remaining songs on the Victor label are discontinued except for "The Frog Song," which remains in the catalog until 1923.

1922 On May 17, after a brief illness, Irwin's son Walter dies in Detroit.

1927 Irwin and her husband, Kurt, sell their Irwin Island home and travel around the world.

1930 On December 21, Irwin's sister, Flo, dies in Los Angeles.

1931 Irwin and Kurt travel to South America.

1933 Harry's wife, Mae, dies. They have no children.

1935 On May 19, May Irwin sings her "Frog Song" to a crowd of ten thousand in Central Park in celebration of the one hundredth anniversary of Mark Twain's birthday.

1938 On October 22, May Irwin dies in NYC of bronchial pneumonia.

1940 On March 31, Kurt Eisfeldt dies after a long illness in Clayton. On July 30, Harry marries Nellie Carton, May's former secretary.

1943 May's grandson William Irwin dies unexpectedly in his sleep while on duty aboard a ship near Hawaii in World War II.

1947 On May 23, Harry Irwin dies in Clayton. He has no children.

1991 May's second grandson dies, leaving two sons, Scott and Todd, with families.

Notes

Introduction

1. Almost every source available lists May Irwin's birth as 1862. However, although Canada did not have an official national census in 1861, the 1871 census indicates May Irwin's birth year as "abt. 1861." (There is an unofficial census of the Ontario area for 1861—and May is not listed as born on that census.) 1871 Census of Canada, s.v., "Georgina Campbell," Whitby, Ontario, accessed through Ancestry.com.

2. The first quotation is from Adolphe Kauber, "A Talk with the High Priestess of Jollity," *New York Times,* November 13, 1904, pt. 4, second magazine section, 2. Irwin is referred to as a "female Falstaff" in Lewis C. Strang, *Famous Actresses of the Day in America,* 175–76; in John Corbin, review of *Mrs. Black Is Back*, *New York Times,* November 13, 1904, 7; and in Norman Hapgood, *The Stage in America,* 99. The third quotation is from Robert Grau, quoted in Anthony Slide, *The Vaudevillians,* 77. The final quotation is from George Odell, *Annals of the New York Stage,* 12:423.

3. *Last Night's Theatres,* review of *Kate Kip, Buyer, Philadelphia Enquirer,* October 11, 1898, Special Collections, Hawn Memorial Library. This collection was simply housed in a few boxes and not organized or with complete information on all materials.

4. Undated review of *Courted into Court,* Special Collections, Hawn Memorial Library; Clayton Hamilton, "Widow by Proxy," *Everybody's,* May 1913, 688.

5. Unidentified clipping, Special Collections, Hawn Memorial Library.

6. Gerald Lenton-Young, "Variety Theatre," in *Early Stages: Theatre in Ontario, 1800–1914,* edited by Ann Saddlemeyer, 207. See also Brian Winter, *Chronicles of a Country Town: Whitby Past and Present.*

7. Slide, *The Vaudevillians,* 72.

8. Sharon Ammen, "Transforming George Moore: Simone Benmussa's Adaptive Art in *The Singular Life of Albert Nobbs,*" *Text and Performance Quarterly* (October

1991): 306–12; Sharon Ammen, "Feminist Vision and Audience Response: Tracing the Absent Utopia in Caryl Churchill's *Top Girls,*" *Utopian Studies* 7 (1996): 86–102.

9. Basic biographical information is available in many sources (although there are errors in some entries). The following examples have good, concise information: Daniel Blum, *Great Stars of the American Stage,* 46; Gerald Bordman, *The Concise Oxford Companion to American Theatre* (Oxford: Oxford University Press, 1987), 237–38; Gale Research, *Who Was Who in the Theatre, 1912–1976,* compiled from *Who's Who in the Theatre* (Detroit: Book Tower, 1978), 3:1273–74; *Notable American Women* (Cambridge, Mass.: Harvard University Press, 1971), 2:206–7; Alice M. Robinson, Vera Mowry Roberts, and Milly S. Barranger, eds., *Notable Women in American Theatre,* 457–59; Slide, *The Vaudevillians,* 77; Garff B. Wilson, *A History of American Acting,* 195–96; William C. Young, *Famous Actors and Actresses of the American Stage,* 563–66.

10. See Jane Robertson Westerfield, "An Investigation of Lifestyles and Performances of Three Singer-Comediennes of American Vaudeville: Eva Tanguay, Nora Bayes and Sophie Tucker."

11. "May Irwin's Tale of Woe," *New York Sun,* February 4, 1900, Robinson Locke Scrapbook, vol. 298. Volumes 297–99 of the Locke Scrapbooks contain clippings of articles and reviews of May Irwin's material. Volume 43 has information on Belle Davis. I was able to look through these scrapbooks by hand and even copy pages during my early visits. Page numbers and details were often missing, but all quotes are taken verbatim from these clippings, and, when possible, I have acquired further information for citation. Any errors are my responsibility only. These notebooks are no longer available to researchers except in microfilm—and on site—because of their condition. See bibliography in this book for microfilm information.

12. May Irwin, "My Views on That Ever-Interesting Topic—Woman," 1057–58.

13. Ellen Terry quoted in Donald Mullin, *Victorian Actors and Actresses in Review,* 267; "Funny May Irwin in *Sister Mary,*" unidentified review, Special Collections, Hawn Memorial Library; E. F. Chase, "Plays and Players," *Boston Journal,* September 7, 1896, Special Collections, Hawn Memorial Library; Douglas Gilbert, *American Vaudeville: Its Life and Times,* 95.

14. Alan Brinkley, *The Unfinished Nation,* A37.

15. Lloyd Morris, *Incredible New York,* 208.

16. Thomas J. Schlereth, *Victorian America: Transformations in Everyday Life, 1876–1915,* 20–27.

17. Bernard Grun, *The Timetables of History,* 16.

18. Olive Logan, *Apropos of Women and Theatre,* 15.

19. Benjamin McArthur, *Actors and American Culture,* 29.

20. Albert Auster, *Actresses and Suffragists: Women in the American Theatre, 1880–1920,* 4.

21. McArthur, *Actors and American Culture,* 126–27.

22. Auster, *Actresses and Suffragists,* 31.

23. Susan A. Glenn, *Female Spectacle: The Theatrical Roots of Modern Feminism,* 45.

24. For a well-done portrait of Friganza, see Peach Pittenger, "Women in American Popular Entertainment: Creating a Niche in the Vaudevillian Era, 1890s to 1930s."

25. Armond Fields, *Women Vaudeville Stars: Eighty Biographical Profiles,* 128.

26. Information from Pittenger, "Women in American Popular Entertainment"; Fields, *Women Vaudeville Stars;* and M. Alison Kibler, *Rank Ladies: Gender and Cultural Hierarchy in American Vaudeville.*

27. For a complete review of Eva Tanguay's eventful life, see Andrew L. Erdman, *Queen of Vaudeville: The Story of Eva Tanguay.*

29. Pittenger, "Women in American Popular Entertainment," 192.

29. Armond Fields, *Sophie Tucker, First Lady of Show Business.*

30. See Betty Lee, *Marie Dressler, the Unlikeliest Star;* Matthew Kennedy, *Marie Dressler: A Biography with a Listing of Major Stage Performances, a Filmography and Discography;* and Victoria Sturtevant, *A Great Big Girl Like Me: The Films of Marie Dressler.*

31. Albert F. McLean Jr., *American Vaudeville as Ritual,* 176; William Cahn, *The Laugh Makers,* 48.

32. *May Irwin's Home Cooking.*

33. "May Irwin Interviewed," *Pittsburgh Post,* November 25, 1897.

34. Fields, *Women Vaudeville Stars,* 147–51.

35. Kibler, *Rank Ladies,* 130. Kibler's chapter on female coon shouters does include the following sentence: "Unlike many other women who used blackface, Irwin constructed her racial images primarily through the dialect and lyrics" (126). The unfortunate omission of a comma after "women" may be an editing error; even so, this brief note in a chapter titled "The Corking Girls" is likely to be missed by most readers. Importantly, in her recent publication, *Censoring Racial Ridicule,* an excellent study of the controversy over Irish, Jewish, and African depictions during the period of 1890–1930, Kibler notes that May Irwin did not use blackface. Unfortunately, she mistakenly describes Irwin as an "Irish American singer." M. Alison Kibler, *Censoring Racial Ridicule: Irish, Jewish, and African American Struggles over Race and Representation, 1890–1930* (Chapel Hill: University of North Carolina Press, 2015), 23.

36. Pamela A. Brown Lavitt, "First of the Red Hot Mamas: 'Coon Shouting' and the Jewish Ziegfeld Girl," 259.

37. *Three Vaudeville Women: May Irwin, Marie Dressler, and Eva Tanguay.*

38. Eugene McNamara, "The May Irwin–John C. Rice Kiss," *Malahat Review* 36 (1975): 132.

Chapter 1. Never Were There Such Devoted Sisters

1. David Nasaw, *Going Out: The Rise and Fall of Public Amusements* (New York: Harper-Collins, 1993), 14.

2. An even older term, *Vau de Vivre* can be traced to the Valley of Vire in Normandy, France, and fifteenth-century poet Olivier Basselin.

3. Parker Zellers, *Tony Pastor, Dean of the Vaudeville Stage,* 12.

4. For a lucid discussion of early experiments in Vitascope and the use of Vitascope in vaudeville, see Nasaw, *Going Out,* 135–53. For later uses of motion pictures in vaudeville, see ibid., 186–204.

5. In "Vaudeville: A Short History of This Popular Character of Amusement," *Midway* 1 (October 1905): 27, quoted in Robert M. Lewis, ed., *From Traveling Show to Vaudeville: Theatrical Spectacle in America, 1830–1910,* 320.

6. Gillian M. Rodger, *Champagne Charlie and Pretty Jemima: Variety Theater in the Nineteenth Century,* 5.

7. Ibid., 156.

8. Sophie Tucker, *Some of These Days,* quoted in Zellers, *Tony Pastor,* 42.

9. Brinkley, *The Unfinished Nation,* 422.

10. Rosemarie K. Bank, *Theatre Culture in America, 1825–1860,* 114; Richard Butsch, "Bowery B'hoys and Matinee Ladies: The Re-gendering of Nineteenth Century American Theater Audiences," 393.

11. Rodger, *Champagne Charlie and Pretty Jemima,* 149.

12. The law was flouted or circumvented off and on for years. Patrons could certainly drink nearby before the show or between acts. In 1899, when the Victoria Theatre opened to the public, "Smoking and drinking were permitted in the promenade area and alcoholic beverages were served by waiters." Frank Wertheim, *Vaudeville Wars: How the Keith-Albee and Orpheum Circuits Controlled the Big-Time and Its Performers,* 131.

13. For a complete discussion of the Anti-Concert Saloon Bill and its many repercussions, see Gillian M. Rodger, "Legislating Amusements: Class Politics and Theater Law in New York City."

14. Vaudeville's audience still had a mix that included some of society's rougher elements. M. Alison Kibler wryly notes that, as late as 1920, comedian Bert Fitzgibbon was reprimanded for making fun of the pretensions of an audience that included rougher elements in the gallery by calling them "ladies and nuts." Kibler, *Rank Ladies,* 24.

15. Nasaw, *Going Out,* 28.

16. Slide, *The Vaudevillians,* 56.

17. "She ain't no lady, she's my wife." Ibid., 163.

18. W. Colin Crozier, "The Corporal Hugh Campbell Family History," unpublished manuscript (Ancaster, Ontario, Canada, 1994), 94–95, 31, 39–41, appx. G.

19. Brian Winter, Whitby archivist, letter to the author, September 1998, Whitby, Ontario, Canada.

20. Unofficial Whitby, Ontario, Canada, Census of 1861, Jack Brown Scrapbook, 9.

21. Crozier, "Corporal Hugh Campbell Family History," 95.

22. William Wallace quoted in *Oshawa (Ont.) Daily Times,* October 25, 1938, in ibid., appx. R.

23. Strang, *Famous Actresses of the Day,* 175–76.

24. Unidentified newspaper interview with Mrs. Campbell, August 1, 1908, Thousand Islands Museum. Special Collections were originally housed in the Clayton

Opera House and Clayton Museum in one building. They are now in the Thousand Islands Museum.

25. For a time line of Irwin's major life events and performance history, see the chronology.

26. Fields, *Women Vaudeville Stars,* 125–26.

27. Evidence suggests Eva may have exaggerated her family's impoverishment. For a well-researched, entertaining biography of Eva Tanguay, see Erdman, *Queen of Vaudeville.*

28. A. L. Samson, "May Irwin," 155.

29. Unpublished typed manuscript, Special Collections, Hawn Memorial Library.

30. This story appears in a typed manuscript in the Special Collections, Hawn Memorial Library.

31. Strang, *Famous Actresses of the Day,* 176.

32. "The One Sad Spot in May Irwin's Life," *New York Times,* April 13, 1901, 9.

33. Strang, *Famous Actresses of the Day,* 177.

34. Zellers, *Tony Pastor,* 63, 55.

35. Playbill in *New York Clipper,* September 21, 1878, Locke Scrapbook, vol. 297; Strang, *Famous Actresses of the Day,* 177, 178–79.

36. Fields, *Women Vaudeville Stars,* 5, 16.

37. Zellers, *Tony Pastor,* 64, 65.

38. Frank Cullen with Florence Hackman and Donald McNeilly, *Vaudeville, Old and New: An Encyclopedia of Variety Performers in America,* 615.

39. Scene 4, "Burlesque, Revue, and Vaudeville," in *America's Musical Stage: Two Hundred Years of Musical Theatre,* by Julian Mates, 135–63.

40. Ibid., 140–41, 143.

41. Bordman, *Oxford Companion to American Theatre,* 63 (see introduction, n. 9).

42. Lillian Russell, "Lillian Russell's Reminiscences," reprinted in *American Vaudeville as Seen by Its Contemporaries,* edited by Charles W. Stein, 13.

43. Fields, *Women Vaudeville Stars,* 70–71.

44. Strang, *Famous Actresses of the Day,* 179.

45. Robert Grau, *40 Years of Observation of the Music and the Drama,* 236.

46. Strang, *Famous Actresses of the Day,* 182–83.

47. Otis Skinner, *Footlights and Spotlights,* 134.

48. Doris Knowlton Thompson Ranous, *Diary of a Daly Debutante,* 81.

49. Ibid., 53.

50. Mary C. Henderson, *Theater in America,* 244–46.

51. Marvin Felheim, *The Theatre of Augustin Daly* (Cambridge, Mass.: Harvard University Press, 1956), 27–28.

52. May Irwin, "May Irwin on Art in Humor," 68.

53. Skinner, *Footlights and Spotlights,* 139.

54. Ibid., 136.

55. "May Irwin in the Legitimate," *San Francisco Chronicle,* April 23, 1899, 4.

56. Skinner, *Footlights and Spotlights,* 140.

57. Felheim, *Theatre of Augustin Daly,* 43.

58. Skinner, *Footlights and Spotlights,* 270.

59. Joseph Francis Daly, *Life of Augustin Daly,* 362.

60. Clarence J. Webster, "May Irwin, Comedienne, Was Celebrated Figure for Nearly Half Century," *Watertown (N.Y.) Daily Times,* October 24, 1938, Special Collections, Hawn Memorial Library.

61. "May Irwin in the Legitimate," 24.

62. Quoted in Felheim, *Theatre of Augustin Daly,* 180. George Odell wrote his fifteen-volume *Annals of the New York Stage* during the last twenty years of his life. It is still considered the most thorough accounting of eighteenth- and nineteenth-century theater in New York.

63. Anne Hartley Gilbert, *Stage Reminiscences of Mrs. Gilbert,* 186, 187.

64. Unidentified review of *Needles and Pins,* July 1884, British Library Archives; review of *A Night Off, London Times,* May 28, 1886, 5; review of *Nancy and Co., London Times,* July 10, 1886, British Library Archives; "Sarcey Praised May Irwin," unidentified Chicago newspaper, Locke Scrapbook, vol. 297. I have not been able to find Sarcey's direct quote in *Quarante ans de theatre,* the collection of his critiques from 1900 to 1902. Sarcey was critic for *L'Opinion Nationale* in 1860 and for *Le Temps* from 1867 until his death in 1899.

65. Irwin, "May Irwin on Art in Humor," 67.

66. Ada Patterson, "May Irwin on Humor, Home, and Business," 260; Irwin, "May Irwin on Art in Humor," 64.

67. "H. C. Irwin, 65, Son of Comedienne, Expires," *Watertown (N.Y.) Daily Times,* May 23, 1947, Brown Scrapbook, 176.

68. May Irwin, letter to Augustin Daly, 1886, Daly Papers.

69. "Contracts for Actors in Augustin Daly's Company," Special Collections, Harvard Theatre Library; Irwin, letter to Daly, March, 1887, Daly Papers.

70. Strang, *Famous Actresses of the Day,* 180.

71. A. D. Storm, *The Players Blue Book* (Worcester, Mass.: Sutherland and Storm, 1901), 66.

72. Strang, *Famous Stars of Light Opera* (Boston: L. C. Page, 1906), 92.

73. Untitled clipping, *New York Gazette,* December 31, 1898, Special Collections, Hawn Memorial Library.

74. Unidentified article, November 20, 1910, Locke Scrapbook, vol. 298.

75. "Address by Mrs. Kurt Eisfeldt (May Irwin) at Joint Meeting of the Rotary and Kiwanis Clubs at the Hotel Woodruff, Watertown, New York," June 12, 1928, Special Collections, Hawn Memorial Library; also found in Special Collections, *Watertown (N.Y.) Daily Times.* Henceforth cited as "Address by Mrs. Kurt Eisfeldt."

76. Deed of Transfer, September 19, 1893, from Sarah Van Coughnet of Clayton to May Irwin of New York City, for two thousand dollars, section of Club Island, Brown Scrapbook, 66.

77. Stanley Norcom, *Grindstone Island: An Island World Remembered,* 81. Information about Grindstone Island was obtained from Norcom's book. The author moved from Brooklyn to Grindstone Island as a young boy in 1909.

78. McArthur, *Actors and American Culture,* 4–26; Wilson, *History of American Acting,* 60–61.

79. Schlereth, *Victorian America,* 172.

80. Wertheim, *Vaudeville Wars,* 80.

81. Brinkley, *The Unfinished Nation,* 527.

82. Wertheim, *Vaudeville Wars,* 9.

83. Ibid., 30.

84. Stanley Applebaum (text), *The Chicago World's Fair: A Photographic Record* (Mineola, N.Y.: Dover, 1980).

85. Andrew L. Erdman, *Blue Vaudeville: Sex, Morals, and the Mass Marketing of Amusement, 1895–1915,* 70.

86. Brinkley, *The Unfinished Nation,* 492.

87. McArthur, *Actors and American Culture,* 10.

88. Ibid., 170.

89. Ian Whitcomb, *Irving Berlin and Ragtime America,* 57.

90. Untitled article, *New York Times,* September 11, 1887, Brown Scrapbook, 195.

91. Untitled article, *New York Times,* September 15, 1895, Special Collections, Hawn Memorial Library.

92. Untitled article, *New York Times,* September 11, 1887, Brown Scrapbook, 195.

93. This information came out during her accuser's divorce proceedings. "Flo Irwin Named in Divorce Case," *New York Times,* November 24, 1904, 4. Walter Hawley, an actor who had been appearing in many plays opposite Flo, was brought to court by his wife.

94. "May Irwin Married to Hugo Tolland, the San Francisco Millionaire—He Is 26 and She Is 32," *Milwaukee Daily Sentinel,* May 30, 1891, 1; "Only Good Friends," *San Francisco Chronicle,* May 31, 1891, 11.

95. McArthur, *Actors and American Culture,* 140; "Clement Scott Resigns," *New York Times,* December 11, 1898, 1; untitled article, *New York Times,* December 1898, Locke Scrapbook, vol. 297.

96. McArthur, *Actors and American Culture,* 130.

97. Richard de Cordova, *Picture Personalities: The Emergence of the Star System in America,* 103.

98. Quoted in McArthur, *Actors and American Culture,* 140.

99. "What the Players Are Doing," *New York Times,* September 15, 1903, 5.

100. "The Irwin Sisters Disagree," *New York Times,* March 30, 1900, 7.

101. "Proposed Stocking Tariff Raises Ire of May," *Chicago Tribune,* April 11, 1909, B3.

102. Archie Bell, untitled article, *Cleveland Plain Dealer,* April 11, 1912, Locke Scrapbook, vol. 298.

103. Playbill for London Pavilion, June 23, 1913, British Library Archives.

104. George Ade, letter to Florence Irwin, September 20, 1927, in *Letters of George Ade,* edited by Terence Tobin, 124–25; "Flo Irwin, Sister of May, Expires," *Watertown (N.Y.) Daily Times,* December 22, 1930, Brown Scrapbook, 192.

105. *New York Times,* September 17, 1895, Locke Scrapbook, vol. 297.

106. Alan Dale, undated review of *The Widow Jones, New York American,* Locke Scrapbook, vol. 297.

107. "Last Night's Theatres," review of *Kate Kip Buyer, Philadelphia Enquirer,* October 11, 1898, Locke Scrapbook, vol. 297.

108. Webster, "May Irwin, Comedienne."

Chapter 2. Stardom

1. Strang, *Famous Actresses of the Day,* 175–76 (quote 1); James L. Ford, "The Coming Queens of Comedy," 553, 557 (quote 2); E. F. Chase, "Plays and Players," *Boston Journal,* September 7, 1896, Locke Scrapbook, vol. 297 (quotes 3–4).

2. See, for example, John Auerbach, *Body Shots: Early Cinema's Incarnations,* 74–77.

3. Ibid., 75.

4. Sometimes this quote is attributed to Boston critic Herbert Stone. But there is considerable evidence that artist John Sloan may have uttered it. He certainly wrote about his disgust after seeing *The Kiss.* See Janice M. CoCo, *John Sloan's Women: A Psychoanalysis of Vision,* 61–62.

5. Chase, "Plays and Players"; Charles Musser, *The Emergence of Cinema: The American Screen to 1907,* 118.

6. Undated review of *She Knows Better Now, Christian Science Monitor,* Special Collections, Hawn Memorial Library; 1905 Census of New York, May Irwin, accessed through Ancestry.com.

7. For an excellent summary of this development, see Bordman, *Oxford Companion to American Theatre,* 135–210 (see introduction, n. 9).

8. Performance dates have been gathered from many sources. See chronology for details.

9. Chase, "Plays and Players" (emphasis added).

10. Excellent information on early American female theater managers is included in Faye E. Dudden, *Women in the American Theatre: Actresses and Audiences, 1790–1870,* 123–48. For notes on the paucity of female managers in variety theater, see Rodger, *Champagne Charlie and Pretty Jemima,* 159–60.

11. May Irwin, "Nursing the Nerves."

12. *May Irwin's Home Cooking;* untitled article, *Sun,* November 20, 1904, Locke Scrapbook, vol. 298.

13. "May Irwin's Wedding," *Watertown (N.Y.) Daily Times,* May 27, 1907, Brown Scrapbook, 69.

14. Untitled article, *New York Evening Journal,* May 22, 1907, Locke Scrapbook, vol. 298; Alice Rohe, untitled article, *New York Evening World,* May 14, 1907, Locke Scrapbook, vol. 298.

15. "Kurt Eisfeldt, Long Ill, Dies," *Watertown (N.Y.) Daily Times,* May 31, 1940, Brown Scrapbook, 169.

16. John Culhane, *The American Circus,* 144–61.

17. Information on Kurt received from the following: interview with Harold Kendall, town historian, Clayton, New York, July 1994 (like most of my sources who met May Irwin, Mr. Kendall is now deceased); Robert Bertrand, letter to the author, November 1994 (Mr. Bertrand met May Irwin when he was a boy and she stayed at the Herald House in Clayton, now renamed the Thousand Islands Inn); and Scott Irwin, e-mail to the author, February 27, 2013 (Scott is May Irwin's great-grandson).

18. Richard W. Flint, "The Evolution of the Circus in Nineteenth Century America," in *Papers and Proceedings of the Conference of American Popular Entertainment,* edited by Myron Mathieu, 190. For pictures of circus posters and other advertisements for the circus in the late nineteenth century, see Rupert Croft-Cooke and Peter Cotes, *Circus: A World History.*

19. Hartley Davis, "The Business Side of Vaudeville," *Everybody's,* October 1907, reprinted in *Vaudeville as Seen by Its Contemporaries,* edited by Stein, 114.

20. Untitled article, *New York Times,* December 8, 1908, Locke Scrapbook, vol. 298.

21. Unidentified article, January 29, 1914, Locke Scrapbook, vol. 299.

22. Untitled article, *New York Telegraph,* April 8, 1912, Locke Scrapbook, vol. 299.

23. Ada Patterson, "The Players' Christmas."

24. Unidentified article, 1914, Locke Scrapbook, vol. 299.

25. Booth Tarkington, "Actress Makes Free with Comedy Role," *Indianapolis Star,* August 9, 1911, Locke Scrapbook, vol. 299.

26. Peter Milnes, review *of Mrs. Black Is Back, Motion Picture News* (December 12, 1914): 808–9; Mabel Condon, review of *Mrs. Black Is Back, Motography* (November 28, 1914): 736.

27. "Second Thoughts on First Nights," review of *33 Washington Square, New York Times,* October 3, 1915, 6:6; review of *Mrs. Black Is Back, Theatre,* December 1904, 298; undated review of *Madge Smith, Attorney,* Special Collections, Hawn Memorial Library; review of *Kate Kip, Buyer, New York Times,* November 8, 1898, 5.

28. Review of *The Belle of Bridgeport, New York Times,* October 30, 1900, 6; review of *Widow by Proxy, New York Evening World,* February 1913; review of *Widow by Proxy, Variety,* February 28, 1913; review of *33 Washington Square, Brooklyn Eagle,* August 24, 1914, Special Collections, Hawn Memorial Library; Lewis C. Strang, *Celebrated Comedians,* 112.

29. "Dramatics and Music," review of *Madge Smith, Attorney, New York Times,* December 7, 1900, 5.

30. Review of *Getting a Polish, New York Times,* November 9, 1910, 9.

31. Review of *Widow by Proxy,* March 9, 1913, Special Collections, Hawn Memorial Library; review of *Widow by Proxy, Boston Transcript,* September 21, 1913, Locke Scrapbook, vol. 299.

32. Review of *Mrs. Wilson, That's All, New York Times,* November 4, 1906, 4:2; review of *Mrs. Wilson, That's All, New York Globe,* November 6, 1906, Locke Scrapbook, vol. 298.

33. Alan Dale, "Alan Dale Says May Irwin Is a Whole Show in Herself at the Bijou," *New York American,* November 9, 1906, Locke Scrapbook, vol. 298.

34. Schlereth, *Victorian America,* 124; Glenn, *Female Spectacle,* 23.

35. Wilson, *History of American Acting,* 190–93.

36. Strang, *Celebrated Comedians,* 256.

37. Information taken from McArthur, *Actors and American Culture,* 4–26; and Garff B. Wilson, *300 Years of American Drama and Theatre,* 160–61.

38. Bordman, *Oxford Companion to American Theatre,* 199 (on Clayton), 195 (on Templeton), 235 (on Friganza).

39. "The Only One Boss Bully," unidentified article, 1913, Special Collections, Hawn Memorial Library.

40. Florence Yoder, "May Irwin, Comedienne, Insists That She Is a Serious Person," *Washington Times,* September 25, 1915, 13; untitled article, *Boston Transcript,* September 1913, Locke Scrapbook, vol. 299.

41. Bordman, *Oxford Companion to American Theatre,* 167 (on *Santa Maria*), 157 (on *Ollamus*).

42. For an excellent analysis of the iconography of American girls and the "New Woman," see Martha Banta, *Imaging American Women,* 45–91.

43. See "American Girls as the New Woman," in ibid., 145–89.

44. John Cotton, "Comedien [*sic*] Wishes She Could Take Cook Stove on Her Tours," *Minneapolis News,* March 14, 1914.

45. Margaret Bell, "May Irwin—Peeress of Stage Widows."

46. *Toledo Blade,* December 1898, Locke Scrapbook, vol. 298.

47. "May Irwin Sees Pretence as Fair Comedy Target," *Christian Science Monitor,* unclear date, circa 1916, Special Collections, Hawn Memorial Library; May Irwin, "How I Hold My Audience," typed manuscript, Special Collections, Hawn Memorial Library; May Irwin, "Cookbook Plans," 16, Special Collections, Thousand Islands Museum; Rodger, *Champagne Charlie and Pretty Jemima,* 112–26. The "pretence" that May and many Americans of the period loved to mock was often associated with a snobbish upper class.

48. Brooks McNamara, "The Literature of American Popular Entertainment," in *The American Stage: Social and Economic Issues from the Colonial Period to the Present,* edited by Ron Engle, Tice Miller, and Oscar Brocket, 148–49, 155; Linda Martin and Kerry Segrave, *Women in Comedy,* 14; Nancy Reincke, "Antidote to Dominance: Women's Laughter as Counteraction," 36.

49. George Hobart, *Mrs. Wilson, That's All* (1906), 84, microfilm, CR.D9083, Library of Congress.

50. Agnes Louise Crimmins, *She Knows Better Now* (Boston: Baker, 1918), 45.

51. Undated review of *Sister Mary,* Special Collections, Hawn Memorial Library.

52. Ibid. *Sister Mary* is also the title of a very different sentimental play written by Clement Scott and Wilson Barrett and first produced at Wallack's Theatre in 1885–86. Because of Clement Scott's position as a dramatic critic, there is often confusion between the two.

53. Hapgood, *The Stage in America,* 99.

54. Charles Daunton, "Actress Must Have Special License to Drink on Stage and Know When to Stop," *New York Times,* 1908, Locke Scrapbook, vol. 298; see also "May Irwin Wins Applause," *New York Times,* September 30, 1908, 7.

55. Brett Page, *Writing for Vaudeville,* 83, 105.

56. Mikhail Bakhtin, *Rabelais and His World;* Frances Gray, *Women and Laughter,* 31.

57. Sturtevant, *Great Big Girl Like Me,* 35.

58. Gray, *Women and Laughter,* 8.

59. Ruth Bordin, *Women and Temperance,* 3–4; Steven Stark, "Gap Politics," 74.

60. See Harry L. Newton, *Some Vaudeville Monologues,* 91–98.

61. "May Irwin as Suffragist," *Good Housekeeping,* April 9, 1901, Locke Scrapbook, vol. 297.

62. Michael M. Davis Jr., *The Exploitation of Pleasure: A Study of Commercial Recreations in New York City,* 30. See also "New York Theatres, Their Patrons, Their Profits, Their Plays," *New York Times,* May 28, 1911, 2.

63. Kathy Peiss, *Cheap Amusements: Working Class Women and Leisure in Turn-of-the-Century New York,* 143–44.

64. Bordin, *Women and Temperance,* 121.

65. All six songs are available for listening from the Library of Congress online or can be purchased on a CD, along with twenty-one songs sung by Clarice Vance, *The High Priestess of Jollity and the Southern Singer.*

66. I own a copy of this film. As noted in the introduction, the original is at the Thousand Islands Museum.

67. George Hobart, *Mrs. Black Is Back* (1905), microfilm, CR.D6320, Library of Congress.

68. Hobart, *Mrs. Wilson, That's All,* 80.

69. Page, *Writing for Vaudeville,* 435.

70. Untitled article, *Rochester Democrat,* January 1916, Locke Scrapbook, vol. 299.

71. Catherine Chisholm Cushing, *Widow by Proxy* (New York: Richmond Hill, 1930), 56–57.

72. "My First Appearance on the Stage," undated interview, Special Collections, Hawn Memorial Library.

73. Typed manuscript, Special Collections, Hawn Memorial Library.

74. Hapgood, *The Stage in America,* 99.

75. Reviews of *Courted into Court, New York Times,* December 30, 1896, February 20, 1897; untitled article, *New York Journal,* March 26, 1897, Locke Scrapbook, vol. 297.

76. Untitled article, *New York Sun,* March 2, 1913, Locke Scrapbook, vol. 299 (quote 1); review of *Sister Mary, New York Evening Sun,* December 1, 1900, Special Collections, Hawn Memorial Library (quote 2); untitled article, *New York Times,* December 2, 1905, Locke Scrapbook, vol. 298 (quotes 3–4).

77. May Irwin, letter to unidentified playwright, from the Planters Hotel in St. Louis, April 6, 1907, private collection of Karen Killian.

78. "May Irwin Gibes at Bryan," *New York Times,* October 17, 1896, 1.

79. Gray, *Women and Laughter,* 8; Kate Sanborn, *The Wit of Women,* 207.

80. Review of *Kate Kip, Buyer, New York Times,* May 7, 1899; Edward Dithmar, review of *The Swell Miss Fitzwell, New York Times,* November 24, 1897, 4:8; Irwin, "How I Hold My Audience"; "Irwin Sees Pretence."

81. James Bethuel Smiley, *Modern Manners and Social Forms* (1889), quoted in John F. Kasson, *Rudeness and Civility: Manners in Nineteenth Century Urban America,* 242; Kasson, 251.

82. *New York Dramatic Mirror,* May 1913, Locke Scrapbook, vol. 299; *New York Telegraph,* February 15, 1903, Locke Scrapbook, vol. 297.

83. Dale, "Alan Dale Says May Irwin Is a Whole Show." For Alan Dale's review of Clara Morris, see Alan Dale, "Clara Morris," in *Writing on Theater from Washington Irving to Tony Kushner: The American Stage,* edited by Laurence Senelick (New York: Penguin, 2010), 141–49. See also Tice L. Miller, "Alan Dale: The Hearst Critic."

84. Kate Carew, "May Irwin Sketches," review of *The Belle of Bridgeport, New York Times,* November 4, 1900, Locke Scrapbook, vol. 297.

85. Alan Dale, review of *Mrs. Black Is Back, Boston Transcript,* February 27, 1906, Locke Scrapbook, vol. 298.

86. Untitled article, *New York Times,* December 24, 1901, Locke Scrapbook, vol. 298.

87. "Over the Footlights," undated review of *Sister Mary, New York Times,* Special Collections, Hawn Memorial Library. This song's special treatment is also noted by Edward Dithmar in a review of *Sister Mary, New York Times,* October 29, 1899, 14.

88. Harold R. Wynne, *Criterion,* December 25, 1897, Locke Scrapbook, vol. 297.

89. "The Meddler," *Variety,* March 16, 1908, Locke Scrapbook, vol. 298.

90. M'Dougall, cartoons of *Sister Mary, New York Times,* December 11, 1899, Locke Scrapbook, vol. 298.

91. Martin and Segrave, *Women in Comedy,* 38 (on Crabtree); Caroline Caffin, *Vaudeville,* 212 (on d'Armond), 1 (quote).

92. Susan Bordo, *Unbearable Weight, Feminism, Western Culture, and the Body,* 206.

93. For a complete analysis of these ideas, see Jon Stratton, *The Desirable Body: Cultural Fetishism and the Erotics of Consumption* (Urbana: University of Illinois Press, 2001).

94. Jackson Lears, *Fables of Abundance: A Cultural History of Advertising in America,* 104.

95. "May Irwin in Double Bill," *Chicago Journal,* March 20, 1907, Special Collections, Hawn Memorial Library; untitled article, *Dayton (Ohio) Herald,* April 6, 1912,

Locke Scrapbook, vol. 299; untitled article, *Chicago Dramatic Critic,* May 1898, Locke Scrapbook, vol. 297.

96. William Whythe, "Past Laughter," 66; *May Irwin's Home Cooking,* 20.

97. *Watertown (N.Y.) Daily Times,* December 12, 1919 (on fleeting fame); "Address by Mrs. Kurt Eisfeldt" (see chap. 1, n. 75).

98. *Watertown (N.Y.) Daily Times,* January 31, 1917 (quote 1); May Irwin, "Why I Want to Live to Be a Hundred," 446 (quotes 2–3); untitled article, *New York Globe,* February 27, 1913, Locke Scrapbook, vol. 299 (quote 4); "Address by Mrs. Kurt Eisfeldt" (quote 5).

99. "May Irwin in the Legitimate," *San Francisco Chronicle,* April 23, 1899, 24.

100. *May Irwin's Home Cooking,* 180.

101. *Variety,* December 7, 1907, Locke Scrapbook, vol. 298.

102. Review of *She Knows Better Now, Christian Science Monitor,* Special Collections, Hawn Memorial Library.

103. Martin and Segrave, *Women and Comedy,* 56.

104. Review of *Kate Kip, Buyer, Philadelphia Enquirer,* October 11, 1898, Locke Scrapbook, vol. 297.

105. Bordman, *Oxford Companion to American Theatre,* 162 (quotes 1–2); Pittenger, "Women in American Popular Entertainment," 78 (quote 3); Bordman, *Oxford Companion to American Theatre,* 162.

106. Martin and Segrave, *Women and Comedy,* 56; Pittenger, "Women in American Popular Entertainment," 83.

107. Nancy Walker and Zita Dresner, *Redressing the Balance: American Women's Literary Humor from Colonial Times to the 1980s* (Jackson: University Press of Mississippi, 1988), quoted in Linda Morris, ed., *American Women Humorists: Critical Essays,* 43.

108. Ford, "Coming Queens of Comedy," 559 (quote 1); "Seats Too Small for May Irwin," *Watertown (N.Y.) Daily Times,* March 6, 1922, Brown Scrapbook, 136; Ford, "Coming Queens of Comedy," 557 (quote 2); "May Irwin Gains Triumph of Skill," *Boston Herald,* January 20, 1907, Locke Scrapbook, vol. 298 (quote 3); Alan Dale, "How Fat Has Come Back to the Stage," 1898, Locke Scrapbook, vol. 297 (quote 4); "Some of May Irwin's Ideas," *New York Times,* November 19, 1899, 18 (quote 5).

109. Patterson, "Irwin on Home, Humor, and Business," 258 (Mrs. Black); unidentified article mentioning a production of *Sister Mary,* "Fashion behind the Footlights," Special Collections, Hawn Memorial Library; *Billboard,* December 22, 1906, Locke Scrapbook, vol. 298 (Mrs. Wilson).

110. Adolph Klauber, "A Home Talk with High Priestess of Jollity," *New York Times,* November 13, 1904, pt. 4, second magazine section, 2.

111. Undated review of *Mrs. Wilson-Andrews,* Special Collections, Hawn Memorial Library (quotes 1–2); "Homemade Comic Plays," review of *The Widow Jones, New York Times,* September 17, 1895, 5 (quote 3); Dale, "How Fat Has Come Back" (quotes 4–7).

112. Susan Horowitz, "Funny Women: A Study of Female Comedic Personae (Ball, Diller, Burnett, Hawn)," 6. Although Horowitz's dissertation focuses on comediennes from the 1950s–1980s, her ideas can be applied to female comics of any period.

113. For a well-written and entertaining analysis of contemporary female comics, see Linda Mizejewski, *Pretty/Funny.*

114. Ford, "Coming Queens of Comedy," 553.

115. Untitled article, *New York Journal,* March 26, 1897, Locke Scrapbook, vol. 297; unidentified article, *Chicago Dramatic,* May 1898, Locke Scrapbook, vol. 297; "May Irwin Criticizes Herself in *Sister Mary,*" *Broadway,* January 1900, Special Collections, Hawn Memorial Library.

Chapter 3. The Profoundly Troubling History of the Coon Song

1. "Secretary of Laughter," *New York Times,* October 24, 1938, 16; David Pilgrim, *The New Jim Crow Museum: Learning from the Past, Changing Lives.*

2. Leah Cathleen Cothern, "The Coon Song: A Study of American Music, Entertainment and Racism," 76.

3. Ibid., 12–15.

4. A good study of the history of the *N* word is the *Washington Post*'s series in 2014. It is available at http://www.washingtonpost.com/post TV/national/the-n-word-through-history. Quotation marks around *coon* in the text are eliminated hereafter.

5. H. Wiley Hitchcock and Stanley Sadie, eds., *The New Grove Dictionary of American Music,* 4:3–6, 1:343.

6. This edition of "Zip Coon" was published in 1882 by Oliver Ditson and Company in *Minstrel Songs Old and New.* Excellent information on the minstrel era is available in many sources. One of the best is David A. Jason and Gene Jones, *Spreadin' Rhythm Around: Black Popular Songwriters, 1880–1930* (New York: Schirmer Books, 1998), 1–21. A very good online source is the Parlor Songs Academy at "Lessons in America's Popular Music": http://www.parlorsongs.ac. To see the section on minstrelsy, add "/issue/2011-9" to the end of the URL.

7. Jason and Jones, *Spreadin' Rhythm Around,* 9.

8. James H. Dorman, "Shaping the Popular Image of Post-Reconstruction American Blacks: The 'Coon Song' Phenomenon of the Gilded Age," 453. Dorman notes, for example, "If the Man in the Moon Were a Coon" sold three million copies.

9. Whitcomb, *Irving Berlin and Ragtime America,* 112–13.

10. Sigmund Spaeth, *A History of Popular Music in America,* 286.

11. Whitcomb, *Irving Berlin and Ragtime America,* 121.

12. Sam Dennison, *Scandalize My Name: Black Imagery in America Popular Music,* 371.

13. Philip Furia, *The Poets of Tin Pan Alley,* 27.

14. Jason and Jones, *Spreadin' Rhythm Around,* 97–99.

15. Lynn Abbott and Doug Seroff, *Ragged but Right: Black Traveling Shows, "Coon Songs," and the Dark Pathway to Jazz and Blues,* 60–62.

16. Ibid., 23, 28–29.
17. Lavitt, "First of the Red Hot Mamas," 6.
18. For an informative discussion of these acts, see Kibler, *Rank Ladies,* 119–25.
19. Abbott and Seroff, *Ragged but Right,* 19–21.
20. Isaac Goldberg, *Tin Pan Alley,* 150.
21. Whitcomb, *Irving Berlin and Ragtime America,* 111.
22. William J. Schafer and Johannes Riedel, *The Art of Ragtime,* 27; *May Irwin's Songs* (New York: Dempsey, 1897), 1.
23. Undated article, Locke Scrapbook, vol. 297; Amy Leslie, *Some Players;* Henry Austin Clapp, "Jolly May Irwin," *Boston Advertiser,* February 26, 1901, Locke Scrapbook, vol. 297.
24. Hitchcock and Stanley, *New Grove Dictionary of American Music,* 1:494.
25. Ibid.
26. Dennison, *Scandalize My Name,* 347.
27. One of the best books detailing the proliferation of these tunes in late-nineteenth-century America is an old chestnut: Maxwell F. Marcuse, *Tin Pan Alley in Gaslight.*
28. Schlereth, *Victorian America,* 194.
29. Currier and Ives's lithographs can be found on a number of sites. There is a summary article about the "Darktown Comics" at http://campus.albion/edu/library/archives-and-special collections. There are images on many sites, but the central URL for Currier and Ives is simply http://currierandives.com. Henry Ossama Tanner's *The Banjo Lesson* hangs in Hampton University Museum, Hampton, Va.
30. Schlereth, *Victorian America,* 211.
31. Newton, *Some Vaudeville Monologues,* 27; John Strausbaugh, *Black Like You: Blackface, Whiteface, Insult and Imitation in American Popular Culture,* 131.
32. "Paddy McFadden," song quoted in *Champagne Charlie and Pretty Jemima,* by Rodger, 100.
33. Marcuse, *Tin Pan Alley in Gaslight,* 103.
34. Jackson Lears, *Rebirth of a Nation: The Making of Modern America, 1877–1920,* 119.
35. Travis Stewart, *No Applause, Just Throw Money,* 10 (quote). Two of the best histories of Reconstruction and Jim Crow I have read are Eric Foner, *Forever Free;* and Douglas A. Blackmon, *Slavery by Another Name.*
36. Bank, *Theatre Culture in America,* 154–56.
37. Brinkley, *The Unfinished Nation,* 369.
38. Lears, *Rebirth of a Nation,* 15.
39. Ibid., 23–24. For another excellent discussion of the Compromise of 1877, see Brinkley, *The Unfinished Nation,* 425–30.
40. H. W. Brands, *The Reckless Decade: America in the 1890s,* 218.
41. Ibid., 219.
42. John Marshall Harlan, "Dissenting Opinion in *Plessy v. Ferguson*" (1896), in *Great Issues in American History,* edited by Richard Hofstadter, 58. For a good summary of *Plessy v. Ferguson,* see Brands, *Reckless Decade,* 215–53.

43. Paul Barringer, *The American Negro: His Past and Future,* 13, 17; Paulus A. Irving, introductory notes to ibid.

44. Foner, *Forever Free,* 171.

45. Amy Louise Wood, *Lynching and Spectacle: Witnessing Racial Violence in America, 1890–1940,* 3.

46. Frederick Moore, "The Coon's Content," *Strand,* June 1903, reprinted in *Racism at the Turn of the Century: Documentary Perspectives, 1870–1910,* edited by Donald P. DeNevi and Doris A. Holms, 102.

47. Schlereth, *Victorian America,* 280.

48. Barbara C. Cruz and Michael J. Berson, "The American Melting Pot? Miscegenation Laws in the United States," *Magazine of the OAH* 15, no. 4 (2001): 2–3.

49. Nasaw, *Going Out,* 47–48 (see chap. 1, n. 1).

50. Eric Ledell Smith, "Early African-American Broadway Performers: Bert Williams and George William Walker in *In Dahomey* (1903)," *Afro-Americans in New York Life and History* 16, no. 2 (1992): 9.

51. Whitcomb, *Irving Berlin and Ragtime America,* 57.

52. Songs for this period are widely available now online and can be seen at the Music Division of the Library of Congress and the New York Library of the Performing Arts. I own a large selection of these songs, some generously supplied by the late Ragtime Bob Darch (who received many from Janice Cleary of Omaha, Nebraska), in the private collection of Karen Killian. These are all identified in the text.

53. *May Irwin's Songs,* sixteen pages.

54. For an interesting discussion of the Victor recordings, see Jim Walsh, "May Irwin."

55. Edward B. Moogk, *Roll Back the Years: History of Canadian Recorded Sound and Its Legacy.*

56. Elizabeth Surles, liner notes for CD featuring May Irwin and Clarice Vance. See chap. 2, n. 65, for complete information.

57. *Boston Daily Globe,* June 20, 1897, 89.

58. For a study that looks at those two stereotypes separately, see Sam Dennison, "From the Gay '90s through the First World War," chap. 8 in his *Scandalize My Name,* 345–424.

59. Quote marks in the text around names of stereotypes are eliminated hereafter.

60. Furia, *Poets of Tin Pan Alley,* 26.

Chapter 4. The "Only One Boss Bully"

1. Karl Kenneth and Lyn Udall, "Stay in Your Own Backyard" (New York: Whitmark, 1899), Music Division, Library of Congress.

2. See, for example, Joseph S. Nathan and Felix F. Feist, "The Bullfrog and the Coon" (New York: Feist, 1906), ibid. In this number, a black man emulates the wooing of frogs in order to win his lady love, Susan. Many numbers of the period compared blacks to frogs. For example, see Dennison, *Scandalize My Name,* 378.

3. Clarence J. Webster, "May Irwin, Comedienne, Was Celebrated Stage Figure for Nearly Half Century," *Watertown (N.Y.) Daily Times,* October 24, 1938, Special Collections, Hawn Memorial Library.

4. "May Irwin Dead; Comedienne, 76," *New York Times,* October 23, 1938.

5. Dennison, *Scandalize My Name,* chap. 8. He cites coon songs with titles such as "I'm a Lucky Coon" and "I've Got a White Man Running My Automobile."

6. Andrew B. Sterling, "I've Got a White Man Working for Me" (New York: F. A. Mills, 1900), Music Division, Library of Congress.

7. Webster, "May Irwin, Comedienne"; untitled article, *New York Sun,* December 30, 1896, Locke Scrapbook, vol. 297; untitled review of *Kate Kip, Buyer, Philadelphia Enquirer,* October 11, 1899, Locke Scrapbook, vol. 297; Dennison, *Scandalize My Name,* 375.

8. Whitcomb, *Irving Berlin and Ragtime America,* 111.

9. "Story of the 'New Bully,'" *Washington Post,* February 11, 1896, 6.

10. Ibid.

11. The photograph also appears in the article Irwin, "May Irwin on Art in Humor."

12. David Krasner, "'Whose Role Is It Anyway?': Gilpin and the Harlem Renaissance."

13. Foner, *Forever Free,* 220.

14. "Voice from the Past," *Boston Transcript,* March 10, 1925.

15. Performed by the Escorts and Betty, with Hawaiian chords, this version was issued in 1941 by Calumet Music Company in Chicago, from Karen Killian's private collection.

16. "Sang at the Colored Home: May Irwin's Company in a Charitable Entertainment," *New York Times,* February 5, 1897, 12.

17. "May Irwin, Ragtime, and the Cakewalk," review of *The Widow Jones, Boston Transcript,* February 15, 1902.

18. Rudolph Aronson, *Theatrical and Musical Memories,* 160–61.

19. Strausbaugh, *Black Like You,* 105; David Krasner, "Rewriting the Body: Aida Overton Walker and the Social Formation of Cakewalk," *Theatre Survey* 37, no. 2 (1996): 67–92.

20. "S. Coleridge Calls 'Coon Songs' Rot," *Special to New York Times,* November 13, 1904; "Records Racial Melodies as Sung by Members of the Race," *Chicago Defender,* June 4, 1921, 6.

21. Barbara L. Webb, "Authentic Possibilities: Plantation Performance of the 1890s."

22. "Coon Song Craze Soon to Be Ended," *Memphis Scimitar,* reprinted in *Birmingham (Ala.) Age-Herald,* January 18, 1899, 4 (emphasis added to mark the connection with this attitude to the first).

23. "Tom the Tattler," *Indianapolis Freeman,* August 24, 1901, quoted in Abbott and Seroff, *Ragged but Right,* 11.

24. Abbott and Seroff, *Ragged but Right,* 15.

25. Stein, *Vaudeville as Seen by Its Contemporaries,* 152 (on Janis); Erdman, *Queen of Vaudeville,* 166–67 (on West).

26. Unidentified article, December 1899, Locke Scrapbook, vol. 43 (quote 1); unidentified article, February 26, 1899, Locke Scrapbook, vol. 43 (quote 2; emphasis added). Biographical information on Belle Davis is also in Jo A. Tanner, *Dusky Maidens: The Odyssey of the Early Black Dramatic Actress,* 35–36.

27. Unidentified article, February 26, 1899, Locke Scrapbook, vol. 43.

28. Jayna Brown, *Babylon Girls: Black Women Performers and the Shaping of the Modern,* 39.

29. "Coon Songs Must Go," *Indianapolis Freeman,* January 20, 1909, 5.

30. Review of *Kate Kip, Buyer, New York Times,* November 8, 1898, 4; review of "The Bully," *New York Sun,* September 7, 1896, Locke Scrapbook, vol. 297.

31. W. J. Cash, *The Mind of the South,* 84.

32. Frederick Moore, "The Coon's Content," *Strand,* June 1903, reprinted in *Racism at the Turn of the Century,* edited by DeNevi and Holms, 104.

33. Ar-W-T, "The Passing Show in Washington," *Chicago Defender,* August 2, 1911, 6 (Day); "Review," *Chicago Defender,* October 21, 1911, 5 (Ramonde); "Tolliver's Comedy Co.," *Chicago Defender,* May 29, 1915, 6 (Smith); Tony Langston, "Theatrical Review," *Chicago Defender,* June 12, 1915, 6 (black dancers); Daphne A. Brooks, *Bodies in Dissent: Spectacular Performances of Race and Freedom, 1850–1910,* 326–27 (Walker).

34. Kibler, *Rank Ladies,* 126.

35. Micki McElya, *Clinging to Mammy: The Faithful Slave in Twentieth-Century America,* 61, 41.

36. Lears, *Rebirth of a Nation,* 34 (see chap. 3, n. 34); Edith J. R. Isaacs, *The Negro in the American Theatre,* 41.

37. Cash, *Mind of the South,* 83; James Oakes, *The Ruling Race: A History of American Slaveholders,* 195.

38. Rayford W. Logan, *The Betrayal of the Negro,* 225; Abbott and Seroff, *Ragged but Right,* 14.

39. *Sun,* March 20, 1904, Locke Scrapbook, vol. 298.

40. Untitled article, *New York Telegraph,* September 30, 1915, Locke Scrapbook, vol. 299.

41. "May Irwin to Head Laughter Bureau," *New York Times,* September 18, 1915, Locke Scrapbook, vol. 299.

42. Eric Lott, *Love and Theft,* 145, 8.

43. Lears, *Rebirth of a Nation,* 35.

44. McElya, *Clinging to Mammy,* 24.

45. David A. Horowitz, *The People's Voice: A Populist Cultural History of Modern America,* 1–2, 31.

46. Larry Hamberlin, "National Identity in Snyder and Berlin's 'Opera Rag.'"

47. William J. Mahar, "Ethiopian Skits and Sketches: Content and Context of Blackface Minstrelsy, 1840–1890," in *Readings in Nineteenth Century Blackface Minstrelsy,* edited by Annemarie Beane, James V. Hatch, and Brooks McNamara, 179–226.

48. "May Irwin in the Legitimate," *San Francisco Chronicle,* April 23, 1899, 4.

49. Lott, *Love and Theft*, 145; untitled review of *Widow Jones*, December 24, 1901, Locke Scrapbook, vol. 297 (emphasis added).

50. "Voices from the Past"; "Coon Song Craze Soon to Be Ended."

51. Sterling A. Brown, "Negro Characters as Seen by White Authors," *Journal of Negro Education* 2, no. 1 (1933): 184; Thomas Nelson Page, *The Negro: The Southerner's Problem* (1900), 80, quoted in ibid., 187; James Fenimore Cooper, *The Spy* (New York: Scott Foreman, 45); John P. Kennedy, *Swallow Barn*, quoted in S. Brown, "Negro Characters," 188.

52. Lears, *Rebirth of a Nation*, 35.

53. Brinkley, *The Unfinished Nation*, 488, 469. For an astute analysis of this period, see Kahlil Gibran Muhammad, *The Condemnation of Blackness: Race, Crime, and the Making of Modern Urban America* (Cambridge, Mass.: Harvard University Press, 2010).

54. Brinkley, *The Unfinished Nation*, 628.

55. Benjamin Brawley, *A Social History of the American Negro*, 298.

56. Lears, *Rebirth of a Nation*, 21–22 (quote), 92–110.

57. Cash, *Mind of the South*, 116.

58. Ibid., 115.

59. Quoted in Francesca Morgan, *Women and Patriotism in Jim Crow America*, 32.

60. Lears, *Rebirth of a Nation*, 105.

61. Ida B. Wells-Barnett, *A Red Record: Tabulated Statistics and Alleged Causes of Lynchings in the U.S., 1892–93–94, Respectfully Submitted to the 19th Century Civilization in "the Land of the Free and the Home of the Brave"* (Chicago: Hennessey, 1895).

62. Wood, *Lynching and Spectacle*, 52.

63. Whitcomb, *Irving Berlin and Ragtime America*, 112; Dennison, *Scandalize My Name*, 377.

64. Grace Kimball, *Theatres* 6 (emphasis added).

65. Wood, *Lynching and Spectacle*, 98.

66. Manning Marable, "Racism and Sexism," in *Race, Class, and Gender in the United States*, edited by Paula S. Rothenberg, 6th ed. (New York: Worth, 2004), 160–65.

67. Janet Brown, "The 'Coon-Singer' and the 'Coon Song': A Case Study of the Performer-Character Relationship."

68. *May Irwin's Songs*, 1 (on intuition); "May Irwin, Ragtime, and the Cakewalk" (heard singing at hotel); Strang, *Famous Actresses of the Day*, 185–86 (banjo strumming); unidentified article, 1904, Locke Scrapbook, vol. 297 (quote); unidentified and undated article, Locke Scrapbook, vol. 297 (black reception).

69. May Irwin, "Ole Miss Cyarter and the Ghost," *World*, December 9, 1900, Locke Scrapbook, vol. 297.

70. *Los Angeles Examiner*, November 1907, Locke Scrapbook, vol. 297 (quote); Samson, "May Irwin," 154 (caption).

71. "Maids to Stage Women," *New York Times*, February 28, 1897, 11.

72. Ibid.; "May Irwin on Colored Talent," unidentified article (date unclear, ca. 1904), Locke Scrapbook, vol. 298.

73. Raymond Knapp, *The American Musical and the Formation of National Identity,* 12; D. Horowitz, *People's Voice,* 81–82.

74. "A Southern Pastime, First Class Lynching Parties," *Colored American,* February 3, 1900, 1.

Chapter 5. Unbounded Domesticity

1. Anhalt wrote the epigraph poem "while fishing for pike and digesting a meal" during a visit to May Irwin in Clayton during the summer of 1913, according to a note dated May 1913 in Locke Scrapbook, vol. 299.

2. Ann Randolph, "Comedienne and Cook: May Irwin."

3. *New York Sun,* November 20, 1904, Locke Scrapbook, vol. 298; *Denver Times,* May 23, 1913, Locke Scrapbook, vol. 299; *New York Telegraph,* May 26, 1907, Locke Scrapbook, vol. 298.

4. McArthur, *Actors and American Culture,* 72; Helen Ten Broeck, "Motherhood and Art," *Theatre* 24, no. 90 (1916): 372.

5. Butsch, "Bowery B'hoys and Matinee Ladies," 377. For an excellent article on female strategies in going public in the nineteenth century, see Kathy Peiss, "Going Public: Women in Nineteenth Century Cultural History," *American Literary History* 3 (1991): 817–28.

6. Ada Patterson, "At Home with May Irwin"; untitled and undated article, Special Collections, Hawn Memorial Library; "The Stage Woman as Cook," *Variety,* February 26, 1915, Locke Scrapbook, vol. 299.

7. *Boston Herald,* October 24, 1908, Locke Scrapbook, vol. 298.

8. "Stage Woman as Cook."

9. Ibid.; Ada Patterson, "May Irwin's Unique Philosophy of Life"; Patterson, "At Home with May Irwin," 522.

10. "May Irwin a Keen Business Woman," *New York Gazette,* December 31, 1898, Locke Scrapbook, vol. 297.

11. Patterson, "Irwin on Humor, Home, and Business," 259.

12. Ada Patterson, "What They Would Have Been, If They Weren't What They Were," 304.

13. Patterson, "At Home with May Irwin," 529.

14. "May Irwin, "Why Is the Servant Problem?" [*sic*], typed manuscript, Special Collections, Hawn Memorial Library. This section of the manuscript was also reprinted in Patterson, "At Home with May Irwin," 524.

15. "Stage Woman as Cook"; Ada Patterson, "Twenty Years a Star," 236.

16. Untitled article, *Watertown (N.Y.) Daily Times,* June 22, 1920.

17. "Stage Woman as Cook."

18. May Irwin, "Why Is the Servant Problem?" [sic].

19. May Irwin, "How a Woman Can Make and Save Money—Care and Dare," *New York American Journal,* 1915, Special Collections, Hawn Memorial Library.

20. Her impending takeover of the Bijou Theatre, reportedly resulting in her position as the only woman theater manager in New York, was covered in "Various Dramatic Topics," *New York Times,* November 16, 1900, 6.

21. Untitled article, *New York Times,* December 20, 1898, Locke Scrapbook, vol. 297.

22. May Irwin, "How a Woman Can Make and Save Money—Buy a Home, May Irwin Advises Salaried Women," *New York American Journal,* August 24, 1915, Special Collections, Hawn Memorial Library.

23. Auster, *Actresses and Suffragists,* 37.

24. D. Gilbert, *American Vaudeville,* 95.

25. Irwin, "Buy a Home, May Irwin Advises Salaried Women."

26. *Watertown (N.Y.) Daily Times,* February 13, 1922.

27. Untitled article, January 22, 1901, Locke Scrapbook, vol. 298, Special Collections, Hawn Memorial Library.

28. "Prohibition Drives May Irwin Out of the Inn Business," *New York Telegraph,* June 26, 1910, Locke Scrapbook, vol. 298.

29. "Short Talks," September 29, 1906, Locke Scrapbook, vol. 298.

30. Irwin's opinion on divorce is expressed in the column "Characters of the Passing Show," *Philadelphia Enquirer,* 1907, Locke Scrapbook, vol. 298.

31. "Divorce or No Divorce," in *May Irwin's Home Cooking,* 42.

32. Janice Blustein Longone, "'Tried Receipts': An Overview of America's Charitable Cookbooks," in *Recipes for Reading,* edited by Anne L. Bower, 17–28.

33. Other celebrities who joined the organization to aid young actresses included Billie Burke, Frances Starr, and May and Florence Nash. *New York Telegraph,* October 18, 1910, Locke Scrapbook, vol. 298.

34. "'It Takes a Mother to Be a Great Actress,' Says May Irwin," *Chicago Examiner,* March 26, 1913, Locke Scrapbook, vol. 299; Irwin, "My Views," 1062. (This is much the same argument used by actress Blanche Bates in "Motherhood and Art.")

35. Irwin, "My Views," 1062–63.

36. "May Irwin on Bringing Up Boys," January 23, 1905, Special Collections, Hawn Memorial Library.

37. Patterson, "Irwin on Humor, Home, and Business," 260.

38. Irwin, letter to Daly, 1903, Daly Papers.

39. Irwin, letter to Mr. Kenyon, December 5, 1907, from Hotel Woodstock in New York, private collection of Karen Killian; "Race Suicide on the American Stage," *Theatre,* March 1904, 69.

40. "Disks of Dough for Happy Boys," December 10, 1895, Special Collections, Hawn Memorial Library; Patterson, "At Home with May Irwin," 523.

41. Anne Cummings Frye, "'Acting for Movies Good Practice for Stage Folk,' Says May Irwin," Special Collections, Hawn Memorial Library.

42. Irwin's handwritten notes on performance, Special Collections, Thousand Islands Museum.

43. Laurence Senelick, "Consuming Passions: Eating and Stage at Fin de Siècle," 46.

44. *May Irwin's Home Cooking,* cover page.

45. The first two quotations are from reviews of the cookbook published in 1905 and included in the Locke Scrapbook. The third quotation is from the newspaper *On the St. Lawrence* in 1904, reprinted in Special Collections, Hawn Memorial Library.

46. *May Irwin's Home Cooking,* preface.

47. "May Irwin to Give Souvenirs," *New York Times,* December 19, 1904, 9.

48. Anne L. Bower, "Bound Together: Recipes, Lives, Stories, and Readings," in *Recipes for Reading,* edited by Bower, 5.

49. For a detailed analysis of recipes based on setting, character, and plot, see Anne Bower, "Cooking Up Stories: Narrative Elements in Community Cookbooks," in ibid., 29–50.

50. *May Irwin's Home Cooking,* 25, 39, 57, 67, 157, 207, 209.

51. Ibid., 61, 73.

52. Christine M. Mitchell, "The Rhetoric of Celebrity Cookbooks," 530.

53. *May Irwin's Home Cooking,* front pages, 268.

54. Ibid., 175, 227. For a detailed analysis of the language of cookbooks in general, see Colleen Cotter, "Claiming a Piece of the Pie: How the Language of Recipes Defines Community," in *Recipes for Reading,* edited by Bower, 51–71.

55. Ibid., 135, 197.

56. Ibid., 143, 237, 255.

57. Ibid., 168, 38, 40.

58. Ibid., 91 (blatant stereotypes are depicted on at least fifteen other pages: 39, 49, 89, 93, 11, 113, 139, 151, 153, 155, 179, 181, 195, 215, 244).

59. Ibid., 257, 211.

60. Ibid., 267.

61. Quoted in the *Thousand Islands Sun,* May 13, 1981, taken from the file of 1914, Special Collections, Hawn Memorial Library.

62. Cookbook originally owned by cookbook collector Carol Greenberg of Long Island, in Special Collections, Thousand Islands Museum.

63. The *New York Evening Journal* was a supplement to the *New York Times.* Irwin's articles ran periodically (usually biweekly) from March through October 1922. Copies are in Thousand Islands Museum.

64. "May Irwin Dramatizes Potatoes," *New York Evening Journal,* 1922, Thousand Islands Museum.

65. *May Irwin's Home Cooking,* preface.

66. "Address by Mrs. Kurt Eisfeldt" (see chap. 1, n. 75). The address contains the most complete description of her purchase of the island.

67. For example, a series of articles in the *Watertown (N.Y.) Daily Times* in 1914–15 include titles such as "May Irwin to Reside in Long Island Home," "May Irwin Wants a Farm on the River," and "May Irwin to Stay with Us."

68. "Make Breakfast a Festival," *New York Evening Journal,* 1922, Thousand Islands Museum.

69. Untitled article, *New York Telegraph,* April 8, 1912, Locke Scrapbook, vol. 299 (cattle); *New York Dramatic Mirror,* March 8, 1911, Locke Scrapbook, vol. 299 (milk prices); "Picks Chicken in a Minute," *Watertown (N.Y.) Daily Times,* February 11, 1914; "May Irwin Busy Harvesting Hay," *Watertown (N.Y.) Daily Times,* July 25, 1919.

70. "Address by Mrs. Kurt Eisfeldt."

71. From Mari-Jo Buhle, *Women and American Socialism, 1870–1920* (Urbana: University of Illinois Press 1981), 65, quoted in Glenna Matthews, *"Just a Housewife": The Rise and Fall of Domesticity in America,* 86.

72. George Cotkin, *Reluctant Modernism,* 75; Matthews, *"Just a Housewife,"* 36.

73. Catherine Beecher, *The True Remedy of the Wrongs of Women* (1851), quoted in Kathryn Kish Sklar, *Catherine Beecher: A Study in American Domesticity,* 222.

74. Patterson, "What They Would Have Been."

75. Matthews, *"Just a Housewife,"* 151.

76. Schlereth, *Victorian America,* 252.

77. Dorothy Schneider and Carl J. Schneider, *American Women in the Progressive Era, 1900–1920,* 23–24.

78. Irwin, "Why Is the Servant Problem?" [*sic*].

79. Schlereth, *Victorian America,* 73.

80. Ibid., 72.

81. Harvey Green, *The Light of the Home,* 88.

82. Brands, *Reckless Decade,* 55, 59–60.

83. William Leach, *Land of Desire: Merchants, Power, and the Rise of a New American Culture,* 43.

84. L. F. Baum, *The Art of Decorating Dry Goods, Windows, and Interiors* (Chicago, 1900), quoted in ibid., 60.

85. Review of *The Belle of Bridgeport, New York Times,* October 30, 1900, 6, *May Irwin's Home Cooking,* 233; May Irwin's notes for second cookbook, 41.

86. Julian Sivulka, *Soap, Sex and Cigarettes: A Cultural History of American Advertising,* 75–77, 37, 127, 152.

87. Erdman, *Blue Vaudeville,* 71; Irwin, "Buy a Home, May Irwin Advises Salaried Women."

88. Leach, *Land of Desire,* 148.

89. Shari L. Thurer, *The Myths of Motherhood,* 215.

90. Sheila M. Rothman, *Woman's Proper Place,* 22. See also Green, *Light of the Home,* 29–58.

91. Suzanne M. Marilley, "Frances Willard and the Feminism of Fear," 127; *May Irwin's Home Cooking,* 261.

92. Carroll Smith-Rosenberg, *Disorderly Conduct: Visions of Gender in Victorian America,* 177.

93. Irwin, "My Views," 1061.

Chapter 6. Causes and Compromise

1. Irwin, "Why I Want to Live," 446.

2. Information from Brinkley, *The Unfinished Nation*, an excellent source with well-researched information in many areas. One of the best books I have read on the history of the time directly preceding the turn of the twentieth century confines itself to the 1890s, Brands's *Reckless Decade.*

3. Grun, *The Timetables of History,* 16.

4. Leach, *Land of Desire,* 16.

5. Jacob A. Riis, *How the Other Half Lives,* 218 (emphasis added).

6. Rothman, *Woman's Proper Place,* 66.

7. Ibid., 73.

8. Eleanor Flexner, *Century of Struggle* (New York: Atheneum, 1973), 205–6.

9. Charlotte Erickson, *Invisible Immigrants: The Adaptation of Scottish and English Immigrants in Nineteenth Century America.*

10. Kate Sudlicum, "Stars Seen by Day," *Ev'ry Month,* February 1899, Special Collections, Hawn Memorial Library.

11. D. Gilbert, *American Vaudeville,* 97.

12. Sudlicum, "Stars Seen by Day."

13. May Irwin, "The Popular Theater," *New York Dramatic Mirror* 8 (May 1912), Locke Scrapbook, vol. 299.

14. "May Irwin on a Crusade," *New York Times,* August 16, 1915, 9.

15. "The Woman Who Dared."

16. See, for example, "May Irwin in Watertown for Meeting of Jefferson County Dairyman's Leagues," *Watertown (N.Y.) Daily Times,* September 24, 1917.

17. "May Irwin OK's Al in Hylan Fight," *Watertown (N.Y.) Daily Times,* August 7, 1925, Brown Scrapbook, 139.

18. "May Irwin Off Stage for a Time," *Watertown (N.Y.) Daily Times,* June 11, 1921; Wertheim, *Vaudeville Wars,* 230.

19. Wertheim, *Vaudeville Wars,* 110; "Nat Goodwin Will Attempt Shylock," *Chicago Tribune,* January 21, 1901, 9.

20. Bernard Sobel, *A Pictorial History of Vaudeville,* 69.

21. Sean P. Holmes, *Weavers of Dreams, Unite! Actors' Unionism in Early Twentieth-Century America,* 6.

22. "May Irwin Loses and Finds Watch," *Watertown (N.Y.) Daily Times,* February 9, 1922, Brown Scrapbook, 134

23. Patterson, "Irwin's Unique Philosophy of Life."

24. Henderson, *Theater in America,* 169.

25. Frances Starr, "Actors and Managers," *New York Times,* March 29, 1924, 14.

26. Equity timeline, http://www.actorsequity/timeline/timeline-intro.html.

27. Holmes, *Weavers of Dreams, Unite!,* 80.

28. Ibid., 83–84.

29. See, for example, "Prisoners Reach Clayton in Safety," *Watertown (N.Y.) Daily Times,* August 26, 1916, Brown Scrapbook, 115; "Escaped Germans Reach Clayton," *Gananoque (Ont.) Reporter,* August 28, 916, Brown Scrapbook, 17; "Germans Told to Keep Silent," *Watertown (N.Y.) Daily Times,* August 28, 1916, Brown Scrapbook, 118. This is an interesting and strange story. There was a lot of hatred of Germany then. The *Lusitania* had already gone under. The two escaped prisoners tunneled through the garden where inmates were growing vegetables and flowers. Both inmates claimed to have nothing to do with the German army—they were both gainfully employed—one in the United States and one in Canada. But they were accused of being spies. Evidently, Kurt, May's husband, had a wonderful talk with them in German. Newspapers in the area lauded their escape and labeled it "daring" and "thrilling." They were feted all around Clayton and asked to tell the story, especially about the leaky boat that they had to keep dumping water from as they crossed the St. Lawrence River.

30. Patterson, "At Home with May Irwin," 520–22.

31. The information about the girl, Nan Patterson, was in an untitled article, December 31, 1904, Locke Scrapbook, vol. 298. Irwin's comment to Governor Odell was reported in the *Indianapolis News*, December 1, 1906, Locke Scrapbook, vol. 298.

32. Robert Bertrand to the author, August 1995, on recollections of May Irwin; interview with Harold Kendall, town historian, Clayton, N.Y., July 1994.

33. Untitled article, *New York Telegraph,* 1909, Locke Scrapbook, vol. 298.

34. Charles Daunton, "Believe May Irwin: A Woman Can't Outlive Her Sense of Humor," *New York Evening World,* March 1, 1913, Locke Scrapbook, vol. 299.

35. "The Passing Show: The Critic's Saturday Night," undated review of *The Widow Jones, Boston Transcript,* Locke Scrapbook, vol. 297.

36. "Proposed Stocking Tariff Rouses Ire of May Irwin," *Chicago Tribune,* April 11, 1909, B3; Winifred Black, "The Unnecessity of the Blues," undated article, Special Collections, Hawn Memorial Library; "Strong for Vote, Says May Irwin," *Watertown (N.Y.) Daily Times,* June 8, 1916, Brown Scrapbook, 107.

37. Patterson, "At Home with May Irwin," 525.

38. Paula Baker, "The Domestication of Politics: Women and American Political Society, 1780–1920," 90.

39. Ibid., 98.

40. Sue Heinemann, *Timelines of American Women's History* (New York: Roundtable, 1996), 26–51.

41. American Presidential Project, reprint of Republican platform, January 7, 1916, http://www.presidency/ucsh.edu/ws/7pd=29634; Schneider and Schneider, *American Women in the Progressive Era,* 170.

42. This quotation, of a young suffragette marching in a parade down Fifth Avenue in New York in 1915, is from *This Fabulous Century,* vol. 2, *1910–1920* (New York: Time-Life, 1969), 46.

43. Ray Stannard Baker, *Woodrow Wilson: Life and Letters,* 274.

44. August Heckscher, *Woodrow Wilson,* 407; ratifications of U.S. amendments, http://www.usconstitution/net/constamret.html.

45. Francis Power Cobbe, *The Duties of Women* (New York, 1898), 138, quoted in Rothman, *Woman's Proper Place,* 23.

46. Frances E. Willard, *How to Win: A Book for Girls* (New York, 1881), quoted in Heinemann, *Timelines of American Women's History,* 148.

47. Jane Addams, "Why Women Should Vote," *Ladies' Home Journal,* January 1910, quoted in ibid., 41.

48. Irwin, "My Views," 1059; unidentified article, Locke Scrapbook, vol. 298.

49. For a succinct and excellent analysis of the connections between theater and suffragism, see Glenn, *Female Spectacle,* 126–54. See also Auster, *Actresses and Suffragists.*

50. Glenn, *Female Spectacle,* 140–41.

51. "May Irwin in Line," *Chicago Evening American,* May 23, 1916, 6; Irwin, "My Views," 1061.

52. Irwin, "My Views," 1057–58, 1063.

53. "What May Irwin Saw in Europe," *Dayton (Ohio) Journal,* May 24, 1908, Locke Scrapbook, vol. 298.

54. "May Irwin's Tale of Woe," *New York Sun,* February 4, 1900, Locke Scrapbook, vol. 297.

55. Undated verse, Special Collections, Thousand Island Museum.

56. "May Irwin Likes Frank Hitchcock," *Watertown (N.Y.) Daily Times,* June 8, 1916, Brown Scrapbook, 108.

57. May Irwin, "May Sorry for Favorite Sons," *Watertown (N.Y.) Daily Times,* June 10, 1916, Brown Scrapbook, 109.

58. William Hazlitt, "On Wit and Humour" (1819), in *Essays* (London: Walter Scott, 1889), reprinted in Bernard F. Dukore, *Dramatic Theory and Criticism: Greeks to Grotowski* (New York: Holt, Rinehart, and Winston, 1974), 604.

59. John Cotton, "Comedien [*sic*] Wishes She Could Take Cook Stove on Her Tours," *Minneapolis News*, March 14, 1914, Locke Scrapbook, vol. 299; "May Irwin's Tale of Woe."

60. Daunton, "Believe May Irwin."

61. Unidentified article, *Chicago Tribune,* Locke Scrapbook, vol. 297.

62. "May Irwin Sees Pretence as Fair Comedy Target," *Christian Science Monitor,* unclear date, circa 1916, Special Collections, Hawn Memorial Library; Patterson, "Irwin on Humor, Home, and Business," 258; Patterson, "At Home with May Irwin," 525; Florence Yoder, "May Irwin, Comedienne, Insists That She Is a Serious Person," *Washington Times,* September 25, 1915, 12.

63. Henri LaTouche, *Correspondence of Clement XIV and Carlin*, 1827, discussed in Helen O. Borrowitz, "Painted Smiles: Sad Clowns in French Art and Literature," *Bulletin of the Cleveland Museum of Art* 71, no. 1 (1984): 23–25.

64. Whythe, "Past Laughter," 66; unidentified article, January 14, 1905, Locke Scrapbook, vol. 298.

65. Irwin, "May Irwin on Art in Humor," 66.

66. Yoder, "May Irwin, Comedienne," 12.

67. "Strong for Vote, Says May Irwin."

68. "Wants Women to Get City Votes First," *New York Times,* March 26, 1900, Locke Scrapbook, vol. 298.

69. Irwin, "May Sorry for Favorite Sons."

70. "May Irwin to Head Laughter Bureau," *New York Times,* September 18, 1915, Locke Scrapbook, vol. 299.

71. Ada Patterson alludes to this visit in "May Irwin on Popularity," Special Collections, Hawn Memorial Library. The details of the incident are, unfortunately, unavailable.

72. "*33 Washington Square,* May Irwin's Play Anew," *New York Times,* September 28, 1915, 11; *Suffragist,* August 28, 1915, 2.

73. "War and Woman Suffrage," *New York Times,* August 13, 1918, 8.

74. Bordin, *Women and Temperance,* 3–4.

75. "Strong for Vote, Says May Irwin."

76. "May Irwin to Head Laughter Bureau."

77. Untitled article, *New York World,* November 28, 1914, Locke Scrapbook, vol. 299; Yoder, "May Irwin, Comedienne," 12.

78. "Have Dry Zone, Says May Irwin," *Watertown (N.Y.) Daily Times,* February 1922, Special Collections, Hawn Memorial Library.

79. Schlereth, *Victorian America,* 11.

80. Woodrow Wilson's "Appeal for Neutrality," August 19, 1914, in *Great Issues in American History,* edited by Richard Hofstadter, 205; Brinkley, *The Unfinished Nation,* 609.

81. Whythe, "Past Laughter," 64.

82. "May Irwin Dead; Comedienne, 76," *New York Times,* October 23, 1938, 41; "May Irwin Scores Hit," *Washington Herald,* September 25, 1915, 3; "May Irwin, Laugh Winner," *Washington Post,* September 25, 1915, 5; "Wilson Sees May Irwin," *New York Times,* September 25, 1915, 12–13.

83. Appointment book, Friday, September 24, 1915, Woodrow Wilson Presidential Papers; Memorandum Concerning May Irwin to Woodrow Wilson, September 21, 1915, ibid.

84. W. Sargent Epes, "Memories of May Irwin, Dead at 76."

85. "May Irwin Backs Wilson," *Washington Bee,* September 24, 1915, 4.

86. Yoder, "May Irwin, Comedienne," 13; Frances H. Early, *A World without War: How US Feminists Resisted World War I,* 100–101.

87. Brinkley, *The Unfinished Nation,* 610.

88. Woodrow Wilson, telegram to May Irwin, April 3, 1917, Wilson Presidential Papers.

89. "May Irwin, Comedienne, Was Celebrated Stage Figure for Nearly Half Century," *Watertown (N.Y.) Daily Times,* October 24, 1938, Special Collections, Hawn Memorial Library.

90. "The Business of Stage as Career," *Cosmopolitan,* April 1900, 657.

91. She recalled this kindness in detail in her address on June 12, 1928, to the joint Rotary and Kiwanis Clubs of Watertown, N.Y., Special Collections, Watertown Library, 6.

92. Early, *World without War,* 100–101.

93. Draft registration papers of Walter and Harold Irwin, accessed through Ancestry.com. Both of Irwin's sons did register for the draft, but neither served in the war.

94. "May Irwin Says Actresses Must Have Special License to Drink on Stage and Know When to Stop," undated article, Locke Scrapbook, vol. 298.

95. Cartoon, "May Irwin Asks President Wilson to Establish Department of Laughter," *St. Louis Democrat,* September 2, 1915, Locke Scrapbook, vol. 299; untitled article, April 1907, Locke Scrapbook, vol. 298.

96. Walter Lippmann, "Today and Tomorrow," *Herald Tribune,* January 28, 1936, Special Collections, Hawn Memorial Library.

Chapter 7. The Road to Rainbow's End

1. Irwin, "Why I Want to Live," 444.

2. "May Irwin Sees Self in Movie," *Watertown (N.Y.) Daily Times,* August 9, 1918. Information on Watertown and on F. W. Woolworth can be seen at http:/www.watertown-ny.gov/. This site includes many wonderful photographs of buildings and people from the 1880s to 1900.

3. "Farewell Tour? No, Says May- -Miss Irwin Indignant at Idea—Why, I'm Only a Girl," *Watertown (N.Y.) Daily Times,* April 10, 1919.

4. "Irwin Benefit Wins Acclaim," *Watertown (N.Y.) Daily Times,* August 30, 1927, Brown Scrapbook, 143.

5. Many theaters during this time used the term *opera house* to give their theaters a more respectable tone, even though their fare was seldom, if ever, opera and often consisted only of vaudeville acts. The Clayton Opera House featured a variety of entertainment, including a film showing of May Irwin's *Mrs. Black Is Back.*

6. "Clayton Opera House, Clayton," opening page of the website Theater, Museums, and Festivals, http://www.thousandislandslife.com.

7. "Harry C. Irwin," *New York Times,* May 24, 1947, 15.

8. Untitled article, November 20, 1910, Locke Scrapbook, vol. 298.

9. Untitled article, *New York Telegraph,* February 11, 1912, Locke Scrapbook, vol. 299.

10. These endeavors are referred to in several articles in the Special Collections, Hawn Memorial Library.

11. Irwin's obituary in the *Watertown (N.Y.) Daily Times* sets the price at $605,000. Clarence J. Webster, "May Irwin, Comedienne, Was Celebrated Figure for Nearly

Half Century," *Watertown (N.Y.) Daily Times*, October 24, 1938, Special Collections, Hawn Memorial Library.

12. "May Irwin Sells," *New York Times*, March 21, 1920, 45.

13. Unidentified article, November 8, 1905, Locke Scrapbook, vol. 298.

14. Untitled article, *New York Telegraph*, March 17, 1909, Locke Scrapbook, vol. 298.

15. "May Irwin Asks for Waist Injunction," *New York Times*, September 21, 1916, 14.

16. "May Irwin Sued for Loss by Fire," *New York Dramatic Mirror*, November 16, 1918, Locke Scrapbook, vol. 299; "Sue May Irwin for Fire," *New York Times*, November 2, 1918, 11.

17. "May's Summer Home," *Gananoque (Ont.) Reporter*, September 4, 1915, Brown Scrapbook, 96.

18. "Prohibition Drives May Irwin Out of the Inn Business," *New York Telegraph*, June 26, 1910, Locke Scrapbook, vol. 298; "New Actors' Home," *New York Times*, September 19, 1915, Brown Scrapbook, 98; "Irwin Isle Home for Actors," *Gananoque (Ont.) Reporter*, September 18, 1915, Brown Scrapbook, 97.

19. "May Irwin Would Quit the Islands," *Watertown (N.Y.) Daily Times*, September 26, 1913; "May Irwin Wants a Farm on River," *Watertown (N.Y.) Daily Times*, April 24, 1915.

20. "May to Have Summer Bungalow on Mason's Point," *Watertown (N.Y.) Daily Times*, September 24, 1917; "Secures Possession of Charles G. Emery Farm," *Watertown (N.Y.) Daily Times*, June 26, 1917.

21. These articles are collected in the Special Collections, Thousand Islands Museum.

22. "Actress to Auction Island Estate," *New York Times*, August 11, 1927; "May Irwin Farm Goes for $16,000," *Watertown (N.Y.) Daily Times*, August 22, 1927; "May Irwin's Island Sold," *Gananoque (Ont.) Reporter*, August 25, 1927, Brown Scrapbook, 141.

23. Norcom, *Grindstone Island*, 85.

24. "Paid Notice: Deaths Haxall, Elizabeth Dodge Rains, Ford," *New York Times*, February 9, 1998, http://www.newyorktimes.com/1998/02/09. Elizabeth was the granddaughter of Cleveland H. Dodge of the famous Dodge family, the wealthy owners of the Copper Queen Consolidated Mining Company. See Robert Glass Cleland, *A History of Phelps Dodge* (New York: Alfred A. Knopf, 1952).

25. "Delightful Day at the Islands," *Watertown (N.Y.) Daily Times*, August 21, 1909.

26. "May Irwin Here, Goes to Clayton," *Watertown (N.Y.) Daily Times*, May 3, 1920.

27. Unidentified article, Special Collections, Hawn Memorial Library.

28. "Address by Mrs. Kurt Eisfeldt" (see chap. 1, n. 75).

29. "Seats Too Small for May Irwin," *Watertown (N.Y.) Daily Times*, March 6, 1922, Brown Scrapbook, 136.

30. Untitled article, *Watertown (N.Y.) Daily Times*, January 14, 1922.

31. "W. C. Irwin to Be Buried in New York Mausoleum," *Detroit News*, May 18, 1922, 2.

32. May bought the tomb in 1915. A copy of the record of interments includes all eight members of the family. My copy includes handwritten notes to the side of the names. "May Helen Irwin" is identified as May's niece—but the burial dates coincide with Harry Irwin's wife's death. May herself is listed as "George Eisfeldt." Copy procured from Special Collections, Thousand Islands Museum.

33. Photograph in *Theatre*, July 1927.

34. Webster, "May Irwin, Comedienne."

35. "May Irwin to Return to Footlights at 72," *New York Times*, August 2, 1934, Brown Scrapbook, 154.

36. "May Irwin, Sticking to Farm, Lauds Playhouse," *Watertown (N.Y.) Daily Times*, August 11, 1934, Brown Scrapbook, 155.

37. "Puny Jumps Make a Frog Champion," *New York Times*, May 20, 1935, Brown Scrapbook, 156–57.

38. "May Irwin Film Projected in New York," *Watertown (N.Y.) Daily Times*, July 11, 1935; bulletin from the Museum of Modern Art in 1936, with May's handwritten comment, Special Collections, Thousand Islands Museum.

39. "May Irwin Celebrates 72nd Birthday," *On the St. Lawrence*, June 28, 1934, Special Collections, Hawn Memorial Library.

40. Webster, "May Irwin, Comedienne."

41. *Sun Dial, New York Times Supplement*, March 16, 1936, Special Collections, Thousand Islands Museum.

42. "May Irwin Gains after Stroke," *New York Times*, May 12, 1937, Brown Scrapbook, 162; "May Irwin Dead; Comedienne, 76," *New York Times*, October 23, 1938, 41; Epes, "Memories of May Irwin"; "Old Stage Friends Pay Tribute to May Irwin," *Watertown (N.Y.) Daily Times*, October 25, 1938, Brown Scrapbook, 164; "May Irwin's Will Is Filed," *Watertown (N.Y.) Daily Times*, November 4, 1938, Brown Scrapbook, 165.

43. The dispensation of the will is discussed in "Kurt Eisfeldt Left Estate of $77,604" and "Brother Willed Eisfeldt Estate," *Watertown (N.Y.) Daily Times*, June and November 1940, Brown Scrapbook, 173.

44. "Sgt. Wm. Irwin, Aged 24, Dies," unidentified Clayton, N.Y., newspaper, July 19, 1943, Special Collections, Thousand Islands Museum.

45. Scott Irwin, e-mail to Karen Killian, February 25, 2013; "Sgt. Wm. Irwin, Aged 24, Dies"; Scott Irwin, e-mail to Killian.

46. "Harry C. Irwin," *New York Times*, May 24, 1947, 15.

47. In my research at the Special Collections, Thousand Islands Museum, I came upon a newspaper clipping titled "May Irwin Once Star of 'Widow by Proxy,'" with a handwritten date of "November 8 [?] 1953" announcing a production of the play at the Watertown Little Theater.

48. See the following articles from the magazine *Thousand Islands:* Kim Lunman, "May Irwin and Her Keeper," April 13, 2009; Karen Killian, "May Irwin, Historical

Discoveries, Compiled by Karen Killian," May 2010; Karen Killian, review of *May Irwin's Home Cooking,* January 13, 2013; and reprint from the *Toronto Daily Star,* September 17, 1927, "May Irwin Gives Up Home to Join Hubby at Farming," March 2013. The magazine is available for free online at http://www.thousandislandslife.com.

49. Reprint of "May Irwin Planned to Build Bungalow," *Thousand Islands Sun,* October 4, 1917, in *Thousand Islands Sun,* July 15, 2015, 13; Sharon Bourquin, "Thousand Islands Museum News," *Thousand Islands Sun,* August 19, 2015, 17.

50. Robert Bertrand, letter to the author, November 1994.

51. "May Irwin Is Going to Build a Skyscraper in Chicago," *Chicago Tribune,* April 13, 1901.

52. Undated home films of May Irwin (which appear to be from the late 1920s or early 1930s), original film owned by the Thousand Islands Museum.

53. "Another Legend about May Irwin," *On the St. Lawrence,* December 8, 1950, Special Collections, Hawn Memorial Library.

54. Reginald Blyth, *Humor in English Literature: A Chronological Anthology* (London: Folcroth, 1959), 15, quoted in Gray, *Women and Laughter,* 7.

55. S. Horowitz, "Funny Women," 22. Although Horowitz's dissertation focuses on mid- to late-twentieth-century comediennes, her ideas can be applied to female comics of any period.

56. Martha Bensley Bruere and Mary Ritter Beard, eds., *Laughing Their Way: Women's Humor in America,* vi.

57. McLean, *American Vaudeville as Ritual,* 15.

58. J. S. Bratton, "Irrational Dress," in *The New Woman and Her Sisters: Feminism and Theatre, 1850–1914,* edited by Vivien Gardner and Susan Rutherford, 89.

59. Frederick Moore, "The Coon's Content," *Strand,* June 1903, reprinted in *Racism at the Turn of the Century,* edited by DeNevi and Holms, 105.

60. Dorman, "Shaping the Popular Image," 466.

61. Lott, *Love and Theft,* 40 (quote), 5, 6.

62. See, for example, Gloria T. Hull et al., *All the Women Are Black, All the Blacks Are Men, but Some of Us Are Brave;* and Nicole-Claude Mathieu, "'Woman' in Ethnology: The Other of the Other and the Other of the Self."

63. Dennison, *Scandalize My Name,* 394–97.

64. Moore, "The Coon's Content," reprinted in *Racism at the Turn of the Century,* edited by DeNevi and Holms, 105.

65. May Irwin, Clayton, New York, letter to Miss Ewing, 192?, Special Collections, Thousand Islands Museum.

Epilogue

1. For an excellent summary of theories of performance and reception, see Susan Bennett, *Theatre Audiences: A Theory of Production and Reception.*

2. Marco de Marinis, "New Theatrology and Performance Studies," translated by Marie Pecorari, *Drama Review* 55, no. 4 (2011): 68.

3. Pilgrim, *New Jim Crow Museum.*

4. Willfried Passow, "The Analysis of Theatrical Performance: The State of the Art," *Poetics Today* (1981): 217–54.

5. Stanley Fish, *"Is There a Text in This Class?"* (Cambridge, Mass.: Harvard University Press, 1980).

6. For a sharp and penetrating analysis of the idea of performing racism and sexism in ironic comedy, see Dustin Bradley Goltz, "Ironic Performativity: Amy Schumer's Big (White) Balls."

Selected Bibliography

Special Collections and Archives

British Library Archives. Colindale, England.

Brown, Jack, Scrapbook. Mallorytown, Ontario, Canada.

Cozier, W. Collin. "The Corporal Hugh Campbell Family." Unpublished manuscript, 1994. Ancaster, Ontario, Canada.

Daly, Augustin, Papers. Folger Shakespeare Library, Washington, D.C.

Harvard Theatre Library, Cambridge, Mass.

Hawn Memorial Library, Clayton, N.Y.

Houghton Library, Harvard University, Cambridge, Mass.

Hutton, Jack. "Is There a Canadian Ragtime?" Notes for Montreal Ragtime Festival, early 1980s.

Killian, Karen. Private clippings and letter collection, Clinton, N.Y.

Killian, Karen, Janice Cleary, and Ragtime Bob Darch. Private sheet music collections.

Levy, Lester S. Collection of Sheet Music. Sheridan Libraries, John Hopkins University, Baltimore, Md.

Library of Congress, Washington, D.C.

Locke, Robinson, Scrapbooks. NAFR, vols. 297–99. Series I, Reel 26, Zc528. New York Library of the Performing Arts, New York.

Music Division, Library of Congress, Washington, D.C.

Music Division, New York Library of the Performing Arts, New York.

Thousand Island Museum, Clayton, N.Y.

Watertown Daily Times Morgue, Watertown, N.Y.

Watertown Library, Special Collections, Watertown, N.Y.

Whitby Archives. Whitby, Ontario, Canada.

Wilson, Woodrow, Presidential Papers. Special Collections, Manuscript Division, Library of Congress, Washington, D.C.

Film

Irwin, May. *Hearts and Jerseys* (1918). Thousand Island Museum Archive, Clayton, N.Y.

Irwin, May, and John Rice. *The Kiss.* Produced in Thomas Edison's Vitascope, 1896. Special Collections in both the Library of Congress and the New York Public Library of the Performing Arts.

Irwin, May, with friends and family. Videocassette of silent home movies, circa late 1920s, early 1930s. Author's copy procured from private collection of Bob Darch.

Pilgrim, David, narrator. *The New Jim Crow Museum: Learning from the Past, Changing Lives.* DVD. Big Rapids, Mich.: Ferris State University Media Productions, 2004.

Three Vaudeville Women: May Irwin, Marie Dressler, and Eva Tanguay (2008). Directed by Kathleen Golden. Edinboro, Pa.: Edinboro Media.

Scripts

Some additional scripts available in multiple libraries.

Du Souchet. *The Countess de Cagiac.* (Renamed *The Swell Miss Fitzwell* for performance, 1897). TMs. Rare Book Collections, Library of Congress, Washington, D.C.

Ade, George. *Mrs. Peckham's Carouse* (1899).

Daly, Augustin. *After Business Hours* (1886).

———. *Love on Crutches* (1884).

———. *A Night Off* (1885).

———. *Red Letter Days* (1884).

Hobart, George. *Mrs. Black Is Back* (1905).

———. *Mrs. Wilson, That's All* (1906).

Scripts on microfilm. Manuscript Room, Library of Congress, Washington, D.C.

Sound Recordings

The High Priestess of Jollity and the Southern Singer. Archeophone 5015. Produced by Richard Martin and Meagan Hennessey, 2011.

Music Division, Library of Congress, Washington, D.C.

Other Sources

Abbott, Lynn, and Doug Seroff. *Ragged but Right: Black Traveling Shows, "Coon Songs," and the Dark Pathway to Jazz and Blues.* Jackson: University Press of Mississippi, 2007.

American Heritage Cookbook. New York: Simon and Schuster, 1964.Aronson, Rudolph. *Theatrical and Musical Memories.* New York: McBride, Nast, 1913.

Auerbach, John. *Body Shots: Early Cinema's Incarnations.* Berkeley: University of California Press, 2006.

Aunt Babette's CookBook. New York: Bloch, 1909.

Auster, Albert. *Actresses and Suffragists: Women in the American Theatre, 1890–1920.* New York: Praeger, 1984.

Austin, Mary. "The Sense of Humor in Women." *New Republic,* November 26, 1924, 10–13.

Baker, Paula. "The Domestication of Politics: Women and American Political Society, 1780–1920." In *Unequal Sisters,* edited by Vicki L. Ruiz and Ellen Carol DuBois, 85–110. 2nd ed. New York: Routledge, 1994.

Baker, Ray Stannard. *Woodrow Wilson: Life and Letters.* Vol. 6. Garden City, N.Y.: Doubleday, 1931.

Bakhtin, Mikhail. *Rabelais and His World.* Translated by Helene Iswolsky. Cambridge, Mass.: MIT Press, 1971.

Bank, Rosemarie K. *Theatre Culture in America, 1825–1860.* Cambridge: Cambridge University Press, 1997.

Banta, Martha. *Imaging American Women.* New York: Columbia University Press, 1987.

Barreca, Regina R. "Hate and Humour in Women's Writing: A Discussion of Twentieth Century Authors." Ph.D. diss., City University of New York, 1987.

———. *Last Laughs: Perspectives on Women and Comedy.* New York: Gordon and Breach, 1988.

———. *They Used to Call Me Snow White . . . but I Drifted.* London: Penguin, 1992.

Barringer, Paul. *The American Negro: His Past and Future.* Raleigh, N.C.: Edward and Boughton, 1900.

Beane, Annemarie, James V. Hatch, and Brooks McNamara, eds. *Readings in Nineteenth Century Blackface Minstrelsy.* Middletown, Conn.: Wesleyan Press, 1996.

Bell, Margaret. "May Irwin . . . Peeress of Stage Widows." *Mclean's,* October 1913, 99.

Bennett, Susan. *Theatre Audiences: A Theory of Production and Reception.* 2nd ed. London: Routledge, 2003.

Blackmon, Douglas A. *Slavery by Another Name.* New York: Random House, 2009.

Blum, Daniel. *Great Stars of the American Stage.* New York: Greenburg, 1952.

———. *A Pictorial History of American Theatre: 100 Years, 1860–1960.* New York: Crown, 1960.

Bordin, Ruth. *Women and Temperance.* 1981. Reprint, New Brunswick, NJ: Rutgers University Press, 1990.

Bordo, Susan. *Unbearable Weight: Feminism, Western Culture, and the Body.* Berkeley: University of California Press, 1995.

Bower, Anne L., ed. *Recipes for Reading.* Amherst: University of Massachusetts Press, 1997.

Brands, H. W. *The Reckless Decade: America in the 1890s.* New York: St. Martin's, 1995.

Brawley, Benjamin. *A Social History of the American Negro.* New York: Macmillan, 1970.

Brinkley, Alan. *The Unfinished Nation.* New York: Alfred A. Knopf, 1993.

Brooks, Daphne A. *Bodies in Dissent: Spectacular Performances of Race and Freedom, 1850–1910.* Durham, N.C.: Duke University Press, 2006.

Brown, Janet. "The 'Coon-Singer' and the 'Coon Song': A Case Study of the Performer-Character Relationship." *Journal of American Culture* 7 (Spring–Summer 1984): 1–8.

Brown, Jayna. *Babylon Girls: Black Women Performers and the Shaping of the Modern.* Durham, N.C.: Duke University Press, 2008.

Brown, T. Allston. *A History of the New York Stage, 1732–1901.* 3 vols. 1903. Reprint, New York: Blom, 1964.

Bruere, Martha Bensley, and Mary R. Beard, eds. *Laughing Their Way: Women's Humor in America.* New York: Macmillan, 1934.

Bunkers, Suzanne L. "Why Are These Women Laughing? The Power and Politics of Women's Humor." *Studies in American Humor* 4, nos. 1–2 (1985): 82–93.

Butsch, Richard. "Bowery B'hoys and Matinee Ladies: The Re-gendering of Nineteenth Century American Theater Audiences." *American Quarterly* 46 (September 1994): 374–405.

Caffin, Caroline. *Vaudeville.* New York: Mitchell Kennerley, 1914.

Cahn, William. *The Laugh Makers.* New York: Putnam, 1957.

Carlson, Susan. *Women and Comedy.* Ann Arbor: University of Michigan Press, 1991.

Cash, W. J. *The Mind of the South.* 1941. Reprint, New York: Random House, 1991.

Chafe, William H. *The American Woman.* Oxford: Oxford University Press, 1972.

Chinoy, Helen Krich, and Linda Walsh Jenkins, eds. *Women in American Theatre.* New York: Theatre Communications Group, 1987.

Clark, Larry D. "Female Characters on the New York Stage in the Year of Suffrage: Enter Advocacy, Quietly, Stage Left." *Theatre History Studies* 7 (1987): 61–72.

Clemens, Samuel, and Charles D. Warner. *The Gilded Age.* New York: Harper and Row, 1899.

CoCo, Janice M. *John Sloan's Women: A Psychoanalysis of Vision.* Cranberry, N.Y.: Associated University Press, 2004.

Cordova, Richard D. *Picture Personalities: The Emergence of the Star System in America.* Urbana: University of Illinois Press, 1990.

Cothern, Leah Kathleen. "The Coon Song: A Study of American Music, Entertainment and Racism." Master's thesis, University of Oregon, 1990.

Cotkin, George. *Reluctant Modernism.* New York: Twayne, 1992.

Cott, Nancy F., ed. *The Grounding of Modern Feminism.* New Haven, Conn.: Yale University Press, 1987.

———. *Roots of Bitterness: Documents of the Social History of American Women.* New York: E. P. Hutton, 1972.

Croft-Cooke, Rupert, and Peter Cotes. *Circus: A World History.* New York: Macmillan, 1977.

Culhane, John. *The American Circus.* New York: Henry Holt, 1990.

Cullen, Frank, with Florence Hackman and Donald McNeilly. *Vaudeville, Old and New: An Encyclopedia of Variety Performers in America.* Vol. 1. New York: Routledge, 2007.

Daly, Joseph Francis. *Life of Augustin Daly.* New York: Macmillan, 1917.
Davis, Michael M., Jr. *The Exploitation of Pleasure: A Study of Commercial Recreations in New York City.* New York: Department of Child Hygiene of the Russell Stage Foundation, 1911.
Davis, Tracy. *Actresses as Working Women.* London: Routledge, 1991.
DeNevi, Donald P., and Doris A. Holms, eds. *Racism at the Turn of the Century: Documentary Perspectives, 1870–1910.* San Rafael, Calif.: Leswing, 1973.
Dennely, Thomas Edward. "Social Reform and the American Theatre, 1880–1920." Ph.D. diss., Michigan State University, 1974.
Dennison, Sam. *Scandalize My Name: Black Imagery in American Popular Music.* New York: Garland, 1982.
Dorman, James H. "Shaping the Popular Image of Post-Reconstruction American Blacks: The 'Coon Song' Phenomenon of the Gilded Age." *American Quarterly* 40 (Dec 1988): 450–67.
Dreiser, Theodore. *Sister Carrie.* New York: Doubleday, 1900.
Dudden, Faye E. *Women in the American Theatre: Actresses and Audiences, 1790–1870.* New Haven, Conn.: Yale University Press, 1994.
Early, Frances H. *A World without War: How US Feminists Resisted World War I.* Syracuse, N.Y.: Syracuse University Press, 1997.
Eaton, Walter Prichard. *Plays and Players.* Cincinnati: Stewart and Kidd, 1916.
Engle, Ron, Tice Miller, and Oscar Brocket, eds. *The American Stage: Social and Economic Issues from the Colonial Period to the Present.* Cambridge: Cambridge University Press, 1993.
Epes, W. Sargent. "Memories of May Irwin, Dead at 76." *Variety,* October 26, 1938, 26.
Erdman, Andrew L. *Blue Vaudeville: Sex, Morals, and the Mass Marketing of Amusement, 1895–1915.* Jefferson, N.C.: McFarland, 2004.
———. *Queen of Vaudeville: The Story of Eva Tanguay.* Ithaca, N.Y.: Cornell University Press, 2012.
Erickson, Charlotte. *Invisible Immigrants: The Adaptation of Scottish and English Immigrants in Nineteenth Century America.* Ithaca, N.Y.: Cornell University Press, 1972.
Ewen, David. *The Life and Death of Tin Pan Alley.* New York: Funk and Wagnalls, 1964.
Fields, Armond. *Sophie Tucker, First Lady of Show Business.* Jefferson, N.C.: McFarland, 2003.
———. *Women Vaudeville Stars: Eighty Biographical Profiles.* Jefferson, N.C.: McFarland, 2006.
Foner, Eric. *Forever Free.* New York: Random House, 2006.
Ford, James L. "The Coming Queens of Comedy." *Everybody's,* June 1903, 553–60.
Freidl, Bettina, ed. *On to Victory: Propaganda Plays of the Woman Suffrage Movement.* Boston: Northeastern University Press, 1987.
Freidman, Sharon. "Feminism as Theme in Twentieth Century Women's Drama." *American Studies* 25 (Spring 1984): 69–89.
Furia, Philip. *The Poets of Tin Pan Alley.* New York: Oxford University Press, 1990.

Gardner, Vivien, and Susan Rutherford, eds. *The New Woman and Her Sisters: Feminism and Theatre, 1850–1914.* Ann Arbor: University of Michigan Press, 1992.

Gilbert, Anne Hartley. *Stage Reminiscences of Mrs. Gilbert.* Edited by Charlotte M. Martin. New York: Scribner, 1901.

Gilbert, Douglas. *American Vaudeville: Its Life and Times.* New York: Dover, 1940.

Glenn, Susan A. *Female Spectacle: The Theatrical Roots of Modern Feminism.* Cambridge, Mass.: Harvard University Press, 2000.

Goldberg, Isaac. *Tin Pan Alley.* New York: John Day, 1930.

Goltz, Dustin Bradley. "Ironic Performativity: Amy Schumer's Big (White) Balls." *Text and Performance Quarterly* 35, no. 4 (2015): 266–85.

Grau, Robert. *40 Years of Observation of the Music and the Drama.* New York: Broader, 1909.

———. "When They Were Twenty-One." Pts. 1 and 2. *Theatre,* April 1915, 191–92; June 1915, 307.

Gray, Frances. *Women and Laughter.* Charlottesville: University Press of Virginia, 1994.

Green, Harvey. *The Light of the Home.* New York: Pantheon, 1983.

Grossman, Barbara. "Fanny Brice." Ph.D. diss., Tufts University. 1984.

Grun, Bernard. *The Timetables of History.* New York: Simon and Schuster, 1975.

Hall, Margaret. "Personal Recollections of Augustin Daly." Pts. 1–4. *Theatre,* June 1905, 150–53; July 1905, 174–78; August 1905, 188–91; September 1905, 213–15.

Hamberlin, Larry. "National Identity in Snyder and Berlin's 'Opera Rag.'" *American Music* 22, no. 3 (2004): 380–406.

Hamilton, Clayton. "The Players." *Everybody's,* May 1913, 678–88.

Hapgood, Norman. *The Stage in America.* New York: Macmillan, 1901.

Heckscher, August. *Woodrow Wilson.* New York: Scribner, 1991.

Heller, Adele, and Lois Rudnick, eds. *1915: The Cultural Moment.* New Brunswick, N.J.: Rutgers University Press, 1991.

Henderson, Mary C. *Theater in America.* New York: Harry N. Abrams, 1986.

Hitchcock, Wiley, and Stanley Sadie, eds. *The New Grove Dictionary of American Music.* Vols. 1 and 4. New York: Grove, 1986.

Hofstadter, Richard, ed. *Great Issues in American History.* Vol. 2. New York: Vintage, 1958.

Holledge, Julie. *Innocent Flowers: Women in the Edwardian Theatre.* London: Virago, 1981.

Holmes, Sean P. *Weavers of Dreams, Unite! Actors' Unionism in Early Twentieth-Century America.* Urbana: University of Illinois Press, 2013.

Horowitz, David A. *The People's Voice: A Populist Cultural History of Modern America.* Cornwall-on-Hudson, N.Y.: Sloan, 2008.

Horowitz, Susan N. "Funny Women: A Study of Female Comic Personae (Ball, Diller, Burnett, Hawn)." Ph.D. diss., City University of New York, 1988.

Hull, Gloria T., Patricia Bell Scott, Barbara Smith, and May Persey. *All the Women Are Black, All the Blacks Are Men, but Some of Us Are Brave.* New York: Feminist Press, 1982.

Hymowitz, Carol, and Michaele Weissman. *A History of Women in America.* New York: Bantam Books, 1978.

Irwin, May. "The Business of the Stage as a Career." *Cosmopolitan,* April 1900, 655–60.

———. "May Irwin on Art in Humor." *Home,* January 1900, 64–69.

———. *May Irwin's Home Cooking.* New York: Stokes, 1904.

———. "My Views on That Ever-Interesting Topic—Woman." *Green Book,* December 1912, 1057–63.

———. "Nursing the Nerves." *Green Book Album,* July 2, 1904, 152–56.

———. "Why I Want to Live to Be a Hundred." *Green Book,* September 10, 1913, 441–46.

Isaacs, Edith J. R. *The Negro in the American Theatre.* New York: Theatre Arts, 1947.

Kasson, John F. *Rudeness and Civility: Manners in Nineteenth Century Urban America.* New York: Hill and Wang, 1990.

Kelly, Fred C. *George Ade, Warmhearted Satirist.* New York: Bobbs-Merrill, 1947.

Kelly, Joan. *Women: History and Theory.* Chicago: University of Chicago Press, 1984.

Kennedy, Matthew. *Marie Dressler: A Biography with a Listing of Major Stage Performances, a Filmography and Discography.* Jefferson, N.C.: McFarland, 2006.

Kerr, Walter. *The Silent Clowns.* New York: Alfred A. Knopf, 1979.

Kibler, Alison. *Rank Ladies: Gender and Cultural Hierarchy in American Vaudeville.* Chapel Hill: University of North Carolina Press, 1999.

Kimball, Grace. *Theatres* 17 (January 1897): 6.

Knapp, Raymond. *The American Musical and the Formation of National Identity.* Princeton, N.J.: Princeton University Press, 2005.

Kraditor, Aileen S., ed. *Up from the Pedestal: Selected Writings in the History of American Feminism.* Chicago: Quadrangle Books, 1968.

Krasner, David. "'Whose Role Is It Anyway?': Gilpin and the Harlem Renaissance." *African American Review* 29, no. 3 (1995): 483–96.

Kuehn, Eileen Karen. "Maude Adams, an American Idol: True Womanhood Triumphant in the Late Nineteenth and Early Twentieth Century Theatre." Ph.D. diss., University of Wisconsin–Madison, 1984.

Lahue, Kalton, and Samuel Gill. *Clown Princes and Court Jesters.* New York: Barnes, 1970.

Lavitt, Pamela A. Brown. "First of the Red Hot Mamas: 'Coon Shouting' and the Jewish Ziegfeld Girl." *American Jewish History* 87, no. 4 (1999): 253–90.

Leach, William. *Land of Desire: Merchants, Power, and the Rise of a New American Culture.* New York: Random House, 1993.

Lears, Jackson. *Fables of Abundance: A Cultural History of Advertising in America.* New York: HarperCollins, 1994.

Lee, Betty. *Marie Dressler, the Unlikeliest Star.* Lexington: University Press of Kentucky, 1997.

Lerner, Gerda. *The Majority Finds Its Past.* New York: Oxford University Press, 1981.

Leslie, Amy. *Some Players.* Chicago: Strong, 1899.

Lewis, Robert M., ed. *From Traveling Show to Vaudeville: Theatrical Spectacle in America, 1830–1910.* Baltimore: John Hopkins University Press, 2003.

Logan, Olive. *Apropos of Women and Theatres.* New York: Carleton, 1869.

Logan, Rayford W. *The Betrayal of the Negro.* New York: Collier Books, 1965.

Long, Linda Sue. "The Art of Beatrice Hereford, Cissie Loftus, and Dorothy Sand." Ph.D. diss., University of Texas, 1982.

Lott, Eric. *Love and Theft.* New York: Oxford University Press, 1993.

Malpede, Karen, ed. *Women in Theatre: Compassion and Hope.* New York: Drama Book, 1983.

Marcuse, Maxwell F. *Tin Pan Alley in Gaslight.* Watkins Glen, N.Y.: Century House, 1959.

Marilley, Suzanne M. "Frances Willard and the Feminism of Fear." *Feminist Studies* 19 (Spring 1993): 123–46.

Marks, Edward. *They All Sang: From Tin Pan Alley to Abbott J. Liebling.* New York: Viking, 1935.

Martin, Linda, and Kerry Segrave. *Women and Comedy.* Secaucus, N.J.: Citadel, 1986.

Mates, Julian. *America's Musical Stage: Two Hundred Years of Musical Theatre.* Westport, Conn.: Greenwood Press, 1985.

Mathieu, Myron, ed. *Papers and Proceedings of the Conference of American Popular Entertainment.* Westport, Conn.: Greenwood Press, 1977.

Mathieu, Nicole-Claude. "'Woman' in Ethnology: The Other of the Other and the Other of the Self." *Feminist Issues* 8, no. 1 (1988): 3–13.

Matthews, Glenna. *"Just a Housewife": The Rise and Fall of Domesticity in America.* New York: Oxford University Press, 1987.

May Irwin Songs. New York: Dempsey, 1897.

Mayo, Edith, ed. *American Material Culture.* Bowling Green, Ohio: Bowling Green State University Press, 1984.

McArthur, Benjamin. *Actors and American Culture.* Philadelphia: Temple University Press, 1984.

McElya, Micki. *Clinging to Mammy: The Faithful Slave in Twentieth-Century America.* Cambridge, Mass.: Harvard University Press, 2007.

McLean, Albert F., Jr. *American Vaudeville as Ritual.* Lexington: University Press of Kentucky, 1965.

McNamara, Brooks, ed. *American Popular Entertainment.* New York: Performing Arts Journal, 1983.

Miller, Tice L. "Alan Dale: The Hearst Critic." *Educational Theatre Journal* 26 (March 1974): 69–80.

Mitchell, Christine M. "The Rhetoric of Celebrity Cookbooks." *Journal of Popular Culture* 43, no. 3 (2010): 524–40.

Mizejewski, Linda. *Pretty/Funny.* Austin: University of Texas Press, 2014.

Moogk, Edward B. *Roll Back the Years: History of Canadian Recorded Sound and Its Legacy.* Ottawa: National Library of Canada, 1975.

Morgan, Francesca. *Women and Patriotism in Jim Crow America.* Chapel Hill: University of North Carolina Press, 2005.

Morris, Linda A., ed. *American Women Humorists: Critical Essays.* New York: Garland, 1994.

Morris, Lloyd. *Incredible New York.* New York: Random House, 1951.

Morrow, Lee Alan. "Elsie Janis: A Compensatory Biography." Ph.D. diss., Northwestern University, 1988.

Mullin, Donald. *Victorian Actors and Actresses in Review.* Westport, Conn.: Greenwood Press, 1983.

Musser, Charles. *The Emergence of Cinema: The American Screen to 1907.* New York: Charles Scribner and Sons, 1990.

Nasau, David. *Going Out.* New York: Basic Books, 1993.

Nash, Elizabeth. *The Luminous Ones: A History of the Great Actresses.* New York: Lang, 1991.

Newton, Harry L. *Some Vaudeville Monologues.* Chicago: T. S. Denison, 1917.

Norcom, Stanley. *Grindstone: An Island World Remembered.* Edited by Norvin Hein. New Cumberland, Pa.: Robert Edwards, 1993.

Oakes, James. *The Ruling Race: A History of American Slaveholders.* New York: Random House, 1982.

Odell, George. *Annals of the New York Stage.* 16 vols. New York: Columbia University Press, 1949.

Page, Brett. *Writing for Vaudeville.* Springfield, Mass.: Writers' Library, 1915.

Patterson, Ada. "At Home with May Irwin." *Green Book Album,* March 1911, 520–25.

———. "May Irwin on Humor, Home, and Business." *Theatre,* October 5, 1905, 257–60.

———. "May Irwin's Unique Philosophy of Life." *Woman's Home Companion,* February 1907, 608.

———. "The Players' Christmas." *Theatre,* December 1912, 196–97.

———. "Players in Business." *Theatre,* October 1916, 202, 250.

———. "Twenty Years a Star." *Theatre,* November 1915, 236–37.

———. "What They Would Have Been, If They Weren't What They Were." *Theatre,* May 1916, 292, 304.

———. "Where They Are Summering." *Theatre,* August 1915, 60–61, 94.

Peiss, Kathy. *Cheap Amusements: Working Class Women and Leisure in Turn-of-the-Century New York.* Philadelphia: Temple University Press, 1986.

Pinter, Nell Irvin. *Standing at Armageddon: The U.S., 1877–1919.* New York: W. W. Norton, 1987.

Pittenger, Peach. "Women in American Popular Entertainment: Creating a Niche in the Vaudevillian Era, 1890s to 1930s." Ph.D. diss, Ohio State University, 2005.

Randolph, Ann. "Comedienne and Cook: May Irwin." *National* (September 1913): 1101–2.

Ranous, Doris Knowlton Thompson. *Diary of a Daly Debutante.* 1910. Reprint, New York: Benjamin Blom, 1972.

Reincke, Nancy. "Antidote to Dominance: Women's Laughter as Counteraction." *Journal of Popular Culture* 24, no. 4 (1991): 27–37.

Riis, Jacob A. *How the Other Half Lives.* 1890. Reprint, New York: Dover, 1971.

Robinson, Alice M., Vera Mowry Roberts, and Milly S. Barranger, eds. *Notable Women in American Theatre.* Westport, Conn.: Greenwood Press, 1989.

Rodger, Gillian M. *Champagne Charlie and Pretty Jemima: Variety Theater in the Nineteenth Century.* Urbana: University of Illinois Press, 2010.

———. "Legislating Amusements: Class Politics and Theater Law in New York City." *American Music* 20, no. 4 (2002): 381–98.

Rothman, Sheila M. *Woman's Proper Place.* New York: Basic Books, 1978.

Russell, Lillian. "Lillian Russell's Reminiscences." *Cosmopolitan,* February 1922.

Ryan, Mary P. *Womanhood in America: From Colonial Times to the Present.* New York: New Viewpoints, 1975.

Saddlemeyer, Ann, ed. *Early Stages: Theatre in Ontario, 1800–1914.* Toronto: University of Toronto Press, 1990.

Sampson, Henry T. *Blacks in Blackface.* Metuchen, N.J.: Scarecrow Press, 1980.

Samson, A. L. "May Irwin." *Metropolitan* (1898): 152–57.

Sanborn, Kate. *The Wit of Women.* New York: Funk and Wagnalls, 1885.

Schafer, William J., and Johannes Riedel. *The Art of Ragtime.* Baton Rouge: Louisiana State University Press, 1973.

Schlereth, Thomas J. *Victorian America: Transformations in Everyday Life, 1876–1915.* New York: HarperCollins, 1991.

Schneider, Dorothy, and Carl J. Schneider. *American Women in the Progressive Era, 1900–1920.* New York: Doubleday, 1994.

Schneir, Miriam, ed. *Feminism: The Essential Historical Writings.* New York: Vintage, 1972

Senelick, Laurence. "Consuming Passions: Eating and Stage at Fin de Siècle." *Gastronomica* 5, no. 2 (2005): 43–49.

Sivulka, Julian. *Soap, Sex and Cigarettes: A Cultural History of American Advertising.* Belmont, Calif.: Wadsworth, 1998.

Skinner, Otis. *Footlights and Spotlights.* New York: Curtis, 1923.

Sklar, Kathryn Kish. *Catherine Beecher: A Study in American Domesticity.* New York: W. W. Norton, 1973.

Slide, Anthony. *The Vaudevillians.* Westport, Conn.: Arlington House, 1981.

Smith, John David, ed. *Anti-Black Thought, 1860–1925.* 7 vols. New York: Garland, 1993.

Smith-Rosenberg, Carroll. *Disorderly Conduct: Visions of Gender in Victorian America.* New York: Oxford University Press, 1985.

Snyder, Robert. *The Voice of the City.* New York: Oxford University Press, 1989.

Sobel, Bernard. *A Pictorial History of Vaudeville.* New York: Citadel, 1961.

Spaeth, Sigmund. *A History of Popular Music in America.* New York: Random House, 1948.

Spitzer, Marian. *The Palace.* New York: Atheneum, 1969.

Stark, Steven. "Gap Politics." *Atlantic Monthly,* July 1996, 71–80.

Stein, Charles W., ed. *American Vaudeville as Seen by Its Contemporaries.* New York: Alfred A. Knopf, 1984.

Stewart, Travis. *No Applause, Just Throw Money.* New York: Faber and Faber, 2005.

Stowell, Sheila. *A Stage of Their Own: Feminist Playwrights of the Suffrage Era.* Ann Arbor: University of Michigan Press, 1992.

Strang, Lewis C. *Celebrated Comedians.* Boston: L. C. Page, 1901.

———. *Famous Actresses of the Day in America.* Boston: L. C. Page, 1899.

Strausbaugh, John. *Black Like You: Blackface, Whiteface, Insult and Imitation in American Popular Culture.* New York: Penguin, 2008.

Sturtevant, Victoria. *A Great Big Girl Like Me: The Films of Marie Dressler.* Urbana: University of Illinois Press, 2009.

Tanner, Jo A. *Dusky Maidens: The Odyssey of the Early Black Dramatic Actress.* Westport, Conn.: Greenwood Press, 1992.

Thurer, Shari L. *The Myths of Motherhood.* New York: Houghton Mifflin, 1994.

Tobin, Terence, ed. *Letters of George Ade.* Lafayette, Ind.: Purdue University Press, 1973.

Toth, Emily Clark. "A Laughter of Their Own: Women's Humor in the United States." In *Critical Essays on American Humor,* edited by William Bedford Clark and W. Craig Turner, 199–215. Boston: G. K. Hall, 1985.

Tucker, Sophie. *Some of These Days.* Garden City, N.Y.: Doubleday, 1945.

Unterbrink, Mary. *Funny Women: American Comediennes, 1860–1985.* Jefferson, N.C.: McFarland, 1987.

Walker, Nancy. *A Very Serious Thing: Women's Humor and American Culture.* Minneapolis: University of Minnesota Press, 1988.

———. "Wit, Sentimentality, and the Image of Women in the Nineteenth Century." *American Studies* 22, no. 2 (1981): 5–22.

Walsh, Jim. "May Irwin." *Hobbies* 68 (July 1963): 32–35.

Webb, Barbara L. "Authentic Possibilities: Plantation Performance of the 1890s." *Theatre Journal* 56, no. 1 (2004): 63–82.

Wertheim, Frank. *Vaudeville Wars: How the Keith-Albee and Orpheum Circuits Controlled the Big-Time and Its Performers.* New York: Palgrave Macmillan, 2006.

Westerfield, Jane Robertson. "An Investigation of Lifestyles and Performances of Three Singer-Comediennes of American Vaudeville: Eva Tanguay, Nora Bayes and Sophie Tucker." Ph.D. diss., Ball State University, 1987.

Whitcomb, Ian. *Irving Berlin and Ragtime America.* London: Century-Hutchinson, 1987.

Whythe, William. "Past Laughter." *Saturday Evening Post,* April 25, 1931, 64–66.

Williams, Susan. *Savory Suppers, Fashionable Feasts: Dining in Victorian America.* New York: Pantheon, 1985.

Wilson, Garff B. *A History of American Acting*. Bloomington: Indiana University Press, 1966.

———. *Three Hundred Years of American Drama and Theatre*. 2nd ed. Englewood Cliffs, N.J.: Prentice Hall, 1982.

Winter, Brian. *Chronicles of a Country Town: Whitby Past and Present*. Whitby, Ontario: Town of Whitby Archives, 1999.

Woloch, Nancy. *Women and the American Experience*. New York: Alfred A. Knopf, 1984.

"The Woman Who Dared." *Munsey's,* January 1900, 591–92.

Wood, Amy Louise. *Lynching and Spectacle: Witnessing Racial Violence in America, 1890–1940*. Chapel Hill: University of North Carolina Press, 2009.

Young, William C. *Famous Actors and Actresses of the American Stage*. Vol. 1, *A–J*. New York: Bowler, 1975.

Zellers, Parker. *Tony Pastor, Dean of the Vaudeville Stage*. Ypsilanti: Eastern Michigan University Press, 1971.

Index

References in *italics* refer to illustrations.

SHARON AMMEN is professor emerita of theatre at Saint Mary-of-the-Woods College, Indiana.

MUSIC IN AMERICAN LIFE

Only a Miner: Studies in Recorded Coal-Mining Songs *Archie Green*
Great Day Coming: Folk Music and the American Left *R. Serge Denisoff*
John Philip Sousa: A Descriptive Catalog of His Works *Paul E. Bierley*
The Hell-Bound Train: A Cowboy Songbook *Glenn Ohrlin*
Oh, Didn't He Ramble: The Life Story of Lee Collins, as Told to Mary Collins *Edited by Frank J. Gillis and John W. Miner*
American Labor Songs of the Nineteenth Century *Philip S. Foner*
Stars of Country Music: Uncle Dave Macon to Johnny Rodriguez *Edited by Bill C. Malone and Judith McCulloh*
Git Along, Little Dogies: Songs and Songmakers of the American West *John I. White*
A Texas-Mexican *Cancionero*: Folksongs of the Lower Border *Américo Paredes*
San Antonio Rose: The Life and Music of Bob Wills *Charles R. Townsend*
Early Downhome Blues: A Musical and Cultural Analysis *Jeff Todd Titon*
An Ives Celebration: Papers and Panels of the Charles Ives Centennial Festival-Conference *Edited by H. Wiley Hitchcock and Vivian Perlis*
Sinful Tunes and Spirituals: Black Folk Music to the Civil War *Dena J. Epstein*
Joe Scott, the Woodsman-Songmaker *Edward D. Ives*
Jimmie Rodgers: The Life and Times of America's Blue Yodeler *Nolan Porterfield*
Early American Music Engraving and Printing: A History of Music Publishing in America from 1787 to 1825, with Commentary on Earlier and Later Practices *Richard J. Wolfe*
Sing a Sad Song: The Life of Hank Williams *Roger M. Williams*
Long Steel Rail: The Railroad in American Folksong *Norm Cohen*
Resources of American Music History: A Directory of Source Materials from Colonial Times to World War II *D. W. Krummel, Jean Geil, Doris J. Dyen, and Deane L. Root*
Tenement Songs: The Popular Music of the Jewish Immigrants *Mark Slobin*
Ozark Folksongs *Vance Randolph; edited and abridged by Norm Cohen*
Oscar Sonneck and American Music *Edited by William Lichtenwanger*
Bluegrass Breakdown: The Making of the Old Southern Sound *Robert Cantwell*
Bluegrass: A History *Neil V. Rosenberg*
Music at the White House: A History of the American Spirit *Elise K. Kirk*
Red River Blues: The Blues Tradition in the Southeast *Bruce Bastin*
Good Friends and Bad Enemies: Robert Winslow Gordon and the Study of American Folksong *Debora Kodish*
Fiddlin' Georgia Crazy: Fiddlin' John Carson, His Real World, and the World of His Songs *Gene Wiggins*
America's Music: From the Pilgrims to the Present (rev. 3d ed.) *Gilbert Chase*
Secular Music in Colonial Annapolis: The Tuesday Club, 1745–56 *John Barry Talley*
Bibliographical Handbook of American Music *D. W. Krummel*
Goin' to Kansas City *Nathan W. Pearson Jr.*

"Susanna," "Jeanie," and "The Old Folks at Home": The Songs of Stephen C. Foster from His Time to Ours (2d ed.) *William W. Austin*

Songprints: The Musical Experience of Five Shoshone Women *Judith Vander*

"Happy in the Service of the Lord": Afro-American Gospel Quartets in Memphis *Kip Lornell*

Paul Hindemith in the United States *Luther Noss*

"My Song Is My Weapon": People's Songs, American Communism, and the Politics of Culture, 1930–50 *Robbie Lieberman*

Chosen Voices: The Story of the American Cantorate *Mark Slobin*

Theodore Thomas: America's Conductor and Builder of Orchestras, 1835–1905 *Ezra Schabas*

"The Whorehouse Bells Were Ringing" and Other Songs Cowboys Sing *Collected and Edited by Guy Logsdon*

Crazeology: The Autobiography of a Chicago Jazzman *Bud Freeman, as Told to Robert Wolf*

Discoursing Sweet Music: Brass Bands and Community Life in Turn-of-the-Century Pennsylvania *Kenneth Kreitner*

Mormonism and Music: A History *Michael Hicks*

Voices of the Jazz Age: Profiles of Eight Vintage Jazzmen *Chip Deffaa*

Pickin' on Peachtree: A History of Country Music in Atlanta, Georgia *Wayne W. Daniel*

Bitter Music: Collected Journals, Essays, Introductions, and Librettos *Harry Partch; edited by Thomas McGeary*

Ethnic Music on Records: A Discography of Ethnic Recordings Produced in the United States, 1893 to 1942 *Richard K. Spottswood*

Downhome Blues Lyrics: An Anthology from the Post–World War II Era *Jeff Todd Titon*

Ellington: The Early Years *Mark Tucker*

Chicago Soul *Robert Pruter*

That Half-Barbaric Twang: The Banjo in American Popular Culture *Karen Linn*

Hot Man: The Life of Art Hodes *Art Hodes and Chadwick Hansen*

The Erotic Muse: American Bawdy Songs (2d ed.) *Ed Cray*

Barrio Rhythm: Mexican American Music in Los Angeles *Steven Loza*

The Creation of Jazz: Music, Race, and Culture in Urban America *Burton W. Peretti*

Charles Martin Loeffler: A Life Apart in Music *Ellen Knight*

Club Date Musicians: Playing the New York Party Circuit *Bruce A. MacLeod*

Opera on the Road: Traveling Opera Troupes in the United States, 1825–60 *Katherine K. Preston*

The Stonemans: An Appalachian Family and the Music That Shaped Their Lives *Ivan M. Tribe*

Transforming Tradition: Folk Music Revivals Examined *Edited by Neil V. Rosenberg*

The Crooked Stovepipe: Athapaskan Fiddle Music and Square Dancing in Northeast Alaska and Northwest Canada *Craig Mishler*

Traveling the High Way Home: Ralph Stanley and the World of Traditional Bluegrass Music *John Wright*

Carl Ruggles: Composer, Painter, and Storyteller *Marilyn Ziffrin*

Never without a Song: The Years and Songs of Jennie Devlin, 1865–1952 *Katharine D. Newman*

The Hank Snow Story *Hank Snow, with Jack Ownbey and Bob Burris*

Milton Brown and the Founding of Western Swing *Cary Ginell, with special assistance from Roy Lee Brown*

Santiago de Murcia's "Códice Saldívar No. 4": A Treasury of Secular Guitar Music from Baroque Mexico *Craig H. Russell*

The Sound of the Dove: Singing in Appalachian Primitive Baptist Churches *Beverly Bush Patterson*

Heartland Excursions: Ethnomusicological Reflections on Schools of Music *Bruno Nettl*

Doowop: The Chicago Scene *Robert Pruter*

Blue Rhythms: Six Lives in Rhythm and Blues *Chip Deffaa*

Shoshone Ghost Dance Religion: Poetry Songs and Great Basin Context *Judith Vander*

Go Cat Go! Rockabilly Music and Its Makers *Craig Morrison*

'Twas Only an Irishman's Dream: The Image of Ireland and the Irish in American Popular Song Lyrics, 1800–1920 *William H. A. Williams*

Democracy at the Opera: Music, Theater, and Culture in New York City, 1815–60 *Karen Ahlquist*

Fred Waring and the Pennsylvanians *Virginia Waring*

Woody, Cisco, and Me: Seamen Three in the Merchant Marine *Jim Longhi*

Behind the Burnt Cork Mask: Early Blackface Minstrelsy and Antebellum American Popular Culture *William J. Mahar*

Going to Cincinnati: A History of the Blues in the Queen City *Steven C. Tracy*

Pistol Packin' Mama: Aunt Molly Jackson and the Politics of Folksong *Shelly Romalis*

Sixties Rock: Garage, Psychedelic, and Other Satisfactions *Michael Hicks*

The Late Great Johnny Ace and the Transition from R&B to Rock 'n' Roll *James M. Salem*

Tito Puente and the Making of Latin Music *Steven Loza*

Juilliard: A History *Andrea Olmstead*

Understanding Charles Seeger, Pioneer in American Musicology *Edited by Bell Yung and Helen Rees*

Mountains of Music: West Virginia Traditional Music from *Goldenseal* *Edited by John Lilly*

Alice Tully: An Intimate Portrait *Albert Fuller*

A Blues Life *Henry Townsend, as told to Bill Greensmith*

Long Steel Rail: The Railroad in American Folksong (2d ed.) *Norm Cohen*

The Golden Age of Gospel *Text by Horace Clarence Boyer; photography by Lloyd Yearwood*

Aaron Copland: The Life and Work of an Uncommon Man *Howard Pollack*
Louis Moreau Gottschalk *S. Frederick Starr*
Race, Rock, and Elvis *Michael T. Bertrand*
Theremin: Ether Music and Espionage *Albert Glinsky*
Poetry and Violence: The Ballad Tradition of Mexico's Costa Chica *John H. McDowell*
The Bill Monroe Reader *Edited by Tom Ewing*
Music in Lubavitcher Life *Ellen Koskoff*
Zarzuela: Spanish Operetta, American Stage *Janet L. Sturman*
Bluegrass Odyssey: A Documentary in Pictures and Words, 1966–86 *Carl Fleischhauer and Neil V. Rosenberg*
That Old-Time Rock & Roll: A Chronicle of an Era, 1954–63 *Richard Aquila*
Labor's Troubadour *Joe Glazer*
American Opera *Elise K. Kirk*
Don't Get above Your Raisin': Country Music and the Southern Working Class *Bill C. Malone*
John Alden Carpenter: A Chicago Composer *Howard Pollack*
Heartbeat of the People: Music and Dance of the Northern Pow-wow *Tara Browner*
My Lord, What a Morning: An Autobiography *Marian Anderson*
Marian Anderson: A Singer's Journey *Allan Keiler*
Charles Ives Remembered: An Oral History *Vivian Perlis*
Henry Cowell, Bohemian *Michael Hicks*
Rap Music and Street Consciousness *Cheryl L. Keyes*
Louis Prima *Garry Boulard*
Marian McPartland's Jazz World: All in Good Time *Marian McPartland*
Robert Johnson: Lost and Found *Barry Lee Pearson and Bill McCulloch*
Bound for America: Three British Composers *Nicholas Temperley*
Lost Sounds: Blacks and the Birth of the Recording Industry, 1890–1919 *Tim Brooks*
Burn, Baby! BURN! The Autobiography of Magnificent Montague *Magnificent Montague with Bob Baker*
Way Up North in Dixie: A Black Family's Claim to the Confederate Anthem *Howard L. Sacks and Judith Rose Sacks*
The Bluegrass Reader *Edited by Thomas Goldsmith*
Colin McPhee: Composer in Two Worlds *Carol J. Oja*
Robert Johnson, Mythmaking, and Contemporary American Culture *Patricia R. Schroeder*
Composing a World: Lou Harrison, Musical Wayfarer *Leta E. Miller and Fredric Lieberman*
Fritz Reiner, Maestro and Martinet *Kenneth Morgan*
That Toddlin' Town: Chicago's White Dance Bands and Orchestras, 1900–1950 *Charles A. Sengstock Jr.*
Dewey and Elvis: The Life and Times of a Rock 'n' Roll Deejay *Louis Cantor*

Come Hither to Go Yonder: Playing Bluegrass with Bill Monroe *Bob Black*
Chicago Blues: Portraits and Stories *David Whiteis*
The Incredible Band of John Philip Sousa *Paul E. Bierley*
"Maximum Clarity" and Other Writings on Music *Ben Johnston, edited by Bob Gilmore*
Staging Tradition: John Lair and Sarah Gertrude Knott *Michael Ann Williams*
Homegrown Music: Discovering Bluegrass *Stephanie P. Ledgin*
Tales of a Theatrical Guru *Danny Newman*
The Music of Bill Monroe *Neil V. Rosenberg and Charles K. Wolfe*
Pressing On: The Roni Stoneman Story *Roni Stoneman, as told to Ellen Wright*
Together Let Us Sweetly Live *Jonathan C. David, with photographs by Richard Holloway*
Live Fast, Love Hard: The Faron Young Story *Diane Diekman*
Air Castle of the South: WSM Radio and the Making of Music City *Craig P. Havighurst*
Traveling Home: Sacred Harp Singing and American Pluralism *Kiri Miller*
Where Did Our Love Go? The Rise and Fall of the Motown Sound *Nelson George*
Lonesome Cowgirls and Honky-Tonk Angels: The Women of Barn Dance Radio *Kristine M. McCusker*
California Polyphony: Ethnic Voices, Musical Crossroads *Mina Yang*
The Never-Ending Revival: Rounder Records and the Folk Alliance *Michael F. Scully*
Sing It Pretty: A Memoir *Bess Lomax Hawes*
Working Girl Blues: The Life and Music of Hazel Dickens *Hazel Dickens and Bill C. Malone*
Charles Ives Reconsidered *Gayle Sherwood Magee*
The Hayloft Gang: The Story of the National Barn Dance *Edited by Chad Berry*
Country Music Humorists and Comedians *Loyal Jones*
Record Makers and Breakers: Voices of the Independent Rock 'n' Roll Pioneers *John Broven*
Music of the First Nations: Tradition and Innovation in Native North America *Edited by Tara Browner*
Cafe Society: The Wrong Place for the Right People *Barney Josephson, with Terry Trilling-Josephson*
George Gershwin: An Intimate Portrait *Walter Rimler*
Life Flows On in Endless Song: Folk Songs and American History *Robert V. Wells*
I Feel a Song Coming On: The Life of Jimmy McHugh *Alyn Shipton*
King of the Queen City: The Story of King Records *Jon Hartley Fox*
Long Lost Blues: Popular Blues in America, 1850–1920 *Peter C. Muir*
Hard Luck Blues: Roots Music Photographs from the Great Depression *Rich Remsberg*
Restless Giant: The Life and Times of Jean Aberbach and Hill and Range Songs *Bar Biszick-Lockwood*

Champagne Charlie and Pretty Jemima: Variety Theater in the Nineteenth Century *Gillian M. Rodger*
Sacred Steel: Inside an African American Steel Guitar Tradition *Robert L. Stone*
Gone to the Country: The New Lost City Ramblers and the Folk Music Revival *Ray Allen*
The Makers of the Sacred Harp *David Warren Steel with Richard H. Hulan*
Woody Guthrie, American Radical *Will Kaufman*
George Szell: A Life of Music *Michael Charry*
Bean Blossom: The Brown County Jamboree and Bill Monroe's Bluegrass Festivals *Thomas A. Adler*
Crowe on the Banjo: The Music Life of J. D. Crowe *Marty Godbey*
Twentieth Century Drifter: The Life of Marty Robbins *Diane Diekman*
Henry Mancini: Reinventing Film Music *John Caps*
The Beautiful Music All Around Us: Field Recordings and the American Experience *Stephen Wade*
Then Sings My Soul: The Culture of Southern Gospel Music *Douglas Harrison*
The Accordion in the Americas: Klezmer, Polka, Tango, Zydeco, and More! *Edited by Helena Simonett*
Bluegrass Bluesman: A Memoir *Josh Graves, edited by Fred Bartenstein*
One Woman in a Hundred: Edna Phillips and the Philadelphia Orchestra *Mary Sue Welsh*
The Great Orchestrator: Arthur Judson and American Arts Management *James M. Doering*
Charles Ives in the Mirror: American Histories of an Iconic Composer *David C. Paul*
Southern Soul-Blues *David Whiteis*
Sweet Air: Modernism, Regionalism, and American Popular Song *Edward P. Comentale*
Pretty Good for a Girl: Women in Bluegrass *Murphy Hicks Henry*
Sweet Dreams: The World of Patsy Cline *Warren R. Hofstra*
William Sidney Mount and the Creolization of American Culture *Christopher J. Smith*
Bird: The Life and Music of Charlie Parker *Chuck Haddix*
Making the March King: John Philip Sousa's Washington Years, 1854–1893 *Patrick Warfield*
In It for the Long Run *Jim Rooney*
Pioneers of the Blues Revival *Steve Cushing*
Roots of the Revival: American and British Folk Music in the 1950s *Ronald D. Cohen and Rachel Clare Donaldson*
Blues All Day Long: The Jimmy Rogers Story *Wayne Everett Goins*
Yankee Twang: Country and Western Music in New England *Clifford R. Murphy*
The Music of the Stanley Brothers *Gary B. Reid*
Hawaiian Music in Motion: Mariners, Missionaries, and Minstrels *James Revell Carr*

Sounds of the New Deal: The Federal Music Project in the West *Peter Gough*
The Mormon Tabernacle Choir: A Biography *Michael Hicks*
The Man That Got Away: The Life and Songs of Harold Arlen *Walter Rimler*
A City Called Heaven: Chicago and the Birth of Gospel Music *Robert M. Marovich*
Blues Unlimited: Essential Interviews from the Original Blues Magazine *Edited by Bill Greensmith, Mike Rowe, and Mark Camarigg*
Hoedowns, Reels, and Frolics: Roots and Branches of Southern Appalachian Dance *Phil Jamison*
Fannie Bloomfield-Zeisler: The Life and Times of a Piano Virtuoso *Beth Abelson Macleod*
Cybersonic Arts: Adventures in American New Music *Gordon Mumma, edited with commentary by Michelle Fillion*
The Magic of Beverly Sills *Nancy Guy*
Waiting for Buddy Guy *Alan Harper*
Harry T. Burleigh: From the Spiritual to the Harlem Renaissance *Jean E. Snyder*
Music in the Age of Anxiety: American Music in the Fifties *James Wierzbicki*
Jazzing: New York City's Unseen Scene *Thomas H. Greenland*
A Cole Porter Companion *Edited by Don M. Randel, Matthew Shaftel, and Susan Forscher Weiss*
Foggy Mountain Troubadour: The Life and Music of Curly Seckler *Penny Parsons*
Blue Rhythm Fantasy: Big Band Jazz Arranging in the Swing Era *John Wriggle*
Bill Clifton: America's Bluegrass Ambassador to the World *Bill C. Malone*
May Irwin: Singing, Shouting, and the Shadow of Minstrelsy *Sharon Ammen*

The University of Illinois Press
is a founding member of the
Association of American University Presses.

Composed in 10.5/13 Adobe Minion Pro
with Archer display
by Lisa Connery
at the University of Illinois Press
Cover designed by Jennifer S. Holzner
Cover illustration courtesy of Karen Killian
Manufactured by Sheridan Books, Inc.

University of Illinois Press
1325 South Oak Street
Champaign, IL 61820-6903
www.press.uillinois.edu